```
HV      Sykes, Richard E.,
8138      1932-
S97        Policing, a so-
1983    cial behaviorist
        perspective
```

POLICING

A Volume in the
Crime, Law, and Deviance
Series

Richard E. Sykes
Edward E. Brent

POLICING
A Social Behaviorist Perspective

Rutgers University Press
New Brunswick, New Jersey

Library of Congress Cataloging in Publication Data
Sykes, Richard E., 1932–
  Policing, a social behaviorist perspective.

  (Crime, law, and deviance)
  Bibliography: p.
  Includes index.
  1. Police—United States. 2. Public relations—United
States—Police. 3. Social interaction—United States—
Mathematical models. 4. Human behavior—Mathematical
models. I. Brent, Edward E., 1949–   II. Title.
III. Series.
HV8138.S97 1983   363.2'3   82-10229
ISBN 0-8135-0971-8

Copyright © 1983 by Rutgers, The State University

All rights reserved

Manufactured in the United States of America

To our families
Ginger, Andrew, and Carrie Sykes
Ruth, Jessica, and Jonathan Brent

Contents

List of Figures	ix
List of Tables	xi
Acknowledgments	xv
Introduction	1

Part One: Perspectives and Definitions

1	*An Alternate Interpretation of Police Work*	11
2	*How Defining the Situation Affects Initial Interaction*	31

Part Two: The Volatile Working Group

3	*The Volatile Working Group and Its Supervision*	51
4	*Getting the Work Done*	75
5	*Patterns of Decisions by Police*	89

Part Three: Police-Civilian Interaction

6	*A Mathematical Model of Symbolic Interaction*	101
7	*Further Explorations of Police-Civilian Dyads*	149
8	*The Model and Multiple-Position Interaction*	177
9	*Exploring Model Implications through Simulation*	195
10	*Using Structural Equation Models to Predict Outcomes*	209

Part Four: Theoretical and Substantive Conclusions
11 *Neo-Social Behaviorism* 227
12 *A Social Psychology of Policing* 247

Appendix: Social Psychologists at Work 261
Bibliography 293
Index 305

List of Figures

2.1	Dendogram of clusters of activities utilizing the complete linkage method	34
2.2	Characterization pairs for police activities	35
2.3	Factor score profile of five clusters of calls	42
2.4	A Wroclow diagram of the five clusters of activities	44
3.1	Schematic of a simple regulatory process	59
7.1	Social acts formed from the permutation of officer-civilian and civilian-officer acts	152
7.2	Digraph of a second-order Markov model of social acts of officers and suspects	156
7.3	Digraph of a second-order Markov model of social acts of officers and complainants	170
8.1	Digraph of the metaprocess of transitions from one dyad to another	182
8.2	Digraph of a second-order Markov model of social acts of officers and civilians in multiple-position encounters	185
8.3	Digraph of officer-officer interaction	188
8.4	Digraph of civilian-civilian interaction	189
8.5	Initiation of new dyadic interactions by officers	191
10.1	Effects of interaction on severity of outcome where both violators and complainants are present	218
10.2	Effects of interaction on severity of outcome where only violators are present	220

List of Tables

2.1	Correlation matrix of the twenty characterization pairs	36
2.2	Factor matrix of variables describing police calls	37
2.3	Euclidean distances between each of twenty-one calls	40
3.1	A schematic of disturbance regulation	65
3.2	Types of regulation used to take charge of a suspect initially (by type of encounter)	67
3.3	Transition probabilities of specific officer responses to specific disturbances by suspects	72
4.1	Percentage of nexial and structural information by phase (N=7,652 strings)	80
4.2	Mean time of occurrence for solutions in reactive encounters (N=256) and on-scene encounters (N=259)	84
4.3	Percentage of information search before and after problem solutions (N=256 suspect-present, reactive encounters)	85
4.4	Percentage of information search before and after problem solutions (N=259 suspect-present, on-scene encounters)	86
5.1	Induced patterns of solutions	91
5.2	Differences between patterns of solutions in reactive and on-scene encounters	92
5.3	Summary transition probabilities for	

	information and solutions based on a 25% random sample of strings (N=2,296)	93
5.4	Information and solution string transitions based on a 25% random sample of sets of utterances (N=2,296)	94
5.5	Nonroutine score means by pattern	96
5.6	Situated identity structure and the means of the nonroutine scale	97
5.7	Order of means of nonroutine index broken down by pattern for traffic-related (N=241) and peacekeeping (N=188) activities	98
6.1	Tests of order, contingency, and role heterogeneity for officer-suspect encounters	120
6.2	Tests of stability and homogeneity for a second-order model of police-suspect interaction	123
6.3	Transition matrix for the second-order Markov model with heterogeneous positions for officer/single-suspect encounters	128
6.4	Expected and observed equilibrium distribution of states for second-order Markov model with heterogeneous roles	131
6.5	Tests of order and role heterogeneity for the single-complainant model	133
6.6	Tests of stationarity for single-complainant encounters	135
6.7	Tests of homogeneity for single-complainant encounters	136
6.8	Transition matrix for the second-order Markov model with heterogeneous positions for officer/single-complainant encounters	138
6.9	Expected and observed distribution of runs for each state of a second-order Markov model with heterogeneous roles (officer-complainant)	142
7.1	Opportunity structures of officers and suspects	

List of Tables xiii

	based on the probability of a particular act by one at time t, given the act of the other at time t-1	164
7.2	Situations for officers and suspects	165
7.3	Opportunity structures for officers and complainants based on the probability of a particular act by one at time t, given the act of the other at time t-1	166
7.4	Situations for officers and complainants	167
7.5	Officers compared, whether interacting with suspects or with violators (dimension 4, top model); and civilians compared, whether officers think they are suspects or complainants (dimension 4, bottom model)	169
7.6	Who has the last word in encounters?	172
7.7	Last social acts of encounters	173
8.1	Substantive significance and frequency of speaker-subject pair sequences	179
8.2	Tests of the order for transitions within "old" civilian-officer dyads	180
8.3	Tests of the order of officer-civilian interaction in officer/multiple-civilian encounters	183
8.4	Tests of the order of officer-officer and civilian-civilian interaction in multiple-position encounters	186
8.5	Comparison of the transition probabilities of officer-officer and civilian-civilian encounters	187
8.6	Tests of order for initiations by new civilians in officer/multiple-civilian interaction	190
9.1	Hypothetical response propensities of demonstrators interacting with officers	200
9.2	Predicted equilibrium distribution for aggregated encounters between demonstrators and officers	200
9.3	Predicted equilibrium distribution for civilian-	

	civilian interaction compared to equilibrium distributions for officer-suspect and officer-complainant interactions (by percentage)	202
9.4	Civilian-civilian confrontation compared to officer-suspect and officer-complainant interactions (eigenvalues)	202
9.5	Transition matrix for hypothetical police-civilian interaction with communication problems (officer-suspect)	205
9.6	Predicted equilibrium distribution of states for simulated encounters in which both officers and civilians misunderstand each other	206
9.7	Predicted eigenvalues for simulated communication problems involving only civilians, involving civilians and officers, and of observed interaction between police and suspects	207
10.1	Interaction indices included in the analysis of outcomes	214
A.1	The interaction code for process	270
A.2	Typology of string summaries	271
A.3	An example of these data: observation number 7008	272

Acknowledgments

Many persons contributed to the research project of which this monograph is one product. The project involved a staff who were asked to do far more than follow instructions. More often than not they were asked to solve difficult problems and create new procedures. Their work involved tremendous amounts of both tedious detail and creativity. This monograph is only a small aspect of their work. The contributions of many who are less evident are nevertheless very important. Therefore, we take this opportunity to thank them publicly, and to detail briefly the nature of their contributions.

This study began in late 1969. We would like to thank the Center for Studies of Crime and Delinquency for their patient and strong support, especially George Weber and Thomas Lalley. The senior author especially appreciated their support during times of trial and difficulty. It is easy enough to support the proven or publicly successful. It is not so easy to support projects that are venturing into areas where a multitude of problems make progress slow. For their support, I owe them an enormous debt of gratitude. The research was supported by Grant 5R01 MH23144, "Comparative Quantitative Studies of Police-Citizen Encounters," and Grant 5T32 MH14673, "Systematic Observation of Criminal Justice Processes," of the United States Public Health Service, National Institutes of Mental Health, Center for Studies of Crime and Delinquency. The senior author also wishes to thank the University of Minnesota for a single quarter leave during which he conceptualized and wrote much of Chapters 1 and 11, and the University of Minnesota Computer Center for support over many years.

In addition to the senior author, obviously, the project owes much to the enthusiasm of John Clark, coprincipal investigator; Duane Wallen, who assisted in preliminary fieldwork as early as 1969; and Richard Lundman and James Fox, who were among the first group of observers.

Programming was a continuing challenge. Our work required original programming, often of a kind involving unseen hazards. Paul Steinbeck and David Doren made great contributions. William Briggs and William Geery also assisted.

The project would not have been possible without the assistance of Robert Scarlett, Beverly Mains, and Dana Drennan. Robert Scarlett did most of the day-to-day administration during the data-collection phase of the project (1970–1973) and continually showed his expertise at maintaining good human relations with the departments we were studying. He also did his best to teach the senior author how to do things in an orderly and systematic manner, though with limited success. First Beverly Mains, and then Dana Drennan faced the vital task of processing on a continuous basis immense amounts of coded information, keeping track of this information, tracing down equipment problems, working with observers to edit printouts, and the like. Ms. Drennan probably reviewed a million and a half codes with continuous and highly responsible attention to detail. But in addition, she and Ms. Mains with the programmers designed the entire data-handling and file-management systems at a time when few "canned" systems were available.

Because we had many problems with the equipment we were using, a good deal of originality had to be manifested in solving them. Both Ms. Mains and Ms. Drennan provided great assistance in this regard, but they required the assistance of someone with engineering expertise. First Sheldon Mains and then David Madigan provided this expertise and designed and built modifications of the original equipment, which made our work much easier.

The training of the observers for the second phase of the

Acknowledgments xvii

project would not have been possible without the assistance of many people in preparing the videotapes of police-civilian encounters. Primarily responsible were James Lorensen, who made most of the arrangements and did the casting, together with David McKenzie, who wrote the scripts. The Media Resources Center of the University of Minnesota did the photography and prepared the tapes. Many actors assisted, and advisers and equipment were provided by the University of Minnesota Department of Police and the Department of Public Safety of the City of St. Paul.

Vijay Gupta prepared an encyclopedic annotated bibliography on American police.

Many other staff members participated in the project. Lewie Holmes, secretary during much of the project, was active in a wide range of areas, including training the observers to use their buttons more accurately, and preparing other training materials. Other staff included Nancy Hoyt, William Graham, Gary Martland, Carol Haugo, David Anderson, Maria Miles, Laurie Ondich, Robert Kyweriga, Peggy Klema, Barbara Shattuck, Pat Burnos, Lynn Masica, Diana Merryman, and Lucile Sukalo. Pat O'Connor, Carol Olson, Steven Clark, and other staff of Minnesota Systems Research also provided assistance.

Of course, the "front line" was manned by the observers. They were on hand for high-speed chases, riots, demonstrations, accidents, a homicide case, and a great many routine events during the period they were observing. One came perilously close to being shot. They were: James Fox, David Hoium, Richard Lundman, Alan Stesin, James Whelpley, Andrew Kozak, Edward Gubman, Steven Sherlock, Carl Stover, Paul Wilkus, Robert Gove, and Ronald Sieloff. Two did their Ph.D. dissertations on this data, one an M.A., and another a Ph.D. dissertation on a project that grew out of his observations. Others have since become physicians, lawyers, politicians, and criminologists.

Several people assisted with the preparation of the final typescript and artwork. We wish to thank Donna Shepherd, Gloria DeWolfe, Marilyn Pindroh Underwood, the late Pearl

Isaacson, and Richard Perlich, but we are especially indebted to Lisa Thornquist, whose expertise with a word processor has been of invaluable assistance.

We also wish to thank Professor David Greenberg, Dr. Susan Martin, and Mr. Robert E. Brown for their very helpful suggestions, and Ms. Marlie Wasserman, Senior Editor, Leslie Mitchner, and the staff of the Rutgers University Press for their conscientious and deeply appreciated assistance.

We also wish to acknowledge permission to reprint material from the following articles:

"The Interactive Bases of Police-Suspect Confrontation: An Empirically Based Simulation" by Edward E. Brent, Jr. and Richard E. Sykes, in *Simulation and Games* 11 (1980):347–363. Reprinted with permission of Sage Publications. Copyright © by Sage Publications.

"A Mathematical Model of the Process of Symbolic Interaction between Police and Civilians" by Edward E. Brent, Jr. and Richard E. Sykes, in *Behavioral Science* 24 (1979):388–402. Copyright © by the General Systems Science Foundation.

"The Regulation of Interaction by Police: A Systems View of 'Taking Charge,'" by Richard E. Sykes and Edward E. Brent, Jr., in *Criminology* 18 (1980):182–197. Copyright © American Society of Criminology. Reprinted by permission of Sage Publications, Beverly Hills/London.

We also want to thank our families, who provided far more than their share of support, encouragement, and patience for the years during which this project was conceived, executed, and interpreted.

Finally, we wish to thank the officers of five police departments for their cooperation, as well as several thousand citizens who together made our study possible. Both necessity and the conventions of research require that they be nameless.

POLICING

Introduction

During the last fifteen years, social scientists have begun to develop an understanding of the police. Several important monographs have been published, most of which focus on the police from a "macro," or occupational, perspective. Little attention was given to the "micro" processes, those interpersonal transactions through which most police work is accomplished. While scholars now understand some of the factors that affect police work, they do not understand the actual detailed process of interpersonal communication and behavior through which it is accomplished.

This book is concerned with the "micro" processes of interaction taking place between police officers and civilians during the course of routine police work. To do justice to this topic we have found it necessary to approach the study of police in a somewhat novel way. Our approach may be defined on at least four levels: (1) our perspective on police and policing; (2) the broader theoretical perspectives that have influenced this work; (3) our methods, particularly our approach to the "data" of police-civilian interaction; and (4) the analysis techniques employed. Examination of the communication processes between police and civilians shows that overt force and coercion are relatively rare in police interaction with civilians. While no scholar has claimed that police depend exclusively on coercion and few have claimed that it is an exclusive prerogative of police, many scholars have tended to emphasize the coercive aspect of policing (the most often cited is Westley, 1953), or the special function of police to use legitimized coercion (Bittner, 1970). We do not wish to deny either that police use legitimate (and sometimes illegitimate) coercion or that it is one of their important resources. Our study of approximately five thousand encounters between police and civilians has led us to conclude that the effectiveness of police action is not usually due to overt coercion. Civilians usually acknowledge police authority without police coercion. We argue that most police work is based on legitimate power, not coercive power (French and Raven, 1959; Tapp and Kohlberg, 1971; Tapp and Levine, 1977). Citizens usually obey police because they recognize the right of police to take charge in disordered situations. Obviously, this is not true in all situations nor of all civilians. Still, it is a very important finding, not the least because to the extent that the public recognizes police power as legitimate, then to that extent overt coercion will be unnecessary. Socrates, by drinking hemlock, made much the same point.

Study also demonstrates that most police activities with civilians consist of verbal and nonverbal communication. Their job is both to constitute a presence and to talk. As the representative of authority, they persuade, argue, cajole, and command. The better they are at this, the less force will be necessary.

Understanding the complex data on which this study is based required a theoretical perspective. More accurately, it required several. We believed that it might be useful to police scholars to present not only a different point of view in regard to the functions of police, but to place the activities of police in a broader perspective. Since most previous studies emphasized what was unique about police, we sought to show how similar their work is to the work of others. We also sought to examine the usefulness of certain traditional concepts, for example, definition of the situation (Thomas, 1923); and to develop new interpretations of old concepts, for example, roletaking (Mead, 1934).

This book at various times uses three different units of analysis. The broadest unit is *the encounter*, which consists of everything that leads up to and goes on during one event in which police and civilians interact. Typical encounters examined in this book include occasions in which a civilian is stopped for a traffic violation, a report is taken from a complainant, or police intervene in a dispute between two or more civilians. We conceive of the police-civilian encounter as an example of a particular kind of work group that we conceptualized here for the first time, *the volatile working group*. Officers are seen as supervisors of such groups. This aspect of the book is partially indebted to general systems theory (Ashby, 1956), but also draws on small group research and sociology of work literature.

The "smallest," most microlevel unit of analysis we employ is the *utterance*. An utterance is all one person says during his or her turn at speaking. Most encounters considered in this study were at least twenty utterances long. The utterance is the unit of analysis for most of this book. We are concerned with the sequence of utterances that occur in police-civilian encounters and the temporal ordering of these utterances as they reflect the relative power and control exerted over the encounter by the participants. This part of the book benefits from the literature on symbolic interaction, general systems theory, and some of the substantive theories of police behavior.

The third and last unit of analysis employed in this book is the *set of utterances* (also called a *string*). A set of utterances is a sequence of adjacent utterances that may be from one to forty or fifty utterances in length, including utterances of different speakers, but all united by focusing on the same topic. Most encounters examined in this study consisted of only six or seven sets of strings. A set of utterances appears to be a reasonable level on which to look for strategies that organize interaction. Strategies may be thought of as broad orienting agenda or decision points which guide the actions of one or more actors in the encounter. While individual utterances constitute the detailed "blow-by-blow" (or more likely, question-answer) process of interaction, the set outlines the encounter in broader brushstrokes, reflecting its general phases. Our examination of sets of utterances was informed by the work in small group research on phases of group problem solving, though as a unit of analysis it is used here for the first time.

While this work has been influenced by a number of theoretical perspectives, without a doubt, the principal influence on the actual collection of data and the conduct of the study is the social behaviorist tradition as exemplified by Mead's work (1934). This study is based on systematic quantitative observations of social interaction in a natural setting. We believe behavior is best understood in the natural context in which it occurs. We conceive of social interaction between police and civilians as a complex interplay between participants in which the actions of officers influence the responses of civilians, and vice versa. Whatever the level of the interaction—whether habitual or, more likely, the outcome of an inner dialogue in which alternate courses of action are considered—it is implemented primarily, if not entirely, through overt acts observable to participants and observers alike.

The social behaviorist perspective is very compatible with the study of police-civilian interaction. Although few scholars have studied the process in detail, they are agreed that most police work involves peacekeeping and service activities of which interpersonal communication is an intrinsic and necessary part. They are also agreed that law enforcement duties require the exercise of discretion by officers, and that this is also frequently a function of the interaction between officers and civilians. Neither has access to the other's private thoughts, but only to the other's overt verbal and nonverbal behavior. This behavior must be the basis for their attributions. Civilians and officers, in regard to each other, are not unlike the scientific observers who study them. Each has no other source of information than the other's behaviors. Understanding the process of their behavior depends upon an analysis of the record of the co-occurring behaviors of both. The social behaviorist perspective, together with recently developed tools of data collection and analysis, permit such an analysis, perhaps for the first time. For the most part, we are concerned in this book with the *form* of social interaction between police and civilians more than its specific content. We do, like Bales (1950), distinguish between interactions with different functions. However, our primary concern is the form that interaction takes, similar to, but not identical with, Simmel's (1955) distinctions between forms of social interaction. We are looking for regularities in social interaction between police and civilians which we hope can help us to understand better the relations that evolve between them during specific encounters. More importantly, we look for regularities which may characterize many types of social interaction that occur outside the specific subject matter of this study.

This book is not just a study of police; the techniques used, the concerns addressed, the concepts, and the theoretical perspectives all pertain to a wider class of phenomena in social psychology of which police-civilian interaction is but one interesting example. This book is a study of social interaction in natural settings. Many features of police-civilian interaction found here are likely to be found in other groups who interact in the course of their everyday lives as a consequence of their social positions.

Hence, this book is also likely to be of interest to readers who have little interest in police per se. It has important implications for the extensive work in social psychology on social interaction. It is of special interest to students of communication. And it contributes to the debate about the nature of symbolic interaction.

The data on which this book is based were gathered by systematic quantitative observation and analyzed using mathematical models. A crucial element of our conception of police-civilian interaction (indeed, of all social interaction) is its dynamic character. Past research on police-civilian interaction and, for that matter, the bulk of research on social interaction, viewed interaction between people as single, discrete events. Yet it is clear that any interaction is not a discrete event, but a series of related events which unfold over time as one person speaks, another responds, the first responds to the second, and on and on. Like the mythical dragon Oroborus who lived by devouring his own tail, social interaction is a complex evolving cycle of action and reaction. Each act is both a response to the prior act by the other participant and a cue that may elicit yet another response.

To say that our focus is on process is not a denial of the importance of structure for understanding social interaction. The search for structures which are useful in understanding social interaction must not focus just on a static snapshot of the interaction process. Those snapshots, which we call states of the system at some particular time, are more useful for understanding interaction to the extent that they persist over time and influence the interaction which occurs. Nor does structure have to be found at the purely static level of states. Persistent structures that describe interaction over time may be found in forms which reoccur throughout the process. Perhaps this point is best made by considering the analog of structure and process in the physical sciences. A car moving at a constant velocity on a road, for example, is simply and concisely described by its constant velocity. That constant velocity may be thought of as a structure describing that system. Falling objects are often described by models that assume constant acceleration. That constant acceleration, although an oversimplification and technically not correct, provides a useful structure to describe falling bodies. Similarly, in social interaction, regularities may be found on any of several levels. Police-civilian interaction may be characterized by constant states, by a constant process of transition from state to state, or perhaps even by constant rate of change in that process.

We believe this process is a fundamental aspect of social interaction that must be explicitly examined in any empirical analysis. Hence, in order to do justice to this phenomenon, we found it necessary to use formal mathematical models that directly address the process of social interaction. Our work in this regard has benefited greatly from the work in three different areas. Our general conception of social interaction draws upon the concepts from general systems theory of dynamic self-regulating systems containing feedback (Bertalanffy, 1968; Ashby, 1956; Fisher, 1982). Those conceptions have been expressed more formally using Markov models. Finally, the empirical analysis assessing the fit of Markov models to the data has relied upon the use of log-linear models for examining multidimensional contingency tables. These perspectives have played a crucial role in this research, making it possible to examine the process of social interaction between police and civilians as it has never been examined before. At the risk of seeming apologetic for using these techniques, we want to stress their importance for our approach and help the reader to understand the role they play in the analysis.

Although Markov models may be intimidating at first to the reader, they are among the simplest possible models of process and provide a clear baseline against which to assess the process of interaction. Perhaps the best justification for including such formal models is their success in describing most aspects of the observed interaction as reported in Chapters 6 through 8. In Chapter 6 we have included what we hope will be an understandable description of them for readers unfamiliar with finite mathematics.

The fit of the Markov models to the data is assessed using techniques of log-linear analysis for examining multidimensional contingency tables. These techniques, which are still relatively new (Bishop, Fienberg, and Holland, 1975), provide a means for assessing the various hypotheses related to the Markov models within a single unified statistical approach. The reader unfamilar with these techniques or at least with their application to Markov models should be pleasantly surprised with the power they offer for examining process. It is now possible to examine virtually all of the major hypotheses required to assess the fit of a Markov process to data using these widely available techniques. When this research began, such an analysis required the development of costly and complex special-purpose programs with none of the convenience of log-linear models and considerably less statistical sophistication.

Because the data on which this study is based were collected by highly original techniques in actual field observations, the monograph concludes with a methodological appendix reviewing many of the innovations used and the problems encountered. The entire monograph may be more accessible to readers who read the appendix after completing this introduction. Social psychologists and methodologists as well as scholars of policing and social control should find data and ideas relevant to their specialties in the chapters that follow.

PART ONE

Perspectives and Definitions

This monograph is about police working at their main job— talking. In Chapter 1 we outline a perspective on policing quite different from that of most police scholars. We justify our perspective after a critical review of the major theoretical and empirical social scientific literature on policing. In Chapter 2 we immediately concern ourselves with the start of a typical police task, the receipt of a call from the police radio dispatcher by the squad on patrol. While this call results in a preliminary definition of the situation, we show that this preliminary definition has little effect on the initial interaction which takes place.

1

An Alternate Interpretation of Police Work

The last decade of police research was inaugurated by the publication of a small monograph that has become a classic, Egon Bittner's *The Functions of the Police in Modern Society*. Bittner had acquired extensive familiarity with police work during fourteen months of observation and published the analysis of some of his observations in two widely cited articles (1967a, 1967b). He intended to integrate not only his personal experience but the literature available at that time into a coherent interpretation of police and policing. His monograph is not an empirical study but an integration and interpretation of historical documents, prior empirical studies, legal treatises, and then current questions by both police and public. It was written at the end of a decade of turmoil during which the abuses and incompetence of much police work had been revealed each evening to millions of television viewers, and after it had become clear that police administrative techniques were woefully out of date. Not only did police sometimes perform badly, but there was also some question whether in many situations of mass disorder they could perform at all. Even the vaunted FBI had seemed to provide so little adequate domestic intelligence that President Johnson had felt it necessary to mobilize assistance from the military. At the state level the National Guard had to be called to handle many situations.

Bittner sought to reconcile his and other observations of actual policing with his understanding of the rise of the democratic state and the common assumption that police acted under the law. He argued that the modern democratic state came into existence seeking to rule "more and more on voluntary performances of the governed" (Bittner, 1970:18) and less by brute force. Although police did take actions against citizens and enforce the law, observations of police showed that much police activity, even that sought by citizens, was related, not to the law but to more informal desires of the citizenry, politicians, and the police themselves. The law was not fully enforced. It was enforced selectively. Unless a case actually came before the courts, the courts (and by implication, the law) exercised almost no authority or check over police. As often as not, law was used as a convenient resource to justify police intervention, but like many resources, it was used at the discretion of its possessor.

Seeking to reconcile the tendency of modern Western governments to rule with the consent of the governed, with a minimum of force and under law, Bittner sought, with his knowledge of police, to interpret the meaning of the police behavior he had witnessed. He concluded that despite the historical trend toward minimization of force, there always remained situations where consent was not given to the rule of law, which could only be settled by some external mechanism of coercion. The police came into existence to minimize the use of force by civilians against one another or their rulers. The police were to be almost the sole legitimate users of force. Thus Bittner's famous and oft-quoted assertion that *"the role of the police is best understood as a mechanism for the distribution of non-negotiably coercive force employed in accordance with the dictates of an intuitive grasp of situational exigencies"* (46). The phrase "intuitive grasp of situational exigencies" was used deliberately to avoid the empirically incorrect assumption that police use force only or even usually according to law. "Policemen are inevitably involved in activities that cannot be fully brought under the rule of law" (34).

Bittner fully realized that police were not the only persons who could use force. It could be used in self-defense or by such specifically authorized persons as mental-hospital attendants and prison guards (37), but only to a carefully delimited extent. Only the police authorization was essentially "unrestricted." "To say . . . that the police have a monopoly on force means that this is their unique role in society" (34). In sum, the role of police is to address all sorts of human problems when and insofar as their solutions do, or may possibly, require the use of force at the point of their occurrence (44).

If their unique role was to use force, Bittner fully recognized that this did "not entail the conclusion that the ordinary occupational routines consist of the actual exercise of this capacity" (41). "It is very likely, though we lack information on this point, that the actual use of physical coercion and restraint is rare for all policemen" (41).

In a footnote Bittner defined "non-negotiably coercive" as meaning that "when a deputized police officer decides that force is necessary, then, within the boundaries of this situation, he is not accountable to anyone, nor is he required to brook the arguments or opposition of anyone who would object to it" (41).

THE ORTHODOX VIEW OF POLICING

We believe it is fair to suggest that much of Bittner's monograph was preoccupied with the police use of force, but this would be accurate only if we add that the preoccupation was fully as much with minimizing and controlling *excessive* use of force by police as with force itself. Bittner criticized the military model of police and the image of their activities as "a war on crime"; suggested that police should become true professionals who use force only minimally and when necessary; should receive more extensive training; and should be taught interpersonal skills of negotiation that would make resort to force unnecessary (98).

We have chosen to focus on Bittner's statement, not only because it is probably the most succinct statement of what many scholars before and since have believed to be the role of the police, but also because it has been highly influential. Even though it cannot be tested empirically, there is evidence that might be used to bolster it. Thus, in his 1971 summary of his extensive data, *The Police and the Public*, Reiss found that there was "an almost 2 in 5 chance that police officers will have to restore order when they are dispatched to handle complaints from citizens, but that in most cases they do *not* do so by arrest" (73). He observed that police did not interpret most of their activities as criminal matters, that is, as matters coming under the criminal statutes. On the other hand, he reported that in handling disputes, "the police tended to rely on negotiated settlements and 'cooling out' the participants rather than using coercive authority" (76). While Reiss agrees with Bittner that police possess a virtual monopoly on the legitimate use of force, he appears to emphasize the importance of the law more than Bittner. "Fundamentally, the police mediate between the community and the legal system" (1). This description of their role is difficult to reconcile with Reiss's own finding that police view only a minority of civilian complaints as actually related to the law. On the other hand, clearly, nearly two-thirds of *citizens* believe their complaints to be law-related (73).

In March 1972 the American Bar Association (ABA) published *The Urban Police Function*. Bittner's monograph was included in the selected bibliography. The enumeration of responsibilities of police did not focus exclusively on the actual or potential use of coercion. Of the eleven current responsibilities listed (9), most might occasionally involve coercion. Like Bittner, the ABA committee emphasized that the use of force should be minimized (10) and alternate methods used (11).

In his monograph *Policing a Free Society*, published in 1977, Herman Goldstein, who had also taken a very active part in the work of the American Bar Association's Advisory Committee on the Police Function, introduced his chapter on the police function with the assertion that "the police function is incredibly complex" (21). Nevertheless, he asserted that "the most sophisticated explanation for the myriad duties assigned to police has been developed by Egon Bittner" (27). Goldstein agreed with Bittner that to understand police "it is essential to break through the confining criminal justice framework" (32), and that their activities involve "the use of varying degrees of authority and coercion" (33). Goldstein did tend to use the term "authority" (e.g., 38) rather more than "coercion" or "force". He acknowledged the difficulty implicit in use of the term because many police methods lack clear legal authorization (38).

Despite his dramaturgical perspective and his attempt to apply that perspective in all its subtlety to the social organization of policing, Manning (1977:40) accepted Bittner's definition of police agencies and of the only partial articulation between the law and policing. His later, more complete description is obviously indebted to Bittner though it goes beyond it. "Policing can be seen as (1) being a representation of coercive potential and its enactment, the application of force to everyday affairs; (2) being backed by law and conventional institutional structure in the community; and (3) reflecting the interests of those who control and define situations requiring the application of authority" (101–102). Manning emphasized the import of legitimization by the citizenry of the state which the police symbolize (105), as well as the historical differences that have affected the citizen's reaction to police in America and Britain. American police, in his view, have a more problematic "symbolic canopy of authority" (92) than English police, and therefore came to have both a more violent and legalistic dimension (89).

Jonathan Rubinstein's book, *City Police*, is widely recognized as the best ethnological description of uniformed police patrol work ever written. Because Rubinstein's approach is primarily descriptive rather than theoretical, it is difficult to compare to Bittner's work. Nonetheless, a substantial part of his book, especially the chapter entitled "Cops' Rules," deals with police use of force. Rubinstein wrote that "the policeman's principal tool is his body" (267). He continued: "Every encounter the policeman has in public, except when he is called to aid someone, must begin with an abridgement of personal freedom" (269). "The moment he accepts the responsibility of being a policeman, he assumes the risks of physical combat" (272).

Unlike Bittner, Rubinstein recognized that cops sometimes lose. While his descriptions of police behavior fully recognized the coercive nature of many police activities he modified this by emphasizing that the officer "must also learn how to establish and express his authority by cajoling, requesting, threatening, 'bullshitting them,' as patrolmen say, to avoid using force. He must learn to use his body to express with his whole self the authority represented by the appearance he presents; he must learn to use it as a weapon when the occasion demands" (274).

It is interesting that although officers must use force, they receive almost no training in how to do so (275). "They are urged to understand the difference between a man who is willing to use force and one who is eager to do so" (276). The closest statement of Rubinstein's to Bittner's is that "the police are an instrument for the manipulation of force" (333). He, like Muir, whom we shall deal with next, noted the paradox that "there are many policemen who rarely use force for the simple reason that they appear willing . . . to do almost anything to subdue resistance" (314).

William Ker Muir, Jr.'s *Police: Streetcorner Politicians* is perhaps the most stimulating discussion of policing yet written. Like philosophers of the past, Muir sought an understanding of the good, in this case, the good policeman. Like all those authors we have so far considered, he focused on coercion. In interviewing the officers of Laconia he found that "a critical incident occurred whenever a citizen enjoyed, or could have enjoyed, an initial advantage over the policeman in controlling the course of events" (59). The policeman is engaged in the "extortionate transaction," the use of coercion as "a means of controlling the conduct of others through threats to harm."

Muir perceived much more of the complexity of coercion than any other writer. First, he admitted, perhaps because of his orientation to political science, that "coercive relationships exist everywhere in every society" (37) and that they therefore do not uniquely characterize police. Second, he noted that "the reality and the subtle irony of being a policeman is that, while he may appear to be the supreme practitioner of coercion, in fact he is first and foremost its most frequent victim" (45). "It is the citizen who virtually always initiates the coercive encounter" (45). "The irony of the policeman's lot is that his reasonableness imposes terrible limits on his freedom to react successfully to the extortionate practices of others" (45). This is essentially because the police officer has more to lose than many of those with whom he deals.

Muir clearly described the pitfalls of coercion, especially four paradoxes connected with its use: dispossession, detachment, face, and irrationality. "The less one has, the less one has to lose. The less the victim cares about preserving something, the less the victimizer cares about taking it hostage. The nastier one's reputation, the less nasty one has to be. The more delirious the threatener, the more serious the threat. The more delirious the victim, the less serious the threat" (44).

Since police typically deal with the dispossessed, the detached, and the delirious, their control is continuously problematic. "The policeman is the one who is on the defensive" (45).

Muir also fully recognized that coercion is not the only form of power. There are the powers of the purse and of the word. Police may develop exchange relations with some citizens. Others are amenable to persuasion and exhortation. Often these are insufficient. The officer must use force. The good officer recognizes this; does not fret over it; does not use it unnecessarily; and views those against whom he uses it as persons much like himself. The good police officer accepts the necessity and responsibility of coercion, but sees the ultimate tragedy of many of the situations in which people find themselves. From Manning's dramaturgical perspective, or from that of Rubinstein's officers "bullshitting" citizens, one implication of Muir's analysis is that the officer may present himself as dispossessed, detached, nasty, and irrational precisely so others will be deterred from using coercion against him. His manner is his best protection against the attempts of his antagonist to coerce him.

While Muir was concerned with understanding what characterizes a good policeman, Bittner was concerned with the function of police in society. Muir's level of analysis was the individual, whereas Bittner's was society. Because of their different levels of analysis, their work is not entirely comparable. Nonetheless, there are interesting differences. Muir believed that coercion is everywhere in society; Bittner associated it uniquely with police. Muir saw police as more vulnerable to coercion because they have more to lose than many with whom they deal. Coercion from Muir's viewpoint is not straightforwardly effective. As Rubinstein noted, police do not hesitate to confess that they have been beaten (273). It may be fair to contrast Bittner's and Muir's views in the following way: for Bittner what makes police unique is their right to use coercion; for Muir, on the other hand, coercion is more a protective or defensive reaction police must use to defend themselves from citizens. For Bittner police typically use coercion offensively. For Muir and perhaps even Rubinstein, they use it defensively, or as a last resort.

Another important example of Bittner's influence is a comparative study by David Bayley (1979). Bayley goes even farther than Bittner in emphasizing the import of coercion unconstrained by law.

Subsequent to his 1970 monograph, Bittner (1974) and Rumbaut and Bittner (1979) further specified the function of police. In the latter article they stated that "in stressing the centrality of the police power to coerce provisional solutions by force Bittner does not imply that policing routinely consists of the actual exercise of coercion." "How and how often force is actually used are then *problems for the evaluation, not the definition, of police work*" (267, italics added). *We are here confronted with the real problem of this tradition of interpretation.*

The social scientific study of policing, we would agree, has disclosed "the diversity and complexity of police work, its ambiguous and problematic social context, its role conflict and contradictions" (Rumbaut and Bittner:283). We agree that the combined efforts of Skolnick (1966), Wilson (1968), Bittner (1970, 1974), Reiss (1971), Black and Reiss (1970), Manning (1977), Muir (1977), and Herman Goldstein (1977) have illuminated the paradox that police spend, relative to popular belief, little time enforcing the law and most of their time in peacekeeping and other activities. We further agree that they handle particular incidents with only half an eye to the law, and primarily in terms of the "situational exigencies" involved. The law is one "resource" they use. We agree with Bittner

(1974:235–236) that "the duty of handling nasty criminals devolves on them *because* they have the more general authority to use force *as needed* to bring about desired objectives."

OBJECTIONS TO THE ORTHODOX VIEW

Given that we do not dispute these conclusions, what do we dispute? We dispute the *definition* that has so commonly been accepted. We understand why this definition was proposed, that is, that empirical study of police in America demonstrated that their real activities were much different from merely enforcing the law. However, we do not see how merely *redefining* a word solves a problem. Quite the contrary, it creates as many problems as it solves.

This review of major social scientific monographs on police and policing published during the 1970s has, we hope, demonstrated that, with the possible exception of Rubinstein, the studies have identified the potential or actual police role with the use of force and coercion. None of these scholars *advocate* the use of force, but all admit its occasional necessity and identify the police as the mechanism of its applications.

We respect the insights of all the scholars whose work we have too briefly reviewed. Tentatively we would like to assert a different interpretation of the police role. This interpretation fully acknowledges that police use force, sometimes necessarily, sometimes unnecessarily. It also strongly affirms the view that police perform most of their activities more under the guise than the actual mandate of law. Not only do we reject the conventional view that police are primarily fighters for law and order, engaged in a "war against crime," but we strongly concur with Manning's view (1977) of the basic structural limitations on policing that make the "winning" of any such war impossible.

We believe that all of these scholars have used the terminology of sociology rather imprecisely. Specifically, they have used the terms "force" and "coercion" in vague ways that ultimately make the testing of their propositions very difficult. Thus, does the Reiss data, cited above, validate or invalidate Bittner's view? Like Goldstein, we believe that Bittner's view is very sophisticated, more sophisticated in fact than he was able to express in his brief monograph. He was also consistent in asserting his view of the police role without reference to law, that is, as exercised "in accordance with the dictates of an intuitive grasp of situational exigencies." Unfortunately, for those of us oriented to quantitative social research, the phrase is unclear. Is it fair to rephrase it? "Police use force when they feel it is necessary." This translates to, "Each police officer, given his official and unofficial training, his personality type and his previous experience will use force when he thinks it appropriate." As these various phrasings indicate, including Bittner's original one, there is no "objective" basis for justifying or condemning the use of coercion except the officer's "intuitive grasp of situational exigencies." Both Wilson (1968) and Goldstein (1977) note substantial differences between police departments and therefore, by implication, between the "intuitions" of the officers in those departments.

Recent research that has documented the wide variation by state in use of deadly force (Jacobs and Britt, 1979; Kania and Mackey, 1977) would also seem to confirm the notion that if such "intuitive" grasps exist, they are extremely variable. For one thing, they are highly correlated with the public's rate of violent personal crime. If we may interpolate, where officers deal with a violent citizenry, they will "intuitively grasp" that deadly force will be necessary over a larger number of cases than for a less violent citizenry. But how is this translated into specific situations? And, does the correlation not suggest that officer use of deadly force cannot unilaterally be minimized, since it reflects their estimate of the violence of the citizenry, that is, citizen violence must be reduced before officer violence. The definition by itself takes account of no external standard, neither law nor regulation, so who then feels able to second-guess the intuitive grasp of the officer(s)? Few juries have.

Bittner himself is entirely consistent. He sees professionalism, not law, the courts, or bureaucratic regulations, as the solution; he understands that police must, like all professionals, make complex judgments which cannot be fully justified, because they are based on cues that are often so subtle as to be beyond the conscious awareness of the professional. Some physicians are very good at making correct diagnoses but are unable to explain their ability to do so. The same is undoubtedly true of an experienced police officer making a judgment of when to use force. But, from the point of view of policy, it is not very satisfactory to tell the officer that she or he should use force when he or she thinks it appropriate. Furthermore, evidence already available (Reiss, 1971) indicates that force and excessive force are often used when the officer is insulted or his authority is questioned, if only in a verbal way, by a civilian who, if guilty of any offense, is suspected only of a petty violation, such as public drunkenness. Since these are persons against whom police can and do use force, then are these situations in which their "intuitive grasp of situational exigencies" accounted for or justified their action? As Bittner noted, "the abandonment of the norm-derivative approach to the definition of the role of the police in modern society immediately directs attention to the level of social reality that is unrelated to the ideal formulations" (6). Philosophically, since this is true, there is no basis left upon which to advocate even the minimization of violence, since violence may conceivably be the most cost-effective and "intuitive" way to handle many situations, and certainly the way involving the least effort by the individual officer.

Our main objections to this definition of the police role are (1) that presenting it as a definition makes it impossible to test empirically; (2) that it understates the use and extent of physical force by others in society; (3) that, although quite correctly including coercion as part of the police role, it *identifies* that role with potential or actual coercion. We believe the concepts of police and policing need not be defined in terms of one form of activity. We believe this for three reasons:

First, by making "how and how often force is actually used" a problem of evaluation, not a problem of the definition of police, Rumbaut and Bittner implicitly make their definition immune to criticism. Definitions are not empirically testable, nor are they considered to be either true or false, just more or less useful (Rudner, 1966:28). There is no scientific way to refute or disprove a definition. This is convenient in this case because it has permitted the definition's widespread and uncritical adoption, despite lack of evidence of its usefulness, and indeed, considerable evidence of its inadequacy. Furthermore, certain words that are part of the definition itself, especially the term "coercion," have not been carefully defined by most scholars (though Bittner himself has tried to do so).

Second, the definition underestimates the use of "situationally justified" force by others in society. We believe a dispassionate observer of everyday life in the United States might encounter some problems with this definition. Suppose the observer saw a parent spank his child. May this not be "a mechanism for the distribution of situationally justified force in society" (Bittner, 1970:39)? Suppose our observer spotted a husband slapping his wife's face, or, in the antebellum South, witnessed a master whipping his slave. May these not (historically) have been considered "a mechanism for the distribution of situationally justified force in society"?

Since the definition does *not* assume that force is used strictly according to either the law or any stated policy, suppose our observer watched a lynching in the American South during the period since the Civil War. May this not (historically) have been considered "a mechanism for the distribution of situationally justified force in society"?

Who judges whether any particular use of force is situationally justified? Force, both technically lawful and unlawful, has been widely used in all modern societies, and accepted as normal and legitimate though not used for self-defense, nor by custodial guards, nor by the police. Current attention to battered children and battered husbands and wives makes this abundantly clear.

Third, though the definition emphasizes threatened or actual coercion, there is evidence that would seem to question the usefulness of the definition. It is difficult to know why citizens obey police. There is some evidence that they are *more* apt to be cooperative when police are not overtly coercive. In a field experiment on suspicion stops, Wiley and Hudik (1974) found that citizens were more cooperative when the reason for the stop (e.g., a store in this neighborhood was robbed a few minutes ago) was explained. Such cooperation would not seem to have been based on coercion, but on officers' justifying their actions as reasonable.

Cruse and Rubin (1973) found that there was physical contact of some kind between police and citizens in 20% of the encounters observed. In 7% of these, contact consisted of shaking hands. The remaining 13% included a wide range of coercive contacts (physically restraining, handcuffing, fighting).

Reiss found that 12% of arrested citizens behaved in a violent or aggressive way (54). About half of those arrested challenged the officer's authority at least verbally. Nine percent of offenders were handled with gross force (physical coercion, threat, or handcuffs), an additional 42% experienced some physical contact (holding by the arm, prodding with night stick, etc.). Police, according to Reiss, regard resistance by suspects as routine (55). He also found that resistance by citizens was disproportionately associated with proactive policing (59). The question raised by these figures does not relate to the use of coercion in and of itself. Does not the disproportionate amount of violence in on-view activities suggest that in fact citizens *do* consider police intervention in some situations legitimate but not in others? If this is true then it suggests that police exercise *authority* in many situations both from their own and the citizens' points of view, and that in such situations cooperation is derived not from their coercive power but their authority (for a discussion of widespread acceptance of police legitimacy, see Black, 1980:169ff.).

The reason these findings are important is that they suggest a basis for much police activity other than coercion. Is it not possible that police are called to resolve the problem, not merely as coercive functionaries, but as mediators, arbitrators, or for personal support? Citizens differ in the amount of resources they possess to resolve disputes or resist victimization. When their own resources are inadequate they call for help, but by doing so, neither they nor the police assume that force will be needed. The case of the domestic quarrel in which the wife turns against the police when they lay their hands on her husband is a case in point. She did not wish her husband beaten or arrested, she wanted an additional resource, officially representing society, to help settle the dispute. Perhaps she hoped that the officers' authority, not their coercive power, would be sufficient.

Muir acknowledged that police possess other forms of power based on exchange and upon exhortation. He acknowledged that coercion and probably these other forms of power are widely distributed in society. It is part of the role of many persons in society to exercise these forms of power. Teachers threaten students with bad grades. Employers threaten employees with discharge. Priests threaten even powerful secular rulers with excommunication. Preachers threaten their congregations with Hell, Fire, and Damnation. Lovers threaten each other with loss of love. Consumers threaten businessmen with boycott. Voters threaten to withhold campaign contributions, or vote for a politician's opponent. Employees threaten employers with strikes.

Police themselves threaten the citizenry by noncoercive forms of power. They strike. They campaign against unfriendly politicians. They drive slowly or not at all to locations of complaints which they feel are too dangerous, or where citizens have criticized their service too frequently, or which have not contributed to the annual ball. Their refusal to use coercion can sometimes be a greater exercise of power than coercion itself.

Etzioni (1961) distinguished three types of compliance: alienative, utilitarian, and normative. The first resulted from the use of coercive power. The second, from the use of some good, valued in exchange. The third resulted from the acceptance of the moral authority of the power figure. Is it either empirically valid or wise from the standpoint of public policy to assume that the essence of police work is the use of coercion? We believe there is little evidence to support such an argument, at least in democratic countries, and that from a policy standpoint it holds many dangers. Not the least of these dangers is that police, accepting the definition, will seek to become more expert at its exercise, rather than at other, noncoercive means. If Rubinstein is correct, then, oddly, police now receive little training in methods of physical coercion, other than firearms training. Sailors receive little instruction in swimming. Perhaps the reason is the same. Both police and sailors hope not to use such skills.

Finally, we find this definition of less than optimal use because it may distract scholars from concentrating on how police accomplish *most* of their tasks, that is, by noncoercive means. Social scientists have consistently sought to reduce police violence by seeking to understand the motivations and situations in which violence occurs. Since Westley's (1953) pioneering article, their tendency has been to focus on the occurrence of violence (Chevigny, 1969; Toch, 1969) or on coercion as a unique function of police (Bittner, 1970:74, 79; Manning, 1977; Muir, 1977; Bayley, 1979). One comes to understand violence, not nonviolence, by studying violence. The most important question is, How do potentially violent situations get handled nonviolently? How do police get their work done without using overt coercion?

This focus on violence is analogous to the focus on arrest as a measure of police effectiveness. Both violence and arrest are often measures of police failure to handle properly a situation. A measure of a good police officer is his ability to handle a difficult situation without use of violence, and, in the case of minor violations, without arrest. Every year, every police department should give its highest award to that officer who successfully handled the most potentially violent situation in the least violent way while still accomplishing his or her goal of either peacekeeping or law enforcement. Police and policing need redefinition and coercion, rather than being given a central place in its definition, should simply be recognized as a means that *must* occasionally and regrettably be used. Police should be specialists in its use, but they should be even better specialists at mediation and arbitration. Our focus in this book will be on this less dramatic but more important aspect of police activity.

AN ALTERNATE VIEW

What then are police? What is policing? American police are community functionaries who discharge a special responsibility on a discretionary basis. They are the representatives of the state whose responsibility is to intervene proactively and reactively in a wide range of "disturbances" (see Sykes, 1977a). Routine disturbances include violations of law, custom, the peace, and public health and safety. Policing is the act of intervention and is frequently performed by others than police. Police are professional interveners. On many occasions citizens intervene on their own and the police are never called. Unfortunately, little is known about intervention by others than police, though it is known that only about half of the criminal victimizations which occur are reported to police (McDonald, 1976).

There is no "objective" basis on which to judge whether or not any particular event is a disturbance. We take the position that human beings possess the power to structure their reality both cognitively and behaviorally. Normative cognitive and behavioral orders grow out of human interaction. In any community there are a very large number of such orders. They include, but are not limited to, one for each family, neighborhood, commercial establishment, and public place. The evidence that such orderings exist is so extensive that it is impossible to review. We mention only a few for purposes of illustration. For works relative to families, public places, commercial and other establishments, see: William Foote Whyte's famous classic, *Street Corner Society* (1955) (which, incidentally, deals peripherally with the conflicts police experience mediating between two different normative orders); Eliot Liebow's *Tally's Corner* (1967); and Gerald Suttles's *The Social Order of a Slum* (1968). Many studies of formal organizations describe the normative orders of various work groups (e.g., Dalton, 1959; Roy, 1952; Little, 1964; Goffman, 1961a). Such normative orders exist not only in "straight" but in "deviant" worlds (e.g., Spradley, 1970; Wiseman, 1970; Roebuck and Harper, 1975; Polsky, 1967; Becker, 1963). Most of these normative orders are informal, but they coexist, sometimes in conflict, with many formal social orders including those of the work place, local ordinance, and state and federal rules, regulations, and laws.

Within each sphere of informal or formal order there exist mechanisms of regulation. Most orders and most control are maintained without outside intervention. Regulation is achieved not only by internalization of norms but also by all the means of power—coercion, exchange, and exhortation—which we have previously discussed.

These normative orders are often fragile, changing, incomplete, ambiguous, constantly created and maintained by negotiations between the actors involved in them. There is a range from relatively high consistency between informal and formal orders to very low consistency, at least insofar as *some* of the informal norms of some groups are concerned. Because of this inconsistency it is very hard for some groups to ask for police intervention.

We hypothesize that the resources which members of these many informal social orders possess for purposes of regulation are limited. A husband and a wife, for instance, may negotiate an order, partially based on the power of the husband, which includes occasional beating and physical abuse of the wife. The order is violated only when some threshold of injury or frequency of abuse is exceeded. The wife, even though the threshold is exceeded, has few resources of regulation to bring to bear, or, because of the superior power of the other, fears retaliation from any "extortionate transaction" in which she might engage. The same is true of "disturbances" between neighbors, landlords and tenants, businesses and customers, children or adolescents and adults, and strangers in public places. This is certainly true for both intimates and strangers; victims of criminal acts such as assault, rape, or robbery.

Persons live primarily within the security of their private orders. These orders frequently even include violence (spouse beating, child abuse, "cutting," the various forms of violence by which some young males defend their "honor" and assert their "virility"). The social order of some taverns is quite violent and of others very peaceful. The same may be said of families, neighborhoods, gangs, ethnic groups, and work groups. The practice of violence or other acts is not at issue, only whether it accords with the informal norms of the particular group.

Police intervene in disturbances for no single reason, but for many different reasons, depending upon the disturbance. Reiss (1971) and others have documented that police in almost every country in the West spend a relatively small portion of their time enforcing the law (Bayley, 1979). They are called when the social regulatory resources of members of a particular informal social order are exceeded (Black, 1980:109–192). They are called not as "enforcers" but as "reinforcers." Ordinary people confuse their private informal order with the formal legal order or, perhaps, feel that an alleged violation of the formal legal order is a better justification for requesting police intervention. Thus, a spouse might not feel comfortable calling the police because her husband "beat her more than usual." One is reminded of the police response reported by Parnas (1967): "My boyfriend is threatening to beat me up." "Well, call us again when he does." A call for police assistance requires an appropriate justification and cannot be openly premised on the violation of a private system of order.

Not all disturbances involve violations of informal or formal orders of the interpersonal kind. A traffic jam, an obstruction due to building of a highway, a natural catastrophe such as a heavy windstorm, the mechanical failure of a silent alarm, a rabid animal, or a fire may require police intervention. Some disturbances are more of the routines of everyday life (Harre and Secord, 1972) than of interpersonal normative expectations. Nonetheless, such disturbances require intervention so that the routine may be restored.

Police intervene proactively as well. They may do so for either private or public reasons. Like everyone else, police have been socialized into a multitude of private social orders. They identify their private order with ORDER. Only in time do some learn that many such orders exist, and they learn to "live and let live." In the meantime, they may proactively intervene because others do not observe their own customs. Again, they may, like many citizens, unconsciously assume an identity between their particular private idea of order and the law, or at least feel that they must justify their intervention in those terms (Scott and Lyman, 1968). On other occasions they may in fact intervene proactively because of a disturbance to the formal legal order.

Just as these many orders are usually maintained by internalization, or by the three forms of power—coercion, exchange, or exhortation—the call to police to reinforce these mechanisms is *not* a call to use any one technique. They may appeal to conscience, that is, to the internalizations of the actors. They may use rational persuasion or appeal to self-interest or the interest of others valued by the actors. They may remind actors, when they are known, of their previously negotiated agreements. They may threaten many things, ranging from refusal to come to future calls, to killing, as well as more fanciful if profane consequences. They do not come merely to coerce. They come armed with many sources of power. The means that are nonviolent are by far the most frequently used.

It follows from this perspective that for many reasons the police officer's primary task is talking. His is the responsibility to discover precisely what kind of disturbance is occurring and what the roles of the principal actors are; to appeal to conscience or to prior agreements; perhaps to negotiate a new basis of order; to mediate, arbitrate, cajole, argue, persuade, convince, suggest, order, command, and, if necessary, threaten. If none of these is effective, then he must use force. If his time or patience is limited, he may use force. Often, though, his use of force will be correlated to his inability to talk. As Rubinstein emphasized, "Most shootings occur suddenly, in moments of fear without calculation" (330).

In this book we will be exploring the process through which police intervene in disturbances. Rather than assume police are called upon to exercise coercion, we will document how they normally carry out their duties. We will study their task of talking.

2

How Defining the Situation Affects Initial Interaction

The activities of many workers tend to flow into one another. The boundary between finishing one activity and starting another is often blurred. Alternately, many spend the work day performing similar or repetitive acts. On the other hand, though most of their tasks are routine, the police perform many different activities, and the boundaries between these activities are well marked. Since most police work is reactive (Reiss, 1971), each particular activity begins when an order is received from the dispatcher over the police radio to go to a particular address for a particular reason. In some jurisdictions this reason is implied by a statute number provided by the dispatcher. In other jurisdictions, including those in this study, police used their own argot. The argot succinctly described all the typical activities in which the officers engaged.

"Car 535. DOB's, 1521 South 21st Street."

Here the dispatcher ordered the officers in car 535 to a particular address to respond to a complaint about a group of disorderly boys.

"Car 610. H&R. Possible PI. Corner of Main and Jefferson."

The dispatcher was ordering the officers in car 610 to go to a particular corner because of a hit-and-run automobile-related incident in which there was a possible personal injury.

"Car 712. Heavy domestic. Apartment on second floor of 612 2nd Ave. North."

By specifying that the domestic dispute was "heavy" the dispatcher warned the officers that it was potentially violent and dangerous.

Police encounters begin with such brief labels. An analysis of these labels showed that there were approximately eighty "typical" police activities included in their argot. Unusual or unique events were dispatched using everyday language rather than argot, or sometimes by requesting the squad to call the dispatcher by phone for a special message. The privacy of the phone call permitted discussion of the unusual.

The existence of a police argot specifying a set of activities suggests that officers "typify" the events that they experience (Schutz, 1970). Accidents, fights, disputes, homicides, or robberies become, in this sense, routine. Police activities, like the cases of the prosecutor and public defender (Sudnow, 1965) become "normal." Is it possible to discover whether the definition of these situations by the dispatcher, prior to the officers' arrival on the scene, affects how they initially react when they arrive? Are there differences in how officers subjectively perceive these situations, which could affect their initial interaction?

The very fact that police typify situations, and that most citizen complaints appear to be easily typified into the police argot, suggests that such typifications save effort and are useful. The world the police inhabit is thereby made more meaningful and predictable. On the other hand, at the instant of arrival, sometimes several minutes after receiving the original call, officers have available, even without speaking, many other kinds of data with which to interpret the situation, and perhaps modify the original definition. Are there sounds or sights of conflict? Has a group of bystanders gathered? Is the scene dark and difficult to penetrate? Does the scene appear peaceful, or is there obvious chaos and disorder? Looking, listening, and smelling may transform a typification provided by the dispatcher.

Are there any underlying dimensions or covert definitions of the situation which may affect initial interaction by officers, assuming that a typification has been provided by the dispatcher, and that it has not been changed by sensing nonverbal kinds of information at the time of arrival? If such covert definitions exist, do they result in significant differences in the interaction that takes place at the very beginning of the encounter? Is it true, as Rubinstein (1973:88) suggests, that what the dispatcher relates to him establishes the patrolman's "initial expectation and the manner of his response to the assignment?"

SEEKING DIMENSIONS OF COVERT DEFINITIONS

With data from a previous study (Sykes and Clark, 1975) of over three thousand police-civilian encounters, the nature and distribution of typifications of these activities were analyzed. The study had used a random shift sampling design. There were approximately eighty such typifications. Sixty percent of the activities were classified by dispatchers in twenty-one of these typifications, or close variations of them. These twenty-one typifications are listed in Figure 2.1.

Twenty pairs of descriptive terms were then developed based partly on characterizations of police work such as Skolnick's (1966) and partly on descriptors that might apply to the tasks involved in any job. Each item of a pair was separated from the other by an eight-interval scale, similar to the technique used in semantic differential research. Respondents were instructed to check that interval between each item of the pair which best measured their anticipation of that particular one of the twenty-one activities at the time they received an order from the dispatcher to handle such an activity. In Figure 2.2 is displayed the form that was used for all twenty-one activities.

A police department in a city of approximately 350,000 was asked to mail the twenty-two-page questionnaire (twenty-one pages for the activity-anticipation characterizations plus a small number of other questions) to a random sample of 100 (approximately one-third) of their sworn personnel. The department was very cooperative. Despite the length of the questionnaire, there was a 75% return rate of completed questionnaires. In addition, a few officers returned the questionnaire without filling it out. One officer (who completed the questionnaire) wrote a note on the back which may in fact represent

Distance at Which Cluster Forms

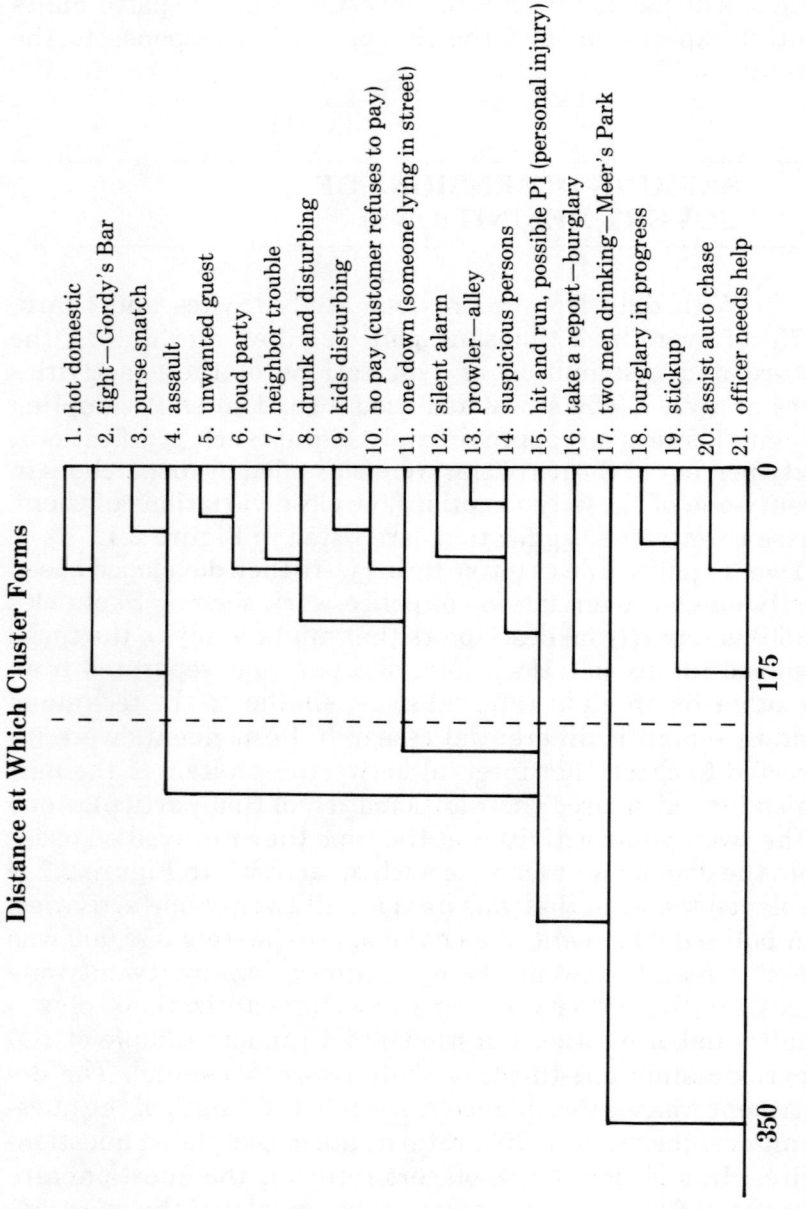

1. hot domestic
2. fight—Gordy's Bar
3. purse snatch
4. assault
5. unwanted guest
6. loud party
7. neighbor trouble
8. drunk and disturbing
9. kids disturbing
10. no pay (customer refuses to pay)
11. one down (someone lying in street)
12. silent alarm
13. prowler—alley
14. suspicious persons
15. hit and run, possible PI (personal injury)
16. take a report—burglary
17. two men drinking—Meer's Park
18. burglary in progress
19. stickup
20. assist auto chase
21. officer needs help

Figure 2.1. Dendogram of clusters of activities utilizing the complete linkage method

Defining the Situation

CALL

1. rush	1__ 2__ 3__ 4__ 5__ 6__ 7__ 8__	take it easy
2. time consuming	1__ 2__ 3__ 4__ 5__ 6__ 7__ 8__	brief
3. dangerous	1__ 2__ 3__ 4__ 5__ 6__ 7__ 8__	safe
4. controllable	1__ 2__ 3__ 4__ 5__ 6__ 7__ 8__	uncontrollable
5. pain-in-the-ass	1__ 2__ 3__ 4__ 5__ 6__ 7__ 8__	OK
6. important	1__ 2__ 3__ 4__ 5__ 6__ 7__ 8__	unimportant
7. dislike	1__ 2__ 3__ 4__ 5__ 6__ 7__ 8__	like
8. confident	1__ 2__ 3__ 4__ 5__ 6__ 7__ 8__	uncertain
9. tense	1__ 2__ 3__ 4__ 5__ 6__ 7__ 8__	relaxed
10. depressing	1__ 2__ 3__ 4__ 5__ 6__ 7__ 8__	enjoyable
11. interesting	1__ 2__ 3__ 4__ 5__ 6__ 7__ 8__	boring
12. violent	1__ 2__ 3__ 4__ 5__ 6__ 7__ 8__	peaceful
13. unusual	1__ 2__ 3__ 4__ 5__ 6__ 7__ 8__	routine
14. satisfying	1__ 2__ 3__ 4__ 5__ 6__ 7__ 8__	dissatisfying
15. initiate	1__ 2__ 3__ 4__ 5__ 6__ 7__ 8__	avoid
16. routine	1__ 2__ 3__ 4__ 5__ 6__ 7__ 8__	unpredictable
17. violation	1__ 2__ 3__ 4__ 5__ 6__ 7__ 8__	service
18. chaotic	1__ 2__ 3__ 4__ 5__ 6__ 7__ 8__	orderly
19. friendly	1__ 2__ 3__ 4__ 5__ 6__ 7__ 8__	hostile
20. take charge	1__ 2__ 3__ 4__ 5__ 6__ 7__ 8__	negotiate

Figure 2.2. **Characterization pairs for police activities**

the unexpressed opinion of many officers. "I personally don't anticipate or have any feelings about the call when it is first received. No preset plan can be laid out regarding these calls except to get there. That is my first consideration. One must approach all calls with a certain amount of caution and observation."

The data were then analyzed using both factor analysis and cluster analysis. These techniques permitted discovery of common factors among the twenty pairs of characterizations as well as the grouping of the twenty-one different types of calls that had similar loadings on the underlying factors.

Factor Analysis of the Semantic Differential Describing Calls

The twenty-item semantic differential type scale describing police expectations regarding the twenty-one calls was analyzed by computing the correlations between each of the twenty variables and then factoring the correlation

Table 2.1. Correlation matrix of the twenty characterization pairs

```
 .65
 .79  .32
-.63 -.18 -.88
-.80 -.62 -.56  .45
 .88  .77  .59 -.44 -.91
-.63 -.45 -.46  .31  .84 -.71
-.54 -.08 -.82  .82  .29 -.27  .17
 .82  .38  .98 -.89 -.62  .66 -.47 -.75
-.38 -.13 -.36  .27  .62 -.40  .84  .23 -.32
 .87  .66  .78 -.67 -.90  .91 -.77 -.45  .83 -.50
 .68  .30  .92 -.86 -.30  .47 -.24 -.78  .92 -.05  .67
 .79  .48  .86 -.84 -.69  .73 -.45 -.59  .93 -.23  .88  .85
 .80  .63  .63 -.51 -.89  .89 -.85 -.25  .70 -.62  .93  .46  .78
 .86  .53  .70 -.62 -.89  .88 -.76 -.33  .79 -.50  .93  .59  .85  .93
-.81 -.35 -.94  .87  .65 -.61  .47  .82 -.94  .37 -.78 -.86 -.86 -.63 -.74
 .58  .47  .61 -.63 -.60  .61 -.56 -.22  .68 -.34  .75  .60  .74  .73  .74 -.56
 .65  .37  .83 -.88 -.36  .45 -.16 -.71  .88  .01  .66  .93  .85  .46  .58 -.83  .63
-.55 -.13 -.88  .87  .32 -.31  .20  .82 -.87  .14 -.56 -.93 -.78 -.37 -.50  .80 -.53 -.88
 .55  .39  .28 -.23 -.76  .70 -.66  .11  .36 -.42  .63  .14  .45  .74  .77 -.31  .62  .15 -.08
```

Defining the Situation

Table 2.2. **Factor matrix of variables describing police calls***

Variable	Factor 1 "Risky"	Factor 2 "Fulfilling"	Factor 3 "Depressing"
Dangerous	**.89**	.35	−.20
Uncontrollable	**.90**	.23	−.13
Uncertain	**.88**	−.06	−.20
Violent	**.94**	.26	.10
Unpredictable	**.86**	.37	−.22
Chaotic	**.89**	.30	.21
Hostile	**.95**	.09	−.04
Time consuming	.11	**.72**	.11
OK	.24	**.84**	−.39
Important	.26	**.92**	−.11
Satisfying	.29	**.87**	−.34
Violation	.43	**.63**	−.08
Take charge	−.02	**.77**	−.23
Dislike	−.10	−.68	**.66**
Depressing	−.08	−.30	**.92**
Rush	.54	**.72**	−.14
Tense	**.87**	.45	−.12
Interesting	.51	**.81**	−.22
Unusual	**.75**	.61	.01
Initiate	.43	**.83**	−.24
Eigenvalue	12.78	3.53	1.13
Variance	63.3(%)	17.6(%)	6.6(%)
Alpha	.96	.92	.89
Total variance explained =	89.1(%)		

*Boldface indicates factors with high loadings.

matrix to identify underlying constructs that might summarize those variables. The correlation matrix for the twenty variables is presented in Table 2.1. The results of the factor analysis of that matrix are presented in Table 2.2.

Principal factor analysis with iterative estimation of communalities followed by varimax rotation to determine interpretable orthogonal factors that account for the maximum amount of variance was used (e.g., see Gorsuch, 1974). Three factors accounted for 89.1% of the variance. After rotation, the first factor accounted for 63.9% of the variance, the second 17.6%, and the third 6.6%. The internal consistency reliabilities of the factors are .96, .92, and .89, respectively, based on the alpha coefficient of internal consistency reliability. Thus, the items in each factor provide rather consistent measures of the same underlying construct within each factor. The first factor dominates the expectations of officers. A single factor might have sufficed since it accounts for so much of the common variance and is so much stronger than the second and third factors. That decision would have been reinforced by a separate smallest-space analysis which we performed. That analysis found that a one-dimensional representation could perfectly replicate the ordinal relationships among these variables.

We elected to retain the second and third factors, because they do account for some additional variance, and because they are helpful in interpreting the differences between specific calls when we distinguish clusters of similar calls in a later section.

By examining the items that have high loadings on each factor, it is possible to "interpret" the factors and provide labels for the covert dimension measured by the pairs. The first factor, which accounts for most of the variance, clearly is a measure of the risk involved in each call, with high scores indicating activities which may endanger the officers' life or limb and low scores indicating very safe activities. It is not insignificant that this element of risk is by far the most important component of the officers' expectations regarding calls. This indicates that at least psychologically the danger and risk involved in police work dominate officers' expectations regarding specific encounters and may have an important effect upon their behavior. Factor two measures the extent to which particular calls provide fulfillment for the officers. High scores are indicative of activities that they find fulfilling, satisfying, and important. Factor three measures the affect the officer feels toward the activity, especially, the extent to which the officer likes or dislikes it. High scores on this variable indicate activities which are depressing and disliked.

Clustering of Calls

To determine whether there were distinguishable clusters of calls around which similar expectations were or-

Defining the Situation 39

ganized by officers, the twenty-one calls were clustered using NT-SYS, the numerical taxonomy system developed by Rohlf, Kishpaugh, and Kirk (1972). The clustering analysis was performed on a matrix of average Euclidean distances between each of the calls (see Table 2.3). Distances rather than correlations were used because differences in the mean values of the variables should be considered as well as differences in the shape of the profiles of these variables (Cronbach, Gleser, and Rajaratnam, 1972).

Three different cluster analyses were performed: single linkage, complete linkage, and the weighted pair group method using arithmetic averages. These methods differ in the criteria used for deciding which activities constitute a single cluster: the closest distance between two points in the separate groups (single linkage), the farthest distance between two points in the separate groups (complete linkage), or the weighted arithmetic mean of distances between points in the separate groups (weighted pair group method using arithmetic averages). One or the other of these techniques may be more appropriate than the others for a particular set of data, depending upon the data and the particular way the calls relate to one another. Each method creates a separate clustering tree or "dendogram," which summarizes the clusters (Sokal and Sneath, 1963). The cophenetic correlation between the clustering tree created by each of these methods and the original distance matrix was used as the criterion to judge the adequacy of each method and was the basis for selecting the reported result. The cophenetic correlations were .750 for the complete linkage method, .719 for the single linkage method, and .624 for the weighted average method. Hence, the complete linkage method results were chosen for interpretation because they most accurately represent the distances observed in the original data. The dendogram obtained through the complete linkage method is presented in Figure 2.1.

The dendogram or clustering tree displays the levels at which different calls would be joined to form clusters. On the right of the diagram each call is a separate cluster. As you move to the left, various calls join at different points to form new clusters. On the far left every call has joined to form one

Table 2.3. **Euclidean distances between each of twenty-one calls**

118																			
121	103																		
160	146	95																	
148	194	129	145																
211	130	146	127	233															
68	136	125	168	116	226														
180	80	156	175	243	112	191													
78	68	121	146	187	156	119	121												
107	40	110	141	186	130	125	82	55											
144	53	121	139	212	102	161	54	82	47										
135	68	96	108	197	96	160	92	84	71	54									
152	219	174	197	86	279	104	266	205	205	237	232								
178	256	209	226	116	317	139	308	238	246	277	265	67							
95	196	62	97	106	158	88	155	105	95	117	104	134	173						
112	103	53	05	108	148	107	157	114	101	121	105	149	184	37					
112	126	88	82	107	155	103	162	117	112	128	114	149	177	49	68				
150	216	156	168	53	239	114	254	199	202	231	217	58	81	120	132	119			
81	67	93	122	160	148	99	114	58	54	75	71	179	213	66	83	84	171		
142	84	123	125	199	103	158	76	90	65	50	63	225	265	108	110	106	214	72	
92	139	109	114	96	186	80	183	118	121	147	135	118	149	58	80	49	95	87	128

Defining the Situation

single cluster. The interpretive task is to decide at which point the activities most alike form clusters. We also wish to avoid joining together activities that are significantly unlike one another.

The level of separation into clusters we have chosen is displayed in Figure 2.1 by the single vertical dotted line. Clusters to the right of that line are reasonable combinations of like elements. Clusters formed to the left of that line are combinations of different elements and hence are ignored.

We find five different clusters of activities. Merely on the basis of intuitive examination there appears to be some face validity to the clusters formed. The calls falling into each cluster appear to be more like one another than calls falling in other clusters.

To obtain a more informed understanding of what the expectations are for each of these calls we examined the mean scores for each of these five clusters on each of the three factors identified earlier. Those mean scores are reported in Figure 2.3 below.

On the basis of these factor score profiles for each cluster, we have given each of the clusters summary names that designate the expectations which appear to characterize the calls within each cluster. Cluster one consists of "hazardous" calls, those for which there is considerable risk and danger, which are not very satisfying and disliked. Cluster two consists of "annoying" calls which though generally not hazardous are unfulfilling and depressing. Cluster three consists of activities which though safe and uneventful are recognized as necessary and important and hence are regarded as fulfilling. Such calls, though not exciting, appear to be regarded as justified activities that the police should undertake. Cluster four consists of very boring and safe activities, not regarded as rewarding but also not regarded as particularly depressing. One of these activities, report taking, is among the most frequent of police activities. Cluster five consists of the most dramatic calls; calls that officers regard as dangerous but also fulfilling and enjoyable. These calls reflect both officers' and many civilians' opinions of what "real" police work is (or ought to be) all about.

Factor Score Profile

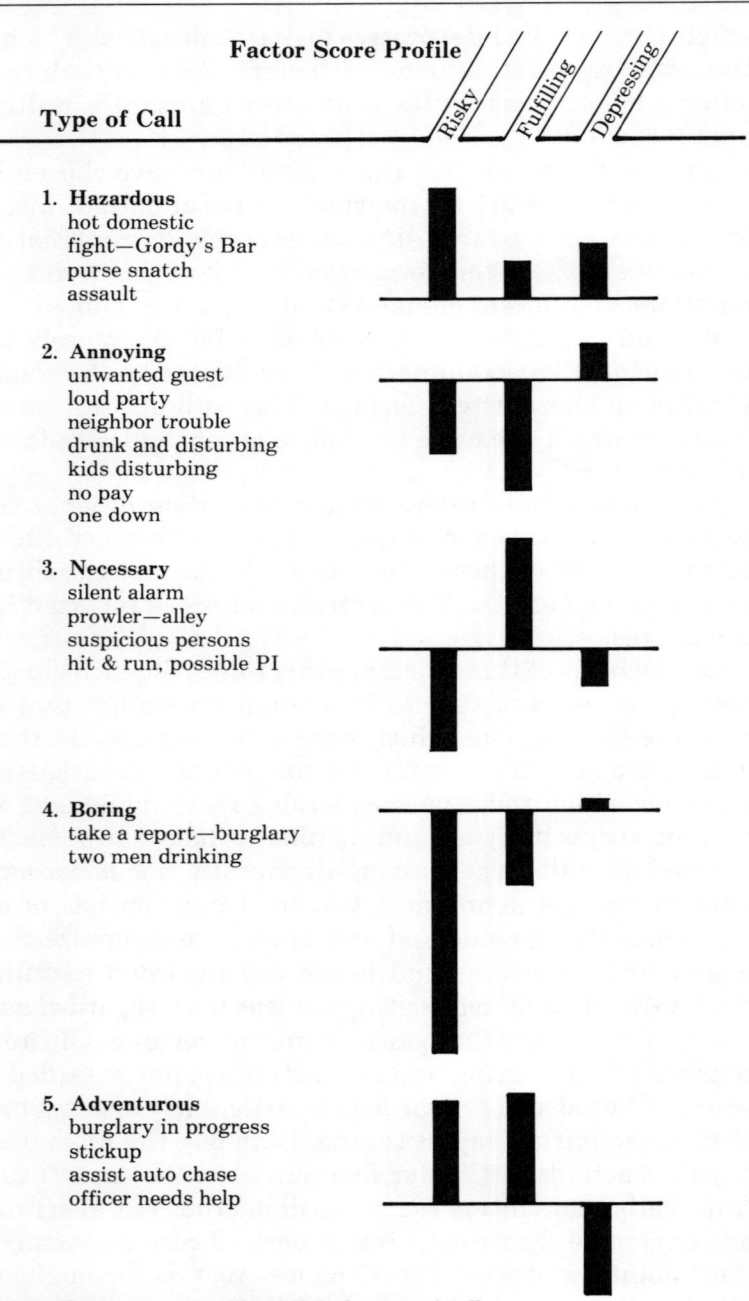

Type of Call — Risky / Fulfilling / Depressing

1. **Hazardous**
   hot domestic
   fight—Gordy's Bar
   purse snatch
   assault

2. **Annoying**
   unwanted guest
   loud party
   neighbor trouble
   drunk and disturbing
   kids disturbing
   no pay
   one down

3. **Necessary**
   silent alarm
   prowler—alley
   suspicious persons
   hit & run, possible PI

4. **Boring**
   take a report—burglary
   two men drinking

5. **Adventurous**
   burglary in progress
   stickup
   assist auto chase
   officer needs help

Figure 2.3. **Factor score profile of five clusters of calls**

Defining the Situation

As a further check on the validity of the clusters found by this method, and as a further aid for interpreting the clusters, a Wrowclaw diagram was created (Sneath and Sokal, 1973), which combines the results of this clustering procedure with the results of a smallest-space analysis of these same data. The Wrowclaw diagram is displayed in Figure 2.4. Smallest-space analysis is a nonmetric multidimensional scaling procedure that attempts to construct a diagram in the smallest dimensional space possible in which particular units (in this case, the calls) are represented by points in some n-dimensional figure, and the distances between those points in that space reproduce the ordinal relationships in the original data matrix. The smallest-space program (in this case the MINISSA program, see Lingoes, 1973) constructs solutions for a range of dimensions, and then those solutions are compared using a stress measure that is a measure of the extent to which the derived configuration differs from the original data matrix. The higher the stress, the poorer the fit. The stress values for this analysis were .18, .05, .03, and .01 for one-, two-, three-, and four-dimensional solutions, respectively. We present here the two-dimensional solution because it has a reasonably low stress value, indicating it is a fairly accurate fit to the data. Reductions in stress through three- and four-dimensional solutions are minor and do not justify the additional complexity involved.

The configuration of points in the figure was provided by the smallest-space analysis program. Superimposed upon that configuration are isolines representing the levels at which various calls unite to form a single cluster. The effect is analogous to a topological map on which lines indicate successive clusters rather than changes in elevation. By examining the levels at which different items cluster and by noting their relative positions in the space we can see that the clusters formed by this technique correspond well with those derived from the completely independent and different smallest-space analysis. The congruence of findings by these distinct techniques provides evidence that the results are not artifacts of individual techniques but are reasonably accurate represen-

44   *Perspectives and Definitions*

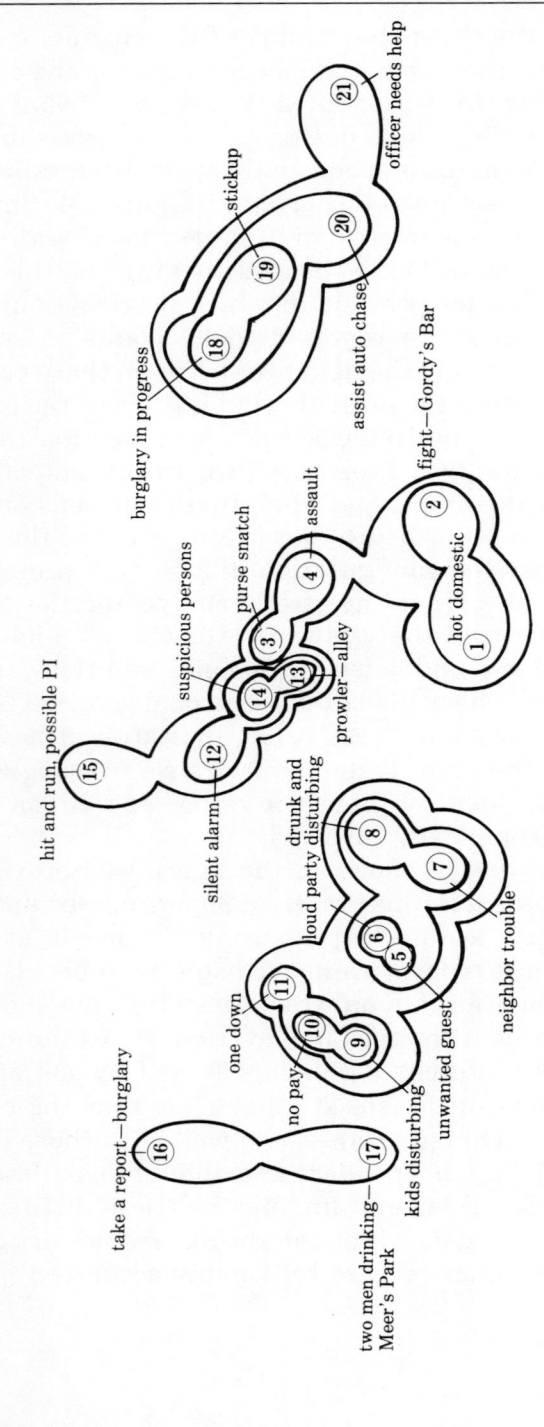

Figure 2.4. **A Wroclow diagram of the five clusters of activities**

tations of the common expectations for different groups of activities.

COVERT DEFINITIONS AND INITIAL INTERACTION

In order to test whether these expectations affected interaction, three samples of encounters were examined: twenty-one hazardous but not satisfying and disliked calls; or dramatic, dangerous, satisfying, and liked calls; eighteen "annoying" calls; and eighteen safe and boring calls. It was necessary to combine the two types of dangerous calls, because several types of dangerous calls possess little interaction or are normally special cases of interaction. High-speed chases, or assisting in such chases, are probably the most frequent dangerous work officers do. In most cases, little interaction results, especially on assists, because either the speeding car is not spotted, or because the officers arrive after it has been stopped. Similarly, when an "officer needs help" call is received, many cars respond and the car containing the observer is unlikely to be the first there. Officers sometimes consider "silent alarms" dangerous, but most are false alarms, no civilians are present, and though side arms and shotguns are routinely carried at the ready, no interaction takes place. These twenty-one calls were chosen because they were contained in the two clusters from which officers expected danger, and because circumstances of these calls permitted the analysis of the interaction. There were many encounters in the other two clusters, and each of the eighteen was chosen on essentially a convenience sampling basis.

When officers are ordered to perform a specific activity by the dispatcher, the only information they have is that provided by the dispatcher and through their own senses at time of arrival. After they arrive, they collect information by means of which they may confirm the dispatcher's original definition, or discover whether the activity is, in fact, dangerous, satisfying, or likeable. Observers riding with the officers entered a code at that time in the encounter when the original definition of the dispatcher was confirmed, or when information or other circumstances required its redefinition. The interaction examined here is limited to that which occurred before this "confirm definition" or "redefinition" code was entered.

First we tested whether there were significant differences between the three types of encounters in the time at which confirmation or redefinition took place. Although the dangerous and boring encounters were significantly longer than the "annoying" encounters, there were no significant differences in the average time at which confirmation or redefinition took place.

We then examined both the distribution of initial sets of utterances that characterized each of the three types, as well as the aggregated totals of sets of utterances that occured before confirmation or redefinition.

We found little difference in the distribution of initial acts by type of encounter. There was a significant difference between first, second, third, and fourth acts over all the encounters, but there was almost no difference between *types* of encounters. Dangerous, annoying, and boring calls all tended to begin with significantly greater amounts of information seeking and imperative supervision, followed by accusations. Suggestions or threats tended to occur several steps into the encounter, not at the beginning.

On the other hand, examining the total aggregated frequencies of acts taking place before confirmation or redefinition, there were significant differences. During the early stages of dangerous calls, but not at the very beginning, significantly less information was sought. Fifteen percent less information was sought than in annoying calls and nearly 40% less than in the safe and boring calls. Conversely, four times as many orders were given in dangerous as in other types of calls, and there were more accusations of civilians' violating proper role expectations. Hostility was also more common as was noncooperation.

These data were puzzling. There was little difference between the three types during the initial acts of the encounter, but a substantial difference in the aggregated types of acts before confirmation or redefinition. These results were apparently contradictory. What could account for the difference?

We asked: Could there be circumstances associated with the dangerous calls that were visible to the officers and affected the interaction, though not necessarily initially, which accounted for the aggregated differences? One obvious difference is the complexity of the role structure of the encounters. They differed not only in number of persons present, but also in types of persons, whether only violators, or violators and complainants, or violators, complainants, and other participants.

We tested whether time of confirmation or redefinition as well as total length of the encounter differed by complexity of role structure. There were substantial significant differences. The more complex the role structure, the longer it took to confirm or redefine the situation, and the longer the encounters themselves lasted. This was especially true of both the dangerous and the boring encounters. The variable mediating between initial definition and interaction was complexity of role structure, something about which officers could have had no knowledge until they arrived. Imperative supervision and regulation, hostility, accusations of violations of role expectations and norms of civility, as well as noncooperation occurred in only those encounters defined ahead of time as dangerous where, officers discovered *after* they arrived, the violators and complainants or other participants were present. The original definition by the dispatcher, for example, "Domestic," might or might not change, but the interaction depended upon the complexity of the role structure discovered at the scene, not the original definition.

During such encounters with suspects and complainants both present, disagreement and disorder occur among civilians. Their number makes effective officer supervision problematic. Disagreement among them makes it more difficult for the officer to define the situation quickly, as he must listen to different accounts. The evolving situation under these circumstances accounts for the differences in the officers' behaviors.

These data are small convenience samples of four of the five types of activities, the dangerous activities combined into one group. Our conclusions for this reason are only tentative, but we believe they support the conclusion that prior definitions of the situation have little effect on initial police behavior. As the officer respondent wrote, "No preset plan can be laid out regarding these calls except to get there." Officer behavior is a response to the actual processes occurring in the situation after he gets there, not a function of prior subjective expectations or definitions of the situations. Officers assert their own definitions of the situation rather than uncritically accepting that of a complainant or dispatcher.

PART TWO

The Volatile Working Group

Police perform their duties in a special kind of working group, one which includes not only officers, but civilians occupying various positions. In working in such groups police are similar to the members of a number of other occupations and professions. Such groups we term volatile *working groups. Police are the supervisors of such groups. We show how officers typically supervise; how they get the main tasks of their groups done through solving certain recurring problems; and what scripts they use in "doing their talk" in routine situations.*

3

The Volatile Working Group and Its Supervision

Everett C. Hughes in *Men and Their Work* (1958) reminds us that "in many occupations there is some category of persons with whom people at work come into crucial contact." Often, he comments, these are other than fellow workers. "Most kinds of work," he writes, "bring people together in definable roles: thus the janitor and the tenant, the doctor and the patient, the teacher and the pupil, the worker and his foreman, the prison guard and the prisoner, the musician and his listener" (53). Hughes might have added: the police officer and the civilian. Officers work with civilians more than with other officers.

The relations between many of these positions have been carefully studied (e.g., doctors and patients; officers and civilians), but these groups have not been identified as special in themselves. They differ from many groups that consist entirely of full-time workers. Such groups always consist of one or more persons who carry on the work full-time, but who must do their work with the active cooperation and participation of "amateurs." These amateurs are necessary for, and actively participate in, the activities of the group. Among such groups are doctors, dentists, or nurses and their patients; lawyers and their clients; other groups such as those mentioned by Hughes; and police and the assortment of complainants, informants, victims, witnesses, onlookers, and suspects with whom they do their daily work.

INTEGRAL AND SITUATED POSITIONS

In such groups we distinguish two types of positions: integral and situated. An integral position is one that an actor occupies for a substantial period of his life, and which he internalizes sufficiently that it becomes part of his self- and other-perceived identity. Occupational and gender positions are integral positions. Situated identities are those perceived by self and other that result from temporary occupancy of a position, sometimes involuntarily, in which the individual finds himself because of a particular set of circumstances or situational contingencies (this usage is different from Goffman's [1961b]). It is not a position that an actor is normally expected to internalize as an important part of his identity. It may also be a position that, because it is relatively temporary, has less specific norms or one, at least, in which the actor has little experience. Situated positions may therefore display greater variation in role behavior, and their incumbents be less predictable.

In this study one integral position is the focus of interest: police officer. Other integral positions including gender, ethnicity, and age will be occasional focuses of study.

Two situated positions will be focuses of interest: alleged violator and complainant (sometimes, victim). There are "professional" violators, although routine police work involves few of them. Civilians temporarily occupy the position because they have been caught speeding, or because they have irked a tavernkeeper or their neighbor. They are seldom happy to be cast in such a position, are relieved to escape it, and certainly do not seek to make it an integral part of their identity (though there are no doubt a few exceptions, e.g., the members of violent gangs). There are even fewer professional victims or complainants, though a small number do get a reputation among police for continuously calling on their services. Nonetheless, while these positions are clearly situated positions, they have a status in the law and in the public mind as well as in the occupational culture of police that makes them clearly recognizable.

In this study we will be concerned with the integral or situated role behaviors of the positions of police officer, alleged violator, and complainant. We will not be concerned with individual differences or personal identities. Our study possesses a sociological, social-psychological emphasis.

An officer and a complainant, or an officer interacting with a person in some other situationally relevant identity, constitute a *working group*. Sometimes we will consider it to be a problem-solving working group. The entire duration during which the members of this working group are engaged in their task will be termed an *encounter* (Goffman, 1961b).

Is it a mistake to consider a police officer giving a ticket to an alleged speeder as a working group? Many integral occupational positions regularly interact with situated positions to carry out their work. The situated position may be the object of work, the occasion for work, the partner in work, or even the source of income from work. Doctors have no work without patients. Clerks need customers. Clergy have none without believers. Lawyers cannot pursue their profession without clients. Similarly, police work would be nothing without complainants, victims, suspects, and alleged violators.

Each of these working groups embraces an integral and a situated identity. In each case the integral identity is superordinate to the situated identity within the working relationship. In each case the situated identity must participate with the integral identity in the task as object, occasion, and partner. Let us term such a group a *volatile working group*. This term seems appropriate because it simultaneously connotes transience, changeability, and the possibility of danger. There is a certain instability that may at any time lead to crisis.

A dentist filling a tooth is working. Is his patient? Few people go to the dentist for recreation. Most who go do so voluntarily, but their volition is strongly related to preventing a future problem or solving a present one. They are active partners in the dentist's work at the same time they are the object and occasion for it and his source of income.

Is a student listening to a lecture and taking notes working? To be a teacher, one must have at least one student. The student is the occasion for teaching. But the complement of teaching is learning. Learning cannot occur unless the student is the active partner of the teacher. This is true even if the course is required and the student is present involuntarily.

Most police work occurs in response to civilian complaints. A person finds that during his absence his home has been burglarized. He calls the police department, which dispatches a patrol officer to take a report. The officer cannot do his job without the complainant. The complainant must actively cooperate in providing information about what was stolen, how entry was gained, and who are possible suspects. Both must "work at" the job of creating a burglary report.

Insufficient attention has been given by sociologists of work to working groups consisting of mixed positions—integral and situated. Instead, sociologists of work have focused on work groups such as those in factories in which all members are full-time employees. Sociologists of occupations and professions have concentrated on individual integral positions, such as that of lawyer, without attending to the group in which the work is situated, or acknowledging the import of persons in situated positions as workers.

If interaction is work-related, then a task must be done. The actors focus their activities on their tasks. This delimits both their activities and their talk. While their conversation may turn to unofficial topics of interest, this diversion is limited by the intimacy of the relation. Fellow workers who are also good friends may chat about many nonwork-related matters, but the relationship between workers, in and of itself, does not demand or even allow broad trespass beyond the work relation. Topics of discussion will tend to remain within the work-relevant domain. This is especially likely if they are strangers.

This limit is accentuated if the relationship is between superordinates and subordinates. The hierarchical nature of the relation lengthens the social distance and limits the breadth of permissible topics. The structural patterns of interaction in such a case are different from those between peers. Superordinates are free to command and to question in a way that subordinates are not. Their right is complemented by the subordinates' obligations to answer or obey. Superordinates have a right to be imperious, uncivil, disagreeable, and abrupt, which subordinates do not. Not that superordinates *should* be ill-mannered, but their station permits them such a privilege. They possess more freedom to be expressively negative interpersonally.

Interaction is influenced not only by its work-related focus and the relationship between the interactants but also by the degree of uncertainty under which it occurs. If both superordinate and subordinate have frequently worked together at a familiar task, then they will not need to exchange much information. If the work is routine the need for work-related interaction is minimized. When the actors confront an uncertain situation they will need to collect and evaluate more information. Then the formally superordinate will express his decisions through explicit guidance, suggestions, and commands directed to the subordinate.

The situation of the actors is like that of the problem-solving groups studied by Bales and Strodtbeck (1951), except that the actors' relations are formal, not informal. The process of leadership development is attenuated. There is a process of problem solving, but it does not invoke to the same extent as in informal groups the development of either a leadership or status structure. Instead of leadership *developing* it is *asserted* by those in integral positions.

It is asserted through its exercise. It is exercised through communications that define for all the actors what is work-related, and by the giving of suggestions and orders, sometimes imperiously. It may also be exercised by explicitly defining and controlling the relationships between the superordinate and subordinate. *Initiation* of all these behaviors may be considered an assertion of formal leadership by the integral role in any working group and may be expected to increase in frequency in groups working under conditions of uncertainty.

Police-civilian encounters have the characteristics of volatile working groups: an integral and situated position, a brief existence, a superordinate-subordinate relation, and a situation that is uncertain. Many are situations which are not routine, at least from the point of view of the situated identity, and which may become routine, but are initially problematic from the point of view of the integral identity. Working occurs during single sessions, and seldom lasts an extended duration with any one particular person incumbent in a situated identity, although sometimes a series of sessions is necessary to complete the work.

Volatile working groups, compared to normal work groups, possess somewhat different characteristics. The integral-position incumbent socializes the neophyte-position incumbents into their roles. This gives an advantage to the veteran who imposes norms on the subordinate. This advantage of the incumbent is due both to higher situationally specific status (Sykes and Clark, 1975) and greater experience.

Efficiency demands quick socialization. The situated-position incumbent often occupies the position briefly or intermittently. Socialization is directive, not only because of the superordinate-subordinate relationship, but also because of the constraints of time. It is obvious that children begin their socialization into the legal system while still very young (Tapp and Levine, 1977); it is just as necessary for those in situated positions as for any neophyte worker.

A police-civilian encounter is the "externalization" of a volatile working group. The superordinate position in such a group socializes the subordinate, situated-position incumbent efficiently and quickly. There is little time for norms to emerge other than those imposed by the person in the integral position. We suggest that the study of police-civilian encounters is an opportunity to initiate the scientific study of volatile working groups.

Clearly, the integral position, the police officer, is the most crucial in the group. This position is one of authority and its incumbent should manifest leadership.

SUPERVISING A VOLATILE WORKING GROUP

In the police literature, the police officer's role as supervisor of a volatile working group has never been recognized. Writers on police, and the police themselves, have emphasized the importance of civilians' recognizing police authority and of "taking charge" in their contacts with civilians. This objective has never been examined in a comparative perspective of other volatile working groups and their supervision. "Authority" and "taking charge" have been treated as unique challenges to police. Are they any less a challenge to an emergency-room nurse, a surgeon, a paramedic, or a lawyer trying to persuade his client to "cop a plea"?

Since encounters have not been conceived of as working groups, little attention has been given to officers as task leaders (though it is possible that sometimes socio-emotional leadership is more needed, and its lack is a chronic source of civilian dissatisfaction), and equally little attention has been given to the specific tasks that officers and civilians together must accomplish.

In this chapter we focus on the police officer as a supervisor, on the tasks his working group must accomplish, and on the exact techniques of supervision that officers use. We have hypothesized that police exercise legitimate authority. That they do so is implied by their perception of a problem whenever it is questioned. Muir (1977) noted that officers he interviewed felt "a critical incident occurred whenever a citizen enjoyed, or could have enjoyed, an initial advantage over the policeman in controlling the course of events." Police expect most civilians to accord them supervisory authority. Civilians display, in Etzioni's terms, calculative and moral involvement with officers, just as they do with many other professionals and bureaucratic functionaries (1961).

Some important questions require answers: How do police supervise the volatile working groups of which they are task leaders? They are taught to "take charge" when interacting, but how do they do this? How do they impart the norms of the police-civilian volatile working group and socialize their workers quickly and efficiently? If their authority is defied by civilians, then what do officers do? In a similar situation, a public or private functionary might threaten to fire the worker or, in extreme cases, even call the police; the police themselves can do neither.

We shall seek to answer these questions from the perspective of general systems theory. Systems theorists have long distinguished between "control" and "regulation." Sociologists have often ignored this distinction, commonly designating as "social control" what we will term regulation. Regulation is possible only after acts of control have taken place (see Sykes, 1977a).

By "control" we mean a decision whereby those involved in any system, in this case, the volatile working group, decide what will be the goals, purposes, ends, or even rules of process of the system. Included are norms that persons believe are necessary to the success and survival of the system. These are the tasks that the working group must accomplish. Control is analogous to policy making.

"Supervision" consists of acts directing the group toward task accomplishment. Supervision is the implementation of policy. "Regulation" consists of acts dealing with disturbances to task accomplishment. The same acts may be supervisory or regulative, depending on where in the process of interaction they occur. Supervisory acts occur before disturbances; regulatory acts, after.

Because the set of tasks that volatile working-group members must achieve is complex, participants, especially those in situated positions in the system, seldom give their attention to any but a small segment of them at any one time, and generally think in terms of a highly simplified model of the system (see, for instance, March and Simon, 1958:169–170). We shall term the entire set of tasks (goals, purposes, ends, rules, and norms) that the supervisor believes necessary to achieve "essential states."

While the actors have tasks to accomplish, their accomplishment is problematic. Changes in the external environment interfere as do deviant or noncooperative acts by those in the work group itself. Any act that frustrates the realization of the essential states of a system we shall term a "disturbance." We use the term much more abstractly than do police, who usually limit its meaning to relatively minor events that destroy the public peace (e.g., loud parties, unpredictable juveniles, minor fights).

A "regulatory" act is any act that is intended to prevent a disturbance from interfering with task realization. "Interfere"

The Group and Its Supervision

means to block their accomplishment, or, in a case where the task is in the process of being accomplished or is already accomplished, to frustrate the process or undo the work already done. The fact of regulation implies that there is some limited set of tasks (essential states) and that the actors seek to achieve them and assure that their achievement is not neutralized.

A very simple regulatory process (taken from Ashby, 1956: 202) is displayed in Figure 3.1. If the actors have already completed an essential task, b, and if, for instance, D(isturbance) 1 occurs, threatening their accomplishment, then R(egulatory) response α is necessary.

Figure 3.1. Schematic of a simple regulatory process

		R		
		α	β	γ
	1	b	a	c
D	2	a	c	b
	3	c	b	a

From the perspectives of both officers and civilians, an encounter may be considered a system. Each interact of a position is both output from and input into a component of the system. Since the encounter is a working group, it has tasks to achieve. Since police possess legitimate authority, and since police-civilian interaction is normatively constrained (see, for instance, Sykes and Clark, 1975), the system possesses essential states subject to both disturbance and regulation.

The Four Essential Tasks

We suggest that officers must accomplish four tasks in every police-civilian encounter. Each of the first three must be accomplished at the start of the encounter if it has not already been accomplished and must remain accomplished throughout the encounter. Realization of the fourth task is contingent upon realization of the first three. Most officers seek these essential states in the midst of interaction itself. Both formal training and customs of police, as well as civilian expectations dictate their import.

First, officers must seek information. Unless they can collect information, they cannot define the situation or the situational identities of the civilians. This is especially true in radio dispatched activities where officers approach the scene with a minimal amount of information, and during on-scene stops for suspicion.

Second, they must attend to the overt behavior of the civilians who are in their presence. Officers insist upon behavioral order. At accident scenes this may merely involve keeping bystanders back. In ordinary encounters it sometimes involves keeping interactional order, e.g., turn taking in conversation. In a domestic dispute it may mean preventing a couple from continuing a battle.

Third, officers must be treated by civilians in a respectful manner, otherwise their supervisory status is threatened. Van Maanan (1978), for instance, speaks of "the attitude test" and Sykes and Clark (1975) of an asymmetrical deference norm. Virtually all effective supervisors have the respect of those they supervise.

Fourth, officers must achieve that outcome or resolution to the encounter which they feel is appropriate. Information, order, respect, and resolution are the essential tasks an officer must achieve in every encounter.

THREE TYPES OF REGULATION
USED TO GET THE JOB DONE

At least since the time of Westley's well-known work (1970), scholars have been fascinated with the violent side of police activities. There is a paradox in this concern, since there is virtually unanimous agreement among scholars that the actual use of unnecessary or brutal force is infrequent (in fact, Westley himself estimated it at only once or twice a year, 1970:136). There is an empirical problem in responding to Muir's book because of his preoccupation with what he terms

The Group and Its Supervision 61

the "extortionate transaction," ultimately based on the threat or actual use of coercion by police to do their jobs. Since no authority estimates that violence occurs in more than a very small percentage of encounters, it would seem inappropriate to focus primarily on coercion in conceptualizing the processes of supervision or regulation. Rubinstein's comment that police must be good at "cajoling, requesting, threatening, bullshitting" civilians seems to get more to the heart of the matter, but not precisely enough.

Supervision is even more subtle than Rubinstein suggests. It is subtle because in most situations the officer initially enacts his role as supervisor and regulates disturbances to the four essential tasks indirectly, almost unconsciously, without any overt show of authority. His weapon is neither a gun nor a club, but rather a technique almost Socratic. The officer takes charge in most encounters by merely asking a question. In asking a question, the officer not only immediately starts to accomplish one essential task, but also focuses the attention of the civilian on the task at hand. By use of the question the officer assumes cognitive regulation, or what we shall term "definitional regulation" or "definitional supervision" over the situation. It is difficult not to answer a question. Even a refusal is often an acknowledgment of a particular cognitive domain and focuses the civilian's attention on that question rather than some other. By paying attention to the question, the civilian inevitably ends by committing himself to the cognitive domain that the officer asserts by merely asking it.

But definitional supervision is not limited to questions. Questions involve both officer and civilian in defining a situation. In some kinds of encounters, not just situations but identities are at stake. Is the suspect an actual violator? Definitional supervision includes the imposition of situational identities, the most salient of which is that of alleged violator. The accusation is the second form of definitional supervision. When the officer informs the driver that he was clocked at 40 mph he is defining him as a violator, and forcing him to respond to that definition. An accused finds it as difficult not to respond to an accusation as to a question.

We suggest then that the most common form of supervision

which police exercise over the interaction process is almost literally "thought control" exercised by information search. By asking questions and making accusations, often in a very subtle and civil manner, they compel civilians to attend the cognitive domain of primary interest to the officer and participate in the task of seeking information. This is completely the opposite from something like nondirective psychotherapy, in which the therapist generally does not direct the stream of consciousness of his client, except to aid the client to clarify his own ideas and feelings. Policemen have agendas; psychiatrists often do not.

Officers probably do not consciously recognize the potency of the question and the accusation as means of taking charge. If a civilian's thoughts can be focused on one cognitive domain, then it is difficult for him to think about or do something else at the same time (Jaffe, 1978). Once he is committed to responding to the officer's questions or accusations, it is difficult to maintain another commitment fully. A couple in a domestic dispute may be diverted from their dispute by having to answer questions. They must focus on the topic of the officer's question, not on some other topic that they might prefer.

The functions of a question may be twofold. Normally it simply focuses on a cognitive domain of interest to the officer and altercasts the civilian in the role of respondent (Weinstein and Deutschberger, 1963). Sometimes it has an additional function: diversion. The question diverts the civilian's attention away from one thing and focuses it on another. Sometimes a long series of the "right kind" of questions may have a "cooling out" function.

Questions and accusations define a cognitive domain, and they have behavioral relevance, but only to the extent that they may weaken the respondent's commitment to some course of behavior because of the difficulty of simultaneously pursuing both. Sometimes officers address behavior directly, most usually by a command or order, or by a nonviolent threat (e.g., "Do this or arrest!"). This we term "imperative regulation" or "imperative supervision." An officer utilizes imperative supervision when he directs traffic; tells a group of complainants all talking at once to keep quiet and take turns; orders a fleeing suspect to stop; commands a civilian to be respectful; or threatens arrest *if* the civilian doesn't do "so and so."

There are numerous situations which are disordered when the officer arrives. Before he can collect information or realize his other goals, he must act very much like a stage manager, telling each civilian where to stand, enforcing turn taking in the telling of explanations, and directing bystanders to "move on." In these cases, his authority is not effective usually or merely because he has the right to use force, but because he acts, quite literally, in a commanding way. His force is in his grammatical form, his tone of voice, his emphasis. He acts as a supervisor and assumes he will be treated as such.

Sometimes neither a question nor a command is sufficient. The threat or actual use of force is necessary. "Coercive regulation" or "coercive supervision" is necessary. It includes the threat of force; restraining force (e.g., holding someone back); or active force (e.g., hitting someone). Threat includes the display of readiness, as when the officer draws a club or a gun to make a possible recourse very clear.

Regulation of Disturbances

The three forms of supervision—definitional, imperative, and coercive—are utilized initially to take charge and also constitute regulatory techniques to prevent interference with the accomplishment of the four essential tasks—information, order, respect, and resolution. The empirical question is: which form of regulation is most likely to be utilized in response to a disturbance of each task? Disturbances may be viewed in the following manner: A disturbance to information search may be conceived of as either a refusal to provide information, or an attempt to assert a cognitive domain different from that implied by the question of the officer. A disturbance to the goal of order may be inferred whenever a civilian disobeys the command of an officer, or when the situation is chaotic. A disturbance to the goal of respect may be inferred whenever a civilian addresses an officer in an uncivil manner. A disturbance to the goal of resolution occurs whenever the civilian refuses to accept the resolution that the officer wishes to impose.

The processes of regulation are displayed in Table 3.1. Each disturbance to task accomplishment is followed by a regulatory response intended to get the work group quickly and efficiently back to task accomplishment.

Some Hypotheses about Regulation

Taking charge (establishing that the officer is the supervisor) occurs minimally once, and in certain encounters many times. In every encounter the officer must *initially* establish his authority. Once he has done so, it may never again be challenged. It must be reasserted on the occasion of each disturbance to the interaction which interferes with the officer's four goals. What strategies may be hypothesized?

1. The officer will use that *type* of regulation consistent with the disturbance. He will use definitional regulation to deal with disturbances to the structuring of the situation and situational identification; imperative regulation to deal with disorder; coercive regulation to deal with the threat or use of force. The principle is more or less analogous to the dictum "an eye for an eye."
2. The officer will be more forceful as the number of goals the disturbance frustrates increases.
3. The longer the disturbance lasts in response to the use of "consistent" regulation, the more likely the officer is to use more forceful regulation. For example, if definitional regulation does not halt the disturbance, then imperative regulation may be tried.
4. The regulatory response of the officer will be related not only to the action of the civilian, but to the extent to which the civilian's action is related to the previous directives of the officer.

These predictions are based on two assumptions: (1) officers will seek to minimize disturbances to their goals; (2) in doing so they will seek to minimize the cost to themselves. "Cost" in

Table 3.1. **A schematic of disturbance regulation**

Police Goal	Type of Disturbance	Definitional	Imperative	Coercive
Information	Redefinition	Citizen redefines or refuses to answer / Officer asks question or makes accusation	Citizen redefines or refuses to answer / Officer gives order	Citizen redefines or refuses to answer / Officer threatens or uses force
	Refusal to answer	Citizen redefines or refuses to answer / Officer asks question or makes accusation	Citizen redefines or refuses to answer / Officer gives order	Citizen redefines or refuses to answer / Officer threatens or uses force
Order	Chaos	Citizen disobeys order or situation in chaos at arrival / Officer asks question or makes accusation	Citizen disobeys order or situation in chaos at arrival / Officer gives order	Citizen disobeys order or situation in chaos at arrival / Officer threatens or uses force
	Disobedience	Citizen disobeys order or situation in chaos at arrival / Officer asks question or makes accusation	Citizen disobeys order or situation in chaos at arrival / Officer gives order	Citizen disobeys order or situation in chaos at arrival / Officer threatens or uses force
Respect	Incivility	Citizen assumes uncivil manner / Officer asks question or makes accusation	Citizen assumes uncivil manner / Officer gives order	Citizen assumes uncivil manner / Officer threatens or uses force
Resolution	Refusal	Citizen rejects officer's resolution / Officer asks question or makes accusation	Citizen rejects officer's resolution / Officer gives order	Citizen rejects officer's resolution / Officer threatens or uses force

Type of Regulation Sequence

this sense is considered broadly relative to the constraints which a reasonable officer would acknowledge in his particular department at the time of the encounter including: (a) norms of officers themselves; (b) department policy regarding the use of force; (c) department concern with police-community relations; (d) effect of publicity, law and other factors external to the department itself.

DATA ANALYSIS

First let us examine from the supervisory perspective 95 police-suspect encounters. Twenty-three percent of the police-suspect encounters were reactive and 77% proactive. Most of the proactive encounters were traffic stops. In Table 3.2 are displayed the types of regulation used to take charge *initially*. Contrary to what some might intuitively assume, officers in both reactive and proactive encounters initially try definitional supervision. Also contrary to what might be inferred from the literature regarding the difficulty of the officer's establishing his legitimacy in proactive encounters, it appears that in such encounters officers take charge in the least forceful way, usually by asking a question. It should also be noted that in over 95% of encounters officers speak *first*, thus preempting situational definition by directing the interaction to topics of interest to themselves. This also suggests acceptance by both officers and civilians of the officer's supervisory responsibility. Coercive regulation occurred initially in none of these encounters, though we would expect its initial use in a very small percentage of a larger set.

The extent of officer domination of the interaction process is evidenced by the fact that, of a total of 2,327 officer acts, 1,093 involved the use of either definitional or imperative supervision or regulation as opposed to only 186 of 2,395 civilian acts. Seventeen percent of the regulatory acts of officers were imperative.

Civilian disturbances to the process of interaction constituted approximately 5% of the total number of utterances in

The Group and Its Supervision

Table 3.2. **Types of regulation used to take charge of a suspect initially (by type of encounter)**

Type of Regulation	Reactive (%)	Proactive (%)
Definitional	65	85
Imperative	35	15
Coercive	0	0

these encounters (234 of 4,722 utterances). One-third of these disturbances were denials of accusations. The second largest category of disturbances (21%) were disagreements by civilians with the officer's interpretation of the situation.

The data from officer-suspect encounters confirm the hypothesis of consistency of regulatory response. Disturbances to the goal of situational structuring and identification were regulated in 93% of cases by definitional means. Nearly 100% of disturbances to order were regulated by imperative means. This implies that the most common technique of regulation of interaction is that of *repetition*. The officer asks a question. The citizen refuses to answer. The officer asks the question again, perhaps in a slightly different way. Then the citizen answers. A common alternate strategy is to ask a question, and then, after the citizen responds, make an accusation of a violation, which the citizen then denies. Then the accusation is repeated and the citizen admits to it. In the event of either a question or an accusation, the most likely response to the civilian's refusal or denial is a repetition or paraphrase that continues the same line of questioning. In the great majority of cases this is sufficient. The same is true of imperative regulation. In over 90% of cases of disobedience to an order that occurred in these encounters, repetition, 75% of the time in a civil manner, was sufficient to achieve compliance. In the remaining cases coercive threat was then resorted to by the officer.

Because of complexities of isolating by computer long sequences of disturbances, we were unable to test quantitatively hypotheses concerning an increase in the forcefulness of regulation as the number or length of the disturbances increases.

Qualitative analysis of the data shows the following kinds of sequences:

Proactive Suspicion Stop
Officer: Civil accusation
Civilian: Civil denial
Officer: Civil repetition of accusation
Civilian: Civil denial
Officer: Civil repetition of accusation
Civilian: Civil denial
Officer: Handcuff, frisk, and arrest civilian

Proactive Auto Stop
Officer: Civil order
Civilian: Refusal to obey
Officer: Repetition of civil order
Civilian: Refusal to obey
Officer: Repetition of order in uncivil manner
Civilian: Refusal to obey
Officer: Repetition of order in uncivil manner, threat of arrest
Civilian: Obedience to order but in an uncivil manner

Such sequences tend to suggest that as the number or length of disturbances increase, the officer gradually escalates the forcefulness of his regulatory response to the point where the civilian gives in.

Officer-Complainant Encounters

Officers do not possess the same authority over complainants that they have over suspects. Even so, in most such encounters a task must be accomplished and the officer must supervise. Even if the argument is accepted that ultimately the basis of the officer-suspect relation is the threat or use of coercion, this argument disregards the approximately 80% of officer activities in which no suspect is present. It also fails to acknowledge that approximately 85% of police activities are reactive—in response to the complaints of civilians—and that police effectiveness depends on the voluntary cooperation of complainants, witnesses, and informants over whom they have no coercive authority. They must work together.

The tasks to be accomplished in an encounter with only a complainant, or complainant and bystanders, present are the same as with a suspect. Officers must obtain from complainants and other witnesses the information necessary to decide whether an event of interest to police has occurred, and, if so, the identities of the participants.

Behavioral order is necessary. In the excitement of crisis, victims, complainants, and bystanders are often upset and fail to observe the courtesies of normal interaction. Officers certainly wish to be treated respectfully, perhaps more in this situation than with a suspect, since they are providing the complainant or victim a positive service.

They must also be able to determine the appropriate resolution. Often, civilians interpret an event as criminal that police do not (Reiss, 1971). The dispute may be civil rather than criminal. If criminal, it may have been a misdemeanor not witnessed by the officers and therefore not subject to their direct authority. The officer must retain sufficient discretion to decide the relevance of the event to police authority and whether, for instance, an official report is warranted. If the tasks are the same, then regulation of disturbances of these tasks is necessary. We see no reason to hypothesize any different processes of regulation except that we expect coercive regulation to occur even less frequently than in police-suspect encounters.

Here we analyze from the supervisory perspective the 177 officer/single-complainant encounters. Very few of these encounters were proactive, and, as would be expected of complainant-officer encounters, most were reactive. In almost all of these encounters, officers initially take charge using definitional supervision. Officers dominate the interaction process with complainants, but to a much lesser extent than with suspects. Of a total of 1,637 officer acts, only 419 involved the use of either definitional or imperative supervision or regulation, nearly 25% fewer than with suspects. Only 3.6% of officer acts with complainants were imperative, 13% less than with suspects. As would be expected, because the tasks that officers and complainants must accomplish are typically more cooperative, there were half as many civilian disturbances. Of 1,634 civilian acts, only 39 involved overt refusal to cooperate.

These data from officer-complainant encounters confirm the hypothesis of consistency of regulatory response, though the data are surprising in some ways. Disturbances to the goal of situational structuring and identification were regulated in 44% of the cases by definitional means, much less than the 93% with suspects. However, 42% were not regulated at all. Instead, the officers accepted the alternate definition of the situation proposed by the citizen. Although the technique of repetition was used, it was much less frequent, and officers were more often willing to allow civilians to influence them. In a small number of cases, the same strain toward consistency pertains to imperative regulation. Where a command by officers was disobeyed by civilians, the command was repeated in 80% of the cases. The supervisory role of officers with complainants is weaker than with suspects.

UNCERTAINTY, AUTHORITY, AND REGULATION

We have asserted that officers are supervisors who have legitimate authority and that in this regard they do not differ from other professionals such as physicians, teachers, or nurses. Crozier (1964), in his comparative study of bureaucracy, proposed that "the power of A over B depends on A's ability to predict B's behavior and on the uncertainty of B about A's behavior." Waitzkin and Stoeckle (1972) hypothesized that "a physician's ability to preserve his own power over the patient in the doctor-patient relationship depends largely on his ability to control the patient's uncertainty."

We would hypothesize that officers are like other bureaucratic functionaries and professionals in relating to civilians. If

The Group and Its Supervision

so, then the actions of officers in response to civilians should be less predictable than of civilians in response to officers. The probability that a particular act by an officer will be followed by some particular act of a civilian, or vice versa, is called a "transition probability." Examination of the transitions for officer-suspects and officer-complainants shows this to be true (see Chapter 7). This is also true of officers interacting with multiple positions (see Chapter 8). The officers' behaviors are always less predictable, and thus keep the civilian "off balance." On the other hand, since civilians are normally very cooperative (predictable), their departure from that norm may appear to the officer unusually sinister, implying much more than similar behavior on the part of the officer. Its very rarity may stimulate officers to attribute more significance to uncooperative behavior than the civilians displaying such behavior intend.

Transition Probabilities Displaying Regulation

Table 3.3, officer/single-suspect encounters, may be examined from the regulatory perspective. This table displays the aggregated probabilities of regulatory responses. We have also examined officer-complainant, and officer/multiple-civilian encounters (data not shown). In officer-complainant, officer-suspect, and officer/multiple-civilian interactions, the transition probabilities from officer definitions of the situation, to an alternate definition proposed by the civilian, to an officer repetition of the original definition, are, respectively, .52, .46, and .39. In the latter case there is also a .38 probability of the officer's accepting the alternate definition offered by the civilian. Similarly, the transitions from imperative regulation by the officer, to disobedience by the civilian, to renewed imperative regulation by the officer are, respectively, .80, .43, and .36. Careful examination of these transitions shows other strategies varying by position of civilian, but these tend to be strategies in which (when the civilians are not suspects) the officers tend to give in to the citizen, or in

Table 3.3. **Transition probabilities of specific officer responses to specific disturbances by suspects**

Police Goal	Disturbance	Type of Regulation	
		Definitional	Imperative
Information	Redefinition	.461	.077
	Refusal to answer	.488	.341
Order	Disobedience	.291	.433

which there is a standoff. In this regard, officer interaction with uncooperative complainants is somewhat like interaction between arguing civilians. Officers usually cannot resort to coercive regulation with complainants and so must overcome by sheer leadership or persuasion, or else give in or leave the scene. The officer's status as supervisor is not secure.

We believe the model of supervision and regulation we propose in this chapter applies to all interaction processes in which the tasks have been identified and in which one position possesses legitimate authority over another. We believe it is especially appropriate to volatile working groups. We have shown that definitional supervision and regulation are usually used by officers. Imperative supervision or regulation is used when the former fails or when the situation is disordered. In many working groups, these officer-supervisors "explain" to subordinates what they are to do—thereby structuring the situation—and thereafter seldom need to give direct orders.

Volatile working groups do differ from ordinary work groups, since the tasks are not routine to the civilians involved. They are rather like new team members for whom more definitional and imperative regulation is necessary. From the viewpoint of the subordinate the work is less routine, so intervention and direction by the officer are more frequent. Routine work groups do not have problems to solve, since procedures for most contingencies are already worked out and familiar to group members. Interaction in such a group is somewhat different from that in a police-civilian encounter.

The Group and Its Supervision

In comparing this particular volatile working group, the police-civilian encounter, with others, such as those involving physicians and patients or lawyers and clients, we speculate that most supervision and regulation is performed by the same means. The physician is likely to begin by asking questions, as is the lawyer. When the patient or client avoids answering, fails to understand, departs from the subject, or rambles, more imperative regulation is likely to be used. This is especially true if, for instance, the patient is not behaving properly during an examination or treatment, or if the client is not cooperating with his counsel in the courtroom. Few coercive alternatives are open to these professionals, except perhaps a threat by the physician to charge more, or to have nothing more to do with the recalcitrant patient; or by the lawyer, to refuse the case.

We should not forget that supervisors in ordinary work groups possess not only authority but the means of coercive regulation. Employees may be fired, fined, suspended, reprimanded, or demoted. They may also fail to receive raises. Although none of these means involves the use of violence, they certainly exceed definitional or imperative regulation and have serious negative effects. Thus most supervisors must resort to essentially coercive means of regulation. It may be that their use of such means is no less frequent in normal work groups than in police-civilian encounters.

4

Getting the Work Done

Discretion was "discovered" by lawyers and sociologists of police only a couple of decades ago. Goldstein (1960) asserted that the most serious problems of discretion were low visibility decisions not to arrest that were made on the street by uniformed officers. Other early legal contributions to the debate were made by Kadish (1962) and LaFave (1965). Herman Goldstein introduced an element of worldly realism into the debate (1967) by pointing out the impossibility of full enforcement, and the need for flexibility. The quantitative studies of Black (1972), Black and Reiss (1970), and Reiss (1971, 1974), provided nearly the first "hard data" on extralegal factors affecting decisions to make an official report or to arrest. Lundman (1974, 1980) focused on other extralegal factors affecting arrest. Sykes, Clark, and Fox (in Niederhoffer and Blumberg, 1976) sought to integrate the legal and extralegal factors into a coherent theory, demonstrating that in making a decision to arrest, officers sought to decide whether a legal violation had occurred; what formal and informal department policy was in regard to the behavior in question; whether the suspect was respectful; and whether the officer's safety was threatened. Recently, Sherman (1980) criticized this view but did not suggest an alternative integration.

All the cited discussions tended to emphasize what was, in effect, a dichotomous dependent variable: arrest—nonarrest. We now know that, except in the case of felonies which the officer has probable cause to believe a particular suspect committed (and even in this instance Reiss documented many nonarrests), most police decisions are part of a set of alternatives to arrest. Virtually no research exists on why one nonarrest alternative rather than another is chosen. Officers may choose to calm the civilians, mediate, or arbitrate their dispute; ask one to leave; structure an interval while they "cool off"; advise one to make a citizen's arrest, or perhaps advise one to go to the prosecutor's office and swear out a complaint; verbally rebuke or warn one or many civilians; or order the civilians to cease and desist whatever activity was the source of complaint. They may also refer them for advice to some agency or professional in the community. The availability of many alternatives suggests that in many encounters arrest is not even a salient option in the officer's mind. More likely, the officer is trying to decide which of the many other alternatives is appropriate. Arrest is a resource to be used primarily as a threat in order to encourage the civilian to accept one of the other alternatives; or, it is a last resort when all else fails.

Not only have the many choices officers have of outcomes been neglected, but the concept of discretion has, itself, been oversimplified. It has been assumed that discretion applies only to choice of outcome. In actual fact the officer, as supervisor of a volatile working group, must make a whole series of decisions from the time the encounter begins until it ends. All of these decisions are complex and discretionary. In this chapter we describe in detail, not the single act, but the process of discretion. In doing so, we also emphasize that not only officers but civilians also must make decisions.

When a police officer approaches an encounter, he must seek answers to somewhat the same questions a newspaper reporter must answer before writing a story: Who? What? When? Where? Why? The officer must ask them in a different order and with a different end in mind. The point is, however, that both reporters and officers have a common fundamental need—information (this point is nicely dealt with by Manning, 1977).

There are three discretionary decisions that the officer must make in every encounter: What happened? What are the situated identities of the civilians (suspect, complainant, victim, witness, bystander)? How should these particular people with their particular situated identities, given that they were involved in what happened, be handled?

The decision about what happened is discretionary because the officer has a choice of typifications. While it has been noted by others (Reiss, for instance, 1971) that many events which are typified as criminal by civilians are not so typified by officers, it has less often been noted that even if the event is typified as criminal, an arrest is not thereby inevitable.

Much of an officer's time is given to eliciting, listening to, and evaluating "accounts" (Scott and Lyman, 1968). His typification of the event as well as his decisions about the situated identities of the civilians are based on these accounts. Choices of typifications might include: whether a missing child is just "missing" or the likely victim of foul play; whether a heavy domestic is "merely" a heavy domestic or an aggravated assault; whether a citizen trying to open a locked car with a coat hanger is the owner, a car thief, a thief of goods inside the car; whether the complainant is too particular; whether a loud party is really loud, or whether the complainant is being unreasonable; whether a driver has had "just one or two" or whether he is really drunk; whether to transport a shoplifter to jail at the request of a store manager, or to persuade the manager to let the suspect go with a warning, given the minimal value of what was taken; whether the civilian with his hands in his pockets is holding a weapon, or whether his hands are cold; or whether a woman reporting having been raped by a man with whom she lives really has been, or whether she is getting even for a recent infidelity.

Not only must the officer decide what happened, but he must also attribute situated identities to the civilians present. Many situations are disordered, include many people, and involve competing claims as to who did what to whom. The officer must refrain from making an accusation until he has heard the stories of the various participants. Even then, he has the discretion to decide that a particular actor is just a little drunk, not really "a criminal," or that the complainant really has nothing to complain about. The officer may even be evaluating the characters of the actors and deciding that one or more is an "asshole" (Van Maanen in Manning, 1978) while others are not.

Finally, given these typifications, the officer must choose from among the many outcomes available to him. Each outcome has implications both for him and the civilian. If he tries to "send" the drunk, will the drunk just return again when he leaves, making a repeat call that evening likely? Will the arrest of a spouse cause him to lose his job and exacerbate an already difficult situation? In short, the officer has not one, but a series of problems to solve, and each solution requires discretionary typification. A police-civilian encounter is a problem-solving group, of which the officer is the supervisor.

Problem-solving groups have been the focus of much social-psychological small-group research. The classic study of such groups (Bales and Strodtbeck, 1951) found that they manifest a phase structure. First, groups collect information; then they evaluate the information; finally, they make a decision to act.

In light of the factors just discussed, we believe that a police-civilian encounter may be best conceived as a problem-solving work group supervised by a police officer. Because the group has three basic problems to solve, rather than one, as in the Bales and Strodtbeck experiments, the phase structure will be cyclic, related to the basic discretionary typifications and outcome decision that the officer must make, as well as to the decisions that the citizens must make. The structure will be more complex.

There is a double process that impinges differently upon officers and civilians. Officers must immediately seek information, in order to define the situation; then to attribute situated identities; then to take action. Civilians need information of a different kind, and this mostly after they find themselves in a situated identity that significantly obligates them within the police jurisdiction. They need information about the implications of being cast in a particular situated identity, and also about the implications for them of the action that the police propose taking. The more deeply involved they become the more such information is needed. We hypothesize that a suspect is more deeply involved than a complainant, and an arrested suspect much more deeply involved, and therefore that suspects and particularly arrested suspects need more such information. In Chapter 3 we have already suggested that one function of this information is to socialize the civilians into their situated identities in the volatile working group.

In the police-civilian interaction code used in this study, two types of information were distinguished:

1. *Legal* (nexial) *or activity-related information*: any communicative act that explicates the nature of the encounter and provides information to be used in the conduct of the police role.
2. *Procedural or role-expectation-related information*: any communicative act which defines or redefines the situational paradigm such that participants can define their expectations or order their behaviors accordingly.

Other factors may affect the distribution of information across an encounter. Chief among these is whether the officer actually witnessed the behavior that is the nexus of the encounter, as is true of many on-scene encounters, notably moving-traffic violations. Having witnessed the violation, the officer does not need to seek much further information about the behavior itself, but may quickly cast the civilian in the situated identity of violator. The civilian is immediately involved in a situated identity in the police jurisdiction, and the primary issue is what that identity entails and what further action the officer is going to take. Such encounters will display a truncated initial situation-defining cycle.

The type of information sought will be located at different points of time in each cycle. Police will tend to seek more information before defining the situation, imposing situated identities; then proposing solutions and seeking momentarily less information after each decision point is reached. The civilian, on the other hand, wanting to know what involvement each decision entails for her or him, will be more apt to seek information after, especially after the imposing of identities and after the solution has been proposed.

The general trends will be as follows: Officers will tend to seek activity-related information during the early phases of the encounter. Civilians will tend to seek procedural-related

Table 4.1. **Percentage of nexial and structural information by phase** (N=7,652 strings)

	Reactive Phase			Proactive Phase		
	1/3	2/3	3/3	1/3	2/3	3/3
Activity-related	74	68	60	82	70	55
Procedural-related	26	32	40	18	30	45

information during the later phases of the encounter. Officers will tend to seek more information before each discretionary decision phase of the encounter (before defining the situation; imposing situated identities; proposing or imposing solutions). Civilians will tend to seek more information after each decision phase of the encounter. Table 4.1 displays data from 256 suspect-present, reactive (civilian-initiated) encounters, and 259 suspect-present, proactive (police-initiated) encounters, divided into thirds, similar to the original Bales and Strodtbeck analysis of the phase hypothesis. It is evident that, as predicted, there is phase movement over these encounters as a whole, but that also, as predicted, nexial and structural information are inversely related.

CYCLIC INFORMATION SEARCH

Our hypothesis is that while police will seek activity-related information before each decision point, civilians will seek procedural information after. Our code distinguished between several kinds of decision points.

A decision point common to all encounters is the confirmation or redefinition of the situation. This is the point where the officer decides what happened. In the case of on-scene encounters, this point is often very near the start of the encounter, since on-scene police encounters are initiated after police have witnessed an act that they interpret as falling in their jurisdiction. Most on-scenes are traffic-related. On the other hand, there may be "suspicion stops" in which considerable

Getting the Work Done

discussion may precede the definition of the situation. Reactive calls almost always involve discussion before the situation is defined.

Situated identities of suspects may be imposed under two different conditions. In the first instance an act has occurred that was performed by the civilian when outside the direct authority of the police. Only after investigation is accusation possible. In other situations police are already present, and the civilian is already subject to their authority, for example, at an accident scene, spectators may be asked to "stand back!" or at a bar fight other patrons will be ordered to "keep out of it!" The search for information will differ under these two conditions. In the first instance, an accusation (imposition of situated identity as a suspect) will occur normally only after information search. In the second case, overt information search will not be as likely, since the violation will have occurred directly in front of the officers and often directly contrary to their explicit order.

Action may also be taken in two ways, though with less hypothetical effect on information search. The officer may attempt to resolve the problem by a suggestion, or a set of alternatives of which one is often explicitly coercive and less desirable to the normal person. "Either you 'take a walk' (leave this place and don't come back tonight) or you go downtown!" The suspect is offered the alternative of leaving the premises or being arrested. Alternatively the officer may simply impose an outcome through a direct order which he expects to be obeyed immediately. "Get out of that car with your hands in the air!" While direct orders may be preceded by discussion and information search, it seems likely that they will be given in situations which are directly monitored by police and in which the information needed is available visually rather than through verbal information search.

These distinctions were made in the code:

1. *Activity-related accusation*: accusation of a legal or quasi-legal violation usually made in reference to activities that occurred before the suspect knew he or she was to be questioned by officers.

2. *Activity-related suggestion*: a proposed solution or resolution of the problem posed by the encounter.
3. *Behavioral accusation*: accusation of a breach of the accepted situational structure or definition of the situation including breach of role.
4. *Command*: direct order affecting behaviors immediately, and assuming the authority and implied coercive power of the officer. No alternatives implied.

We hypothesized phases related to the process of information seeking. We also hypothesized that each of the problems that the officer must solve will typically be confronted at significantly different times in the encounter. First will occur the confirmation or redefinition of the situation. Next, in suspect-present encounters, will occur the definition of situated identities, usually by means of an accusation. Unfortunately we did not include a code indicative of placing the civilian in the situated identity of complainant, though this is implicit where complainants alone are present. Finally, the resolution will be determined either by activity-related suggestions or by command. The location of commands will not always be last. In cases of initial disorder their use may be necessary early in the encounter.

Cycles of information search exist associated with each of the hypothesized decision points described above. Officers will seek more activity-related information immediately before defining the situation than immediately after. Officers will seek more activity-related information before making accusations than immediately after; citizens will seek more procedural information after accusations than before. Officers will seek more activity-related information before suggestions than immediately after; citizens will seek more procedural information after activity-related suggestions than before, since it is only through such information that they can learn about the implications of the alternatives proposed as solutions by the officers for their own situated identities. Officers will sometimes seek activity-related information before making behavioral accusations and less after, but this tendency will be modified by the tendency for such accusations to be appropriate as a result of an act that has been performed directly under the eye, so to speak, of the officer, therefore requiring less verbal information search; civilians will be more apt to seek procedural information after such accusations. Officers will sometimes seek nexial information before commanding civilians and less after, but this tendency will also be modified in situations in which the behavior that was the source of the order occurred directly in front of the officers; civilians will tend to seek more structural information after a command than before.

In order to discover whether officers typically solved problems at different times in the encounter, all sets of utterances in the encounter were ranked from first to last. Tests showed that reactive encounters were significantly longer than on-scene encounters. Thereafter they were treated separately. The rank of each set of utterances in each encounter was then divided by the total number of sets in that encounter in order to provide a standardized measure of the ordered place in which each was located, analogous to the temporal order of their occurrence (hereafter termed "time of occurrence"). Both one-way analyses of variance and t-tests based on separate variance estimates were performed comparing the time of occurrence of the three basic solutions within each type of encounter and between the two types. The hypothesized differences were significant beyond the .001 level in the direction predicted within both reactive and on-scene encounters. The means are displayed in Table 4.2. The only nonsignificant difference was between suggestions and commands in reactive encounters, but no hypothesis had been made regarding such a difference.

Testing differences in time of occurrence between reactive and on-scene encounters resulted in one expected difference and one unexpected but nonhypothesized difference. Taking the mean time of occurrence of only the first accusation (not all accusations as in Table 4.2), first accusations occurred significantly earlier in on-scene encounters, no doubt because, as already suggested, officers have usually directly witnessed the offense. First-suggested resolutions occurred in the predicted order but significantly later in on-scene than reactive encoun-

Table 4.2. **Mean time of occurrence for solutions in reactive encounters (N=256) and on-scene encounters (N=259)**

	Mean Time of Occurrence			
Solution	Reactive	N	On Scene	N
Definition of the situation	.27	256	.29	259
Accusation-imposition of situated identity	.45	355	.46	535
Resolution-suggestion	.58	486	.66	134
Resolution-command	.57	607	.51	393

ters. This difference was not hypothesized, nor do we have an explanation of the difference. There were no other significant differences between time of first occurrence of solutions in the two types of encounters.

It is worth noting the different ratio of solutions in the two types of encounters. Accusations are much more frequent in on-scene encounters. Perhaps civilians need to be persuaded more of their involuntarily assumed situated identities. On the other hand, both suggestions and commands were more common in reactive encounters. Perhaps a traffic ticket, since most on-scene encounters involve traffic violations, is a substitute resolution for either a suggestion or an order.

Obviously, not every encounter contains all the solutions. Every encounter includes a confirmation or redefinition of the situation, but many encounters contain no accusation, suggestion, or command. Despite this, there appears to be an appropriate time for each solution, on the average, if it is made at all.

We now turn to the analysis of the cyclic phase process of activity- and procedural-related information search before and after each of the ordered solutions. These data are displayed in Tables 4.3 and 4.4. The data in Tables 4.3 and 4.4 are based on a count of the three sets of utterances immediately before and the three immediately after the initial solution of each type in each encounter.

The data may be analyzed from two perspectives. One may add up the total of activity-related-information and procedural-information codes, constituting together the total

Getting the Work Done

Table 4.3. **Percentage of information search before and after problem solutions (N=256 suspect-present, reactive encounters)***

| | Information Before | | Information After | |
Problem	Nexial	Structural	Nexial	Structural
Definition of the situation	81 (66)	19 (15)	72 (51)	28 (20)
Activity-related accusation	70 (54)	30 (23)	68 (42)	32 (20)
Activity-related suggestion	75 (57)	25 (19)	63 (38)	37 (22)
Procedural accusation	77 (51)	23 (15)	72 (45)	28 (17)
Procedural command	70 (49)	30 (21)	72 (46)	28 (18)

*Based on the sum of nexial and structural informational strings equalling 100%. Numbers in ( ) represent the percentage of all categories of strings represented by either nexial or structural information at each time.

amount of information sets of utterances, totalling them separately for the three sets of utterances immediately before and immediately after the first of each kind of solution code. The tables then show: The amount of activity-related information always exceeds the amount of procedural information.

Considering activity-related information as a percentage of total information, the trend is as hypothesized in nine of the ten instances. More activity-related information is sought immediately before the solution than after, though the difference is small in two cases (one of five in reactive encounters and one of five on-scene encounters).

The pattern in regard to procedural information is mixed when it is considered as a percentage of all information. The difference is in the direction predicted in four of the five reactive cases and rather substantial in two of these cases, but in the reverse direction in the fifth instance. The same is true of the on-scene encounters—substantial differences in the direction predicted in two instances; and smaller differences in the direction predicted in the three remaining.

Looking at the same tables from the perspective of each type of information as a percentage of *all* sets of utterances, one finds eight of ten instances as predicted for activity-related

Table 4.4. **Percentage of information search before and after problem solutions (N=259 suspect-present, on-scene encounters)***

Problem	Information Before		Information After	
	Nexial	Structural	Nexial	Structural
Definition of the situation	82 (53)	18 (11)	76 (47)	24 (15)
Activity-related accusation	81 (62)	19 (14)	76 (62)	24 (19)
Activity-related suggestion	75 (51)	25 (17)	63 (38)	37 (22)
Procedural accusation	72 (46)	28 (18)	70 (46)	30 (20)
Procedural command	68 (42)	32 (20)	63 (41)	37 (24)

*Based on the sum of nexial and structural informational strings totalling 100%. Numbers in ( ) represent the percentage of all categories of strings represented by either nexial or structural information at each time.

information and two instances where there is no before/after difference. Eight of the ten cases are as predicted for procedural information, while two of the reactive instances are slightly opposite to the predicted trend.

Our prediction was that there would be more information search before activity-related accusations and suggestions than for procedural accusations or commands, since these latter cases often occurred in situations where officers had directly observed the violation and verbal information seeking was unnecessary. Considered as a percentage of all sets of utterances, this hypothesis is strongly supported, but most of this difference has its origin in reactive encounters. In reactive encounters there is a before/after difference of 12% and 19% in amount of information sought, respectively, for reactive activity-related accusations and suggestions, but only a 6% and 3% difference for procedural accusations and commands. On the other hand, there is little before/after difference in regard to activity-related information in on-scene encounters except for suggestions. This may be because most on-scene encounters result from moving-vehicle violations in which accusations follow from the officer's directly witnessing the violation, and therefore require little verbal information search before imposing the situated identity of violator.

In this chapter we hypothesized an overall phase structure of information search in which there was an inverse relation between the search for activity-related and procedural information. This information search was hypothesized to be related to the discretionary solution of three basic problems of every encounter: definition of the situation; definition of situated identities; and resolution (either by suggestion or command). We further hypothesized that each of these solutions occurred at a typically different time in the encounter. Finally, we hypothesized that interacting with the overall phase structure was a cyclic structure related to different kinds of information search before and after each of the solutions. The data confirm our hypotheses, and, while adding to the complexity of the original discoveries made by Bales and Strodtbeck concerning information search and problem solving (a complexity that would be of no surprise to them), strengthen their arguments for the external validity of the original small-group laboratory findings.

Currently, there is a debate not only over the number of phases that decision-making groups manifest, but whether they manifest any phases at all (see Fisher, 1970; Ellis and Fisher, 1975; Hawes and Foley, 1976; and Ellis, 1979). We find nonstationarity to characterize sets of utterances but stationarity to characterize utterances. Differing units of analysis may be partially responsible for differences reported in the literature (see Hatfield and Weider-Hatfield, 1978, for a discussion of the utility and differences in distribution of various units).

These data further strengthen our contention that the exercise of discretion should not be identified with one particular decision made by the officer, but with a series of decisions, each preceded and followed by particular types of information search and involving both the officers and the civilians. The study of discretion requires substantial modification of previous assumptions and definitions.

5

Patterns of Decisions by Police

Officers exercise discretion continually. They do not merely choose between arrest and nonarrest, report or nonreport, but between alternative typifications of the situation, of the situated identities of the civilians, and among many outcomes other than arrest. Choice among these latter alternatives is as much or more of a problem than choice between arrest and nonarrest.

While engaged in the continuous exercise of discretion, they regulate disturbances to the objectives they seek to achieve in their work. Fundamental to this process of discretionary decision making and regulation is the search for information. They must "solve" three problems: What happened? Who did it? What should be done? While officers seek information answering these questions civilians seek information concerning the effect of the officers' decisions on their fate. A cyclic, phase model fits this process.

This phase model is based on analysis of data in the form of *sets* of utterances. Each set consists of two or more adjacent utterances focused on the same topic *and* possessing grammatical complementarity, e.g., question/answer/statement/statement, or command/refusal-to-obey/repetition-of-command/acquiescence. This mode of coding permitted not only analysis of the phases of information search, but also permitted the inference of when officers externalized decisions. Using the utterance set as the unit of analysis, it was possible to infer when officers had decided what had occurred, who did it, and what action was needed.

In the preceding chapter we demonstrated that, on the average, these decisions occurred at particular times in the encounters. However, these averages are merely measures of trends. They are influenced by many factors. In fact, in many encounters the decisions are externalized at different times or in a different order. In some encounters there is no overt externalization of some decisions, while in others all the decisions are externalized.

In routine, proactive traffic stops there is little need for the officer to find out what happened. The officer observed the violation. By accusing the driver of speeding, for example, he altercasts him as a violator, and thus externalizes his decision as to the situated identity of the driver. But the outcome of such a situation is normally a ticket. The officer has no need to persuade, suggest, or order some outcome and, by doing so, verbally externalize it. The civilian is handed the ticket and both go their ways. The situation is defined by the officer prior to the interaction; the identity is externalized by accusation during the interaction; and the writing out and handing over of the ticket are done mostly in silence.

On the other hand, in many routine reactive encounters, the officers must first ask many questions before defining the situation; ask more questions before assigning situated identities; then make suggestions, collect further information, or even negotiate before arriving at some mutually satisfying outcome. The decisions in such instances are verbally externalized and consequently indicated by the interaction code.

It follows that verbalized decisions may display patterns. In different kinds of encounters they will occur in different orders, and will differ in the extent to which they were made explicit in the interaction, and coded by the observers. These patterns may be the result of the situation, as in the examples above. They may reflect different ways officers go about making decisions. They may reflect the routineness of the situation. In very routine encounters, officers may follow a kind of script, repeating lines they have used in similar situations before, and following a familiar strategy. In unusual encounters, they may need to improvise and verbalize much more. They will not be as ready with routine responses or decisions. Here we examine such patterns of decisions. Ex post facto, we iso-

Patterns of Decisions by Police 91

Table 5.1. **Induced patterns of solutions***

Pattern**	N	%
DEF/SUG (DS)	18	3.5
DEF/ID (DI)	66	12.8
DEF/MAND (DM)	23	4.5
DEF/ID/SUG (DIS)	54	10.5
ID/DEF/MAND (IDM)	85	16.5
DEF/MAND/ID (DMI)	88	17.1
DEF/MAND/ID/SUG (DMIS)	83	16.1
OTHER (O)	97	18.9
Total	514	99.9

*Solutions beyond the first listed may assume a different permutation, i.e., DIS may also include DSI.

**DEF = Definition of the situation; ID = Imposition of situated identity or accusation; MAND = direct command or order; SUG = suggested resolution, usually including two or more alternatives. In the following tables only the first letter of each script is used: D = DEF; I = ID; M = MAND; S = SUG. Thus the pattern of scripts DIS includes first a definition of the situation, then an accusation, and finally a suggestion.

lated seven overt, verbal patterns of decisions. Each decision is, in effect, a solution to one of the basic problems of the officer. The remaining encounters do not fall into patterns of sufficient frequency to warrant separate statistical analysis. Each pattern contains a definition of the situation (DEF or D), and may contain an imposition of situated identity (ID or I), a command (MAND or M), and/or a suggested resolution (SUG or S).

The patterns displayed in Table 5.1 are in order of increasing complexity (number of overt decisions) and degree of authority manifest. The first three patterns include only two decisions and are ranked from suggestion to command. The second three patterns involve three solutions and are ranked from imposition of situated identity and suggestion to command and identity imposition. The seventh pattern includes four decisions. The eighth aggregates a wide range of patterns of varying complexity and content but of low frequency.

As anticipated, these patterns differ significantly between dispatch and on-scene encounters. From Table 5.2 it is evident that patterns DM, DMIS, and DS are typical of reactive

Table 5.2. **Differences between patterns of solutions in reactive and on-scene encounters**

Pattern	Reactive (%)	On-Scene (%)
DS	7.0	0.0
DI	8.0	29.0
DM	8.0	0.8
DIS	12.5	12.7
IDM	6.0	14.7
DMI	7.5	10.4
MDI	6.0	12.4
DMIS	21.0	11.6
O	24.0	8.5
Total	100.0	100.1*

*Due to rounding off, total is over 100%.

encounters. Patterns IDM, DI, and MDI are common in on-scene encounters. These latter patterns confirm our prediction that imposition of identity takes place sooner and with no further verbal resolution explicit in the interaction in on-scene encounters. Examination of outcomes of interaction (not shown) confirms that this is due to the significantly higher proportion of tickets associated with these patterns. The DI pattern alone accounts for 39% of all tickets. These three patterns account for 66.7% of all tickets but only 38% of all patterns. Before the encounter begins, the situation is defined as a violation of motor-vehicle law, and this is followed by an accusation putting the driver in the situated identity of violator. Commands may be used to regulate the behavior of the violator, but they do not pertain to the outcome.

Bivariate tests (not shown) display significant differences in pattern by type of activity, mix of situated identities, sex and social class position of situated identities, incivility of officers, noncooperation of civilians, amount of interaction between civilians, and encounter outcome. These differences suggest that officers may choose, or have imposed upon them by circumstances, different patterns and complexities of the decisions regarding the basic problems they must solve. What is the explanation of these differences?

Generally, officers are experienced in their work, whereas

Patterns of Decisions by Police

Table 5.3. **Summary transition probabilities for information and solutions based on a 25% random sample of strings (N=2,296)**

	Information	Solutions
Information	.74	.26
Solutions	.66	.34

the civilians they deal with are not (this is implied in the discussion in Chapter 3 of the different roles of integral and situated identities in volatile working groups). Let us assume that in regard to the events and situations which are repetitive that officers develop "scripts." A script we now define as a stereotyped pattern of announced decisions that officers use in typical encounters which they consider routine. Hypothetically, a pattern of externalized decisions might range from a well-rehearsed script to a complete improvisation. Is there any way to test whether common patterns are associated with routine situations?

One method is to compare data on transition probabilities (for a full discussion of the way these probabilities are calculated, see Chapter 6) between information sets and decision sets of utterances to data relating to kinds of situations. The former data pertain to the process; the latter, since they characterize entire encounters, pertain to parameters that are not dynamic.

Table 5.3 displays summary transition probabilities for legal and procedural information sets combined, and for the four types of decisions combined: activity-related accusations; activity-related suggestions; behavioral accusations; and commands. While there are differences in the probabilities in Table 5.3, there remains a very high probability that a consequent set of utterances will be information-related regardless of whether the antecedent set pertained to either information or a decision. The highest probability, .74, is that a set of utterances containing information will be followed by a similar set of utterances.

If we examine an uncollapsed table, Table 5.4, a clear pattern emerges. Chances are approximately the same for every

Table 5.4. **Information and solution string transitions based on a 25% random sample of sets of utterances** (N=2,296)

	Activity- rel. Accus.	Legal Info.	Suggestion	Bhv. Accus.	Proced. Info.	Com.
Activity-related accusation	.125	.571	.033	.054	.168	.049
Legal information	.095	.468	.050	.063	.250	.073
Suggestion	.080	.482	.153	.066	.175	.044
Behavioral accusation	.091	.379	.052	.209	.196	.072
Procedural information	.057	.522	.035	.051	.254	.081
Command	.093	.397	.044	.029	.250	.186

row of the table, with one exception: in the case of each decision set, the probability is slightly greater that the next decision set will be of the same kind.

For every row in Table 5.4 the highest transition probability relates to legal information; the second highest, procedural information; and the third highest to a similar decision code. This matrix resembles a Markov process approaching equilibrium. The distribution of states has become stable. This matrix suggests that any given consequent *set* of utterances is almost *independent* of any given antecedent *set* of utterances.

Given such a matrix, it seems unlikely that the decision patterns can be explained by reference to the transition probabilities. Apparently the microdynamics within sets of utterances differ from the dynamics between sets of utterances (within-set differences will be examined beginning in Chapter 6). Solution patterns cannot be explained from this matrix. Excluding the two kinds of information, the unweighted average probability of any particular decision following any other decision is rather low, .078.

If the transition matrix provides an inadequate explanation, then is it possible that the difference in patterns reflects a difference between the situations for which officers have common scripts or strategies versus situations in which improvisation is necessary?

Referring back to Table 5.1, the first three patterns are the most simple; the second three are somewhat less simple, and the seventh is most complex while the multitude of patterns included in the eighth are the least frequent. We might hypothesize that patterns seven and eight will be associated with the least routine encounters. Table 5.1 represents a rough ordering from scripted solution patterns to improvised sequences.

If this assumption is true, then there should be an association between the patterns and a measure of the *nonroutine*. The more routine, the more scripted. The less routine, the more improvised. We have already demonstrated that certain of the less complex patterns are associated with a very routine police activity, sanctioning moving-vehicle violations. Is it possible to devise a measure of the nonroutine that might be used to test our general hypothesis?

From Reiss (1971), Cruse and Rubin (1973), and other scholars' research we know that most police-civilian interaction is cooperative and civil. We can hypothesize that generally officers deal with civilians who, whatever they have done, are now, in the presence of the officers, relatively orderly. They do not talk all at once. They direct their remarks to the officers rather than to each other. We also know that officers on routine patrol usually deal with relatively small numbers of civilians in any particular encounter. Small encounters in which civilians are cooperative, polite, and orderly are routine. Quite apart from numbers of civilians, we can also hypothesize that encounters differ in the complexity of the situated identity structure. The most common encounters include either single suspects or single complainants. But encounters can include suspects, complainants, witnesses, interested participants, and bystanders. The more complex the situated identity structure, the less routine.

By utilizing these as separate indexes of the nonroutine, it is possible to combine all except the situated identity structure into a composite index, each variable treated as a single question on a questionnaire, summed so that each "item" counts equally with the other items. The sum of these items is the nonroutine score. The higher the score, the more non-

Table 5.5. **Nonroutine score means by pattern**

Pattern	Mean	N	Rank
DS	2.7778	18	4
DI	1.7278	66	1
DM	3.3478	23	7
DIS	2.5926	54	3
IDM	2.4000	85	2
DMI	2.8636	88	5
DMIS	3.9759	83	8
O	3.1856	97	6

routine. The range of this score is 10. The mean score of the 515 encounters is 2.8716, indicating that, as expected, most are routine. It is possible to treat this score as a criterion variable in a one-way analysis of variance, testing whether there are differences in the means by pattern as well as whether other nominal or ordinal variables contribute to differences in means. Generally, we would hypothesize that the more complex or rare the pattern, that is, the more improvised the solution, the higher the nonroutine score. The more simple the pattern, the lower the nonroutine score.

Table 5.5 displays the means of the nonroutine score by pattern. The differences are significant at a level greater than .0001. Our hypothesis is generally confirmed, though there are exceptions. The hypothesized script, DI, associated primarily with moving-vehicle violations, has the lowest nonroutine mean, whereas the longest and most complex pattern, DMIS, is associated with the highest nonroutine mean. We assume that this is an index of the improvisation required by the nonroutine nature of this set of encounters.

The complexity of the situated identity structure was not included in the summary nonroutine index. A separate analysis of variance of the situated identity structure using the nonroutine index as the criterion variable confirms our hypothesis that different structures are associated with wide differences in the degree of the routine. In Table 5.6 the structure is ordered by complexity of situated identity structure. The least complex includes only a violator (V); the second least complex,

Patterns of Decisions by Police 97

Table 5.6. **Situated identity structure and the means of the nonroutine scale**

Structure	Mean	N
V	1.8792	298
VC	4.0571	105
VCP	5.2439	41
VCPB	3.9286	70

a violator and a complainant (VC); the next, a complainant, violator, and participant (VCP); and the most complex, a violator, complainant, participant, and bystander (VCPB). The differences displayed in Table 5.6 are significant at a level greater than .0001.

If a similar analysis is done sorting the criterion variable by type of activity (crime-related, peacekeeping, service, traffic), situated identity structure, and pattern, the differences are also significant at a level exceeding .0001 (data not shown).

Finally, if one takes the two most frequent activities, peacekeeping and traffic enforcement, and analyzes each separately by pattern, the differences are also significant, the former at the level .0066 and the latter, .0045. The order of the means is displayed in Table 5.7. The mean for all traffic-related activities was 1.8617, and for peacekeeping activities, 3.3320.

In examining these separate activities, it is evident that the predicted rank order is not as close to the observed order as might be hoped. DMIS pattern is consistently ranked highest. It consistently scores highest on the nonroutine measure. The DM pattern is consistently ranked higher than predicted. The simplicity of the pattern is complicated by its including a command. An examination of the specific cases included in the DM pattern shows that most contained some elements of our measure of the nonroutine (the actual means are lower than the mean for all patterns combined), but were mainly typical encounters, many involving DOBs (a group of mildly disorderly boys) who were ordered to make less noise; play ball in the park, not the street; or received and complied with a similar command. Only the first (DS) pattern for which the N is only 2 and the seventh (DMIS) pattern among the traffic

Table 5.7. **Order of means of nonroutine index broken down by pattern for traffic-related (N=241) and peacekeeping (N=188) activities**

Pattern	Traffic Rank	N	Peacekeeping Rank	N
DS	7	2	2	12
DI	2	46	1	17
DM	6	2	6	10
DIS	1	23	5	21
IDM	3	38	3	40
DMI	5	38	4	29
DMIS	8	25	8	41
O	4	14	7	71

encounters possess means above the mean for all suspect-present encounters. On the other hand, six of the eight patterns (excluding only DS and DI) included under peacekeeping have means that exceed the mean for all suspect-present encounters. Since dispatched activities may be more unpredictable, the need for improvisation increases. Alternatively, they may still be scripted, but have different relative anchors where they begin to be perceived as nonroutine.

PART THREE

Police-Civilian Interaction

In Part 3 we turn from consideration of the working group to consideration of the detailed, utterance-by-utterance process of talk between police and civilians. In seeking a basic order to this talk we are simultaneously seeking to find whether the most vital part of police work—talking—has a basic order. We conclude that not only does police-civilian interaction possess a basic underlying order, but that probably most human interaction does.

6

A Mathematical Model of Symbolic Interaction

Most previous research on police assumed that the primary dimension of interaction between police and suspects was demeanor. According to Garrett and Short (1975), evidence of deviance was "pursued by means of a perceptual shorthand in which demeanor, gestures, language, and attire are taken as signs of innocence or culpability." Piliavin and Briar (1964) wrote that "youthful offenders who were fractious, obdurate, or who appeared nonchalant in their encounters with patrolmen were likely to be viewed as 'would-be tough guys' and 'punks' who fully deserved the most severe sanction: arrest." Donald Black (1971) confirmed that arrest rates were much higher for antagonistic or disrespectful suspects. Albert Reiss (1971:47) echoed a similar theme when he wrote that the "most common complaint officers . . . voice about citizens is their failure to show respect for authority." In the structured observation schedule used in the original Reiss study (see Black, 1968:323), under the heading "General Manner" appear such words as "hostile," "nasty," "impersonal."

This tradition of inquiry was formalized by Sykes and Clark (1975) in their theory of deference exchange which posited that toward almost all statuses police adjust their level of deference over the encounter as a whole to just less than that of the civilian. Police expect the civilian to acknowledge that an asymmetrical status norm governs their relations. Failure of the civilian to adjust his or her level of deference to that of the officer leads to confrontation. In Reiss's words (1971:53) "'negative' police conduct is directed to citizens who refuse to defer to their authority."

Despite this extensive and well-documented series of studies, the concepts of demeanor, deference, manner, or respect were not clearly specified. Perhaps the best definition was that of Goffman (1956:477). Deference is that "component of activity which functions as a symbolic means by which appreciation is regularly conveyed *to* a recipient *of* this recipient, or something of which the recipient is taken as a symbol, extension, or agent." Even this definition did not specify the observable cues that constitute deference; nor did Sykes and Clark, who suggested that "such a norm symbolizes some special evaluation of the actor, in this case one in which the officer generally has greater social value and influence than the citizen."

It is not our intent to question the validity of the conclusions cited above, but we mean to suggest that they do not encompass the entire phenomenon of police-civilian interaction. Greater attention must be given to another dimension of their interaction: *symbolic content*. This refers not only to the grammatical form of the utterance, such as question or command, but to the *general* referent of the utterance, such as the problem the police are present to solve, the current behavior of the civilians, the applicability of the law or its procedures. Cues that are interpreted as deference are primarily nonverbal, whereas the verbal content of the interaction and its effects have been neglected. This was evident in the Sykes and Clark study in which data pertaining to the deference/incivility scale were reported, but other scales related to the content of interaction were not. This was also the case in the Reiss study in which manner was distinguished from other dimensions of interaction (Black, 1968:317–334).

Even though inquiries have been few about the symbolic content of interaction rather than its manner, certain scholars have noted its importance. This approach to content we shall term the "symbolic" as opposed to the "deference" approach. The symbolic approach emphasizes that one of the primary problems of both officer and civilian is to express their views clearly and cogently enough to each other so that mutual understanding occurs. The symbolic approach continues to acknowledge the import of deference in police-civilian relations, but it emphasizes that the symbolic factors have equal if not greater influence.

Among studies that acknowledge the symbolic dimension were those of Sacks (1972), McNamara (1967), Hudson (1970), and Wiley and Hudik (1974). Sacks interpreted the relation between officer and suspect as a game in which the suspect sought to conceal as much *information* as possible from the officer, while the officer, playing the same game, gradually acquired sophistication at penetrating beneath the facade to discover those cues to moral character relevant to his/her professional concern.

McNamara was the first scholar to emphasize this dimension. He hypothesized that among the most frequent sources of difficulties encountered by police in face-to-face interaction with citizens were: (1) gathering an adequate amount of relevant *information* about a situation and the citizens in it both prior to and during the interaction; and (2) clarifying police expectations for the citizen (1967:169). Clearly, these are not problems of the manner of officer or civilian, but the manifest symbolic content of their interaction, as evidenced in McNamara's example of the difficulty experienced by officers who spoke only English communicating their expectations to Spanish-speaking civilians (1967:172).

Similarly, Hudson discovered in a study of complaints of alleged police misconduct brought before the Philadelphia Police Advisory Board that, while a civilian challenge to police authority often precipitated a confrontation, the reason the officer's authority was challenged was the civilian's inability to get the officer to *explain* why a particular action was being taken. "The citizen, in short, was unwilling to accept the role of suspect or violator until the situation had been defined to his satisfaction" (Hudson, 1970).

Wiley and Hudik's exchange-theoretic field experiment confirmed that citizens stopped for field interrogation were much more cooperative when the officer provided a *reason* for the interrogation, and that the amount of cooperation increased when the reason given was viewed as appropriate and valuable by members of the community. All of these previous studies suggest that the symbolic dimension of interaction may be as important in police-citizen relations as the deference dimension. Actors must exchange information, explanation, and reasons for their acts, as well as establish identities.

Specifically, the symbolic dimension consists of a continuing process in which information is sought; information is given or withheld; identities are imposed by means of accusation, and accepted or denied; and decisions are implemented through commands, and obeyed or disobeyed. The process is a continuous series of statements of information or opinion, questions, decisions, accusations, and responses such as answers, compliances, admissions, or, conversely, refusals, disavowals, denials, and disobediences. In the data reported here, the content was accompanied by incivility by officers in only 1.4% of the cases, and by the civilians in 1.9%. Clearly, one can command in a civil manner, and deny an accusation with complete deference.

There is a paradox at the heart of police work. Officers *must* collect information and, to do so, must ask questions. They must also, on occasion, "take charge," or accuse a civilian of a violation. These are *necessary* concomitants of police work. Similarly, civilians must decide whether or not to cooperate with the officer on the symbolic dimension. The citizen may deny an accusation if she or he feels innocent. Both accusation and denial may be perfectly civil, yet the disagreement at the symbolic level has negative connotations for both. It is not pleasant to be accused, nor necessarily cheering to have a serious but civil accusation denied. The officer can quite civilly accuse a driver of speeding and the driver both honestly and civilly deny it. It follows that the *content* of interaction has an evaluative implication quite distinct from deference or incivility, and that this evaluative implication may decisively affect the continuing process of the encounter. It is further apparent that while officers may be taught to be polite, they can never entirely avoid asking questions, giving orders, or making accusations. Nor can suspects avoid answers, admissions, or denials. If, then, the *symbolic content* of interaction has an unavoidable evaluative dimension, and this content cannot be avoided, then it follows that there are limits to which police-civilian relations can be amicable.

A SYSTEMS PERSPECTIVE ON SYMBOLIC INTERACTION

Emphasis on symbolic interaction raises several important questions. First, is the temporal sequence of symbolic acts in fact a process, that is, a sequence in which some contingency relation pertains between acts? In the past, the existence of such a process has been assumed, but there is almost no research on such hypothetical processes in natural settings. Second, if it is a process, what kind of process is it? It would seem that identifying the kind of process would have import for understanding the cognitive operations underlying manifest symbolic behavior. Third, if the interaction does constitute a particular kind of process, what does this imply for police and civilians? To answer these general questions, it seemed appropriate to examine data collected during field observations from the perspectives of general systems theory and statistical mathematics.

Let us begin by considering a mathematical representation of a system such as that suggested by Cortes, Przeworski, and Sprague (1974). They suggest that we may represent any system as a set of inputs, a set of outputs, and a transformation rule of the system. Systems take inputs and transform them into outputs. Mathematically, we represent such a system as follows:

$$X(t + 1) = P[X(t)],$$

where $X(t)$ = inputs to the system at time t, $X(t + 1)$ = outputs of the system at a time $t + 1$, and P = a transformation rule characterizing the system and describing the relationship between inputs and outputs.

Hernes (1976) distinguished between three different levels of structure in such systems: output structure, process structure, and parameter structure. The *output structure* for police-civilian interaction consists of the distribution of content categories for officers or civilians at any particular point in time, t, over some set of aggregated encounters. The *process structure* consists of the form of the transformation rule that expresses what the system does to transform inputs into outputs. For example, we will consider a P that is a transition matrix specifying the probability of any particular state, x_j, being output by the system at time $t + 1$ given that some other state, x_i, was the input at time t. The process structure in this case is the transformation matrix and its properties. The *parameter structure* consists of the parameters that describe the process structure. In our example of the transition matrix, the parameters are the specific transition probabilities appearing in each cell of the transition matrix.

Interaction of police and civilians may be conceptualized as the actions of two coupled systems, each characterized by the structures described above. They are coupled because the outputs from one of those systems (e.g., the acts of the social actors considered here in terms of content categories) constitute the inputs to the other system. Each actor takes the inputs and transforms them into outputs. For example, some first act by the officer at time t (e.g., a question) is an out*put* from the officer system. The out*come* corresponding to this act for the civilian serves as the input to the civilian system (i.e., we assume that the civilian evaluates the question and attributes to it a significance in terms of his or her situation). The act of the civilian at time $t + 1$ (e.g., a refusal to answer) is the output of the civilian system at this time and is associated with a corresponding outcome and input to the officer system at the same time.

Utterances may be categorized into broad categories reflecting various aspects of symbolic interaction. For this analysis we consider four such categories. Within any particular encounter, certain topics or lines of interrogation may be established regarding the facts of the case, including what happened and the involvement of the suspect in those events. We shall term the establishment of such lines of interrogation *definitional* acts. Such acts may be performed by either officer or civilian. The effect of a definitional act is to establish cognitively a subject of discourse during a particular phase of the encounter.

There are two related categories of acts. One includes acts

Mathematical Model of Symbolic Interaction 107

that attempt to altercast the other social actor through interaction in a way which goes beyond mere interrogation. A second includes utterances through which such altercasting is resisted. The first, which we shall call *controlling* acts, including accusations, orders, and physical actions such as handcuffing or drawing a weapon, serve to assert the control of one participant over the other in the interaction by imposing on him or her a particular identity. For example, an accusation by an officer results in the civilian's being altercast as a violator. The second, *resistant* acts, are those acts through which such an identification is denied. These acts include refusals to answer a question, denials of accusations, and refusals to obey an order. For example, refusal to answer a question by a civilian challenges the officer's control over the subject of discourse. A final category of acts we consider are *confirming* acts. These are acts of acquiescence, including answering a question, admitting an accusation, or following an order. They allow the interaction to continue and they confirm the definition of the situation and identities asserted by the other social actor.

Logically, resistant and controlling acts are possible for both police and civilians; but empirically, police-civilian interaction displays extensive control by police and resistance by civilians. The converse is seldom displayed by either social actor. For example, officers in the interactions that we examined initiated 423 orders, accusations, and related acts, while civilians initiated only 28. Similarly, officers displayed only 48 refusals to answer questions, denials of accusations, and related acts, while civilians displayed 230.

In addition to the obviously disproportionate use of controlling and resistant acts by officers and civilians, these acts have somewhat different connotations to each social actor. Resistant acts by civilians are attempts to avoid imposition upon them of a distasteful identity. Resistant acts by officers are usually devices to reassert their own control. That is why in this analysis we have considered both acts of control and of resistance by officers to be controlling acts, and acts of control and of resistance by civilians to be resisting acts. Social acts for officers may be definitional, controlling, or confirming; for civilians they may be definitional, resistant, or confirming. Given such a categorization of the utterances of officers and civilians, we suggest hypotheses regarding the structures of the interaction.

Whatever the initial distribution of the categories of either officers or civilians, these will tend toward equilibrium as the encounter unfolds. This tendency will be manifest, because the nature of the police-suspect encounter is different from the normal problem-solving experiment, and, therefore, the phase structure found in such experiments is likely to be different. Within any particular encounter there is not one problem but several, and therefore, it may be less likely that questions and statements of information would occur only at the beginning of the encounter. For instance, the first problem might be to determine whether a violation has taken place. If such a determination is made, then it may be problematic whether the civilian will agree to be cast in the position of violator, and thus a second line of interrogation may begin. And, finally, even if the civilian admits to the accusation, there remains the problem of what to do, which is often subject to negotiation. Not only this, but the sum of acts over some particular period of an encounter—say, the first third—is not identical to the distribution of acts at a particular time, and is independent of the transition probabilities of one kind of act leading to another. We therefore see no compelling reason to believe that the distribution of acts will differ significantly at different *points* in time in the encounter.

Hypothesizing the form of the process structure is more difficult. Despite Cruse and Rubin's claim that the "behavior of the citizen . . . seems to have no statistically measurable effect whatsoever on police behavior" (1973:214), we find this intuitively absurd. At the cognitive level, if one social actor asks a question, both logic and common sense suggest that the other social actor will feel pressure either to answer or refuse to answer the question. Similarly, if a question is answered, then the line of questioning is likely to be pursued in terms of the answer. This suggests *at least* the form of the first-order process, that is, one in which the occurrence of a particular category is contingent on the previous category. Sykes (1974) found that the form of the process of deference exchange was second order. We therefore tentatively hypothesize that the process structure is at least first order in terms of acts, and possibly second or higher order.

Finally, in regard to parameter structure, the authoritative status accorded police suggests that they would be likely to display a greater proportion of definitional and controlling acts, and that civilians would be more likely to display a greater proportion of confirming and resistant acts. In terms of the parameters themselves, a definitional or controlling act by an officer would be more likely to be followed by a compliant act by the civilian, and a resistant act by a civilian more likely to be followed by a controlling act by an officer. Thus, even though we are restricting our purview to the symbolic dimension of interaction, these parameters will be remarkably similar to those of deference exchange.

In this chapter, we limit ourselves to encounters with the simplest structure: single-suspect encounters and single-complainant encounters. Later we will consider encounters involving more than one civilian. Because of the difference in the situated positions of the civilians, each set will be examined separately.

From a total of 1,622 encounters observed during the summer of 1973, 95 single-suspect and 177 single-complainant encounters were analyzed. These were the total of all such encounters that were twenty or more utterances long. We decided that an examination of the process of these encounters required us to focus on those of reasonable length. It is possible that our analysis does not apply to very short encounters.

Most of the single-suspect encounters involved white, male, young adults or adults. About one-third were under the influence of alcohol. They were disproportionately proactive, because single suspects are most frequently involved in moving-vehicle violations. Fifty-eight percent were traffic-related. Thirteen percent were arrested.

Single complainants were mostly white, adult. Half were women. Few were drunk. Most of these encounters were reactive. Observers judged that 20% of the offenses reported by the complainants were felonies; 40% were misdemeanors; and the remainder involved no legal violation.

MARKOV MODELS OF POLICE-CIVILIAN INTERACTION

The fundamental assumption of our view of police-civilian interaction, and one upon which our three hypotheses are based, is that interaction is a process in which acts of each participant at each point in time are, at least in part, contingent upon past acts. It is not enough to say that we expect a process to describe social interaction. A variety of such processes differ from each other substantially. The data to be considered here were collected in both discrete states (e.g., utterances) and discrete time intervals. The simplest mathematical model of a process in discrete space and discrete time is a Markov model. Our three hypotheses describe a particular type of Markov process model. By focusing our analysis on testing the assumptions and predictions of such a Markov model, we not only test the original hypotheses but also may use the known formal properties of Markov models (e.g., see Feller, 1968; Isaacson and Madsen, 1976; Howard, 1971) to generate predictions about many aspects of social interaction between police and civilians.

Markov analysis of communicative processes has gradually developed during the past decade. Among those who tested partial or full Markov models were Hawes and Foley (1973), Sykes (1974), Ellis and Fisher (1975), Hawes and Foley (1976), Cappella (1979), Ellis (1979), and Donohue, Hawes, and Makee (1981). Hewes (1975) described such models and compared them to mean-value models. The need to complement such models with theory was emphasized by Hewes (1979). In Monge and Cappella (1980), there is a useful introduction by Hewes for their use in communication research. While much is yet to be learned about both the possibilities and limitations of Markov models, they have become a useful device for analyzing interaction processes.

The observational language, Police IV, which was used to collect the data, consists of a set of exclusive and exhaustive concepts into which every utterance of a police officer or civilian was categorized. One utterance might have been categorized into the concept "activity-related question"; another into "suggested resolution to the problem posed by the encounter"; or "statement of procedural information." Only one utterance could occur at a time, so the data consist of a series of categories parallel to the actual utterances that occurred in the original encounter. Since officers and civilians usually took turns speaking, every other utterance was spoken by the same position. If the officer initiated the interaction then utterances 1, 3, 5, . . . n were spoken by the officer, and utterances 2, 4, 6, . . . n, by the civilian. The reverse was true if the interaction was initiated by the civilian. An utterance coded into a particular category is said, mathematically, to be in a particular state. Thus, the process of interaction assumes movement of the utterances through time from state to state, for example, from the state of being an activity-related question, to the state of being an activity-related answer, to the state of being a command.

If there is a set of mutually exclusive and exhaustive categories that is equivalent to a set of mutually exclusive and exhaustive states, then it is possible to estimate the probability that if some particular state occurs, then it will be followed by another particular state. For illustration, let us consider an observational language containing only three concepts: question, answer, and command (Q, A, C). Every utterance must be categorized using one and only one of these concepts. Let us suppose that fifteen encounters are observed. Each contains a different number of utterances categorized into these three concepts, but the total number of all utterances in the fifteen encounters is 300. Each utterance may be spoken by either an officer or a civilian (O, C), the officer and civilian always take turns, and their utterances must be either Q, A, or C. The method appropriate to discover the probability of going from one state, say Q, to another state, Q or A or C, is to calculate it from the actual 300 utterances coded in the fifteen encounters. This can be done by writing a computer program that will put the coded utterances in a format which can be conveniently cross-tabulated using a program such as SPSS. Let us take one encounter ten utterances long:

$$\text{OQ, CA, OQ, CA, OA, CQ, OA, CA, OC, CA} \qquad (1)$$

This may be converted to a series of computer cards possessing the following form:

	Variable 1	Variable 2	Variable 3	Variable 4
Card 1	OQ			
Card 2	CA	OQ		
Card 3	OQ	CA	OQ	
Card 4	CA	OQ	CA	OQ
Card 5	OA	CA	OQ	CA
Card n	—	—	—	—

Notice that variable 1 consists of a column of values exactly the same as the row in (1). Variable 2 consists of exactly the same row except that it begins on Card 2. Variable 3 consists of exactly the same row except that it begins on Card 3. A cross-tabulation of Variable 1 with Variable 2 results in a matrix of the frequencies with which each state is followed by each of the other states. This is a 6 × 6 matrix, since there are two positions (O, C) and three categories (Q, A, C). Thus, the matrix takes this form:

| | \multicolumn{5}{c}{Act at Time $t+1$} | Row |
	OQ	OA	OC	CQ	CA	CC	
OQ				n	n	n	1
OA				n	n	n	2
OC				n	n	n	3
CQ	n	n	n				4
CA	n	n	n				5
CC	n	n	n				6

(2)

The upper-left and lower-right quadrants of the matrix are empty because officers and civilians always take turns talking. There are no officer-officer or civilian-civilian pairs.

Mathematical Model of Symbolic Interaction 113

Each cell in *(2)* above contains a count of the number of times a particular state, e.g., OQ, moved to another state, e.g, CQ, or CA, or CC. This matrix of counts may be converted into what is termed a regular stochastic matrix suitable for fitting to a Markov model by transforming each count into a probability. This is done by summing the counts in each row, and dividing each count in a particular row by the sum of counts for that row. The probabilities in each row then add up to 1.00. A row of such probabilities is called a probability vector. The probability in each cell of the matrix is called a transition probability. It is an estimate of the probability that if an utterance is in a particular one of the six possible states at an immediately previous time, it will move to one of the six possible states at the immediately following time. Normally, the previous time is designated t, and the following time, $t + 1$. Notice that every utterance except the first utterance in an encounter is preceded by another utterance and hence can be thought of as occurring at $t + 1$, and every utterance except the last one in the encounter is followed by another utterance and hence can be thought of as occurring at t. On the schematic example of the computer card, variable 2 may signify t and variable 1, $t + 1$.

We have discussed talking both in terms of the form it may possess and its content. Obviously, each concept (Q, A, C) refers to content. To discover whether talking possesses a particular form, it is necessary to create matrices such as the one described above. By examining the probabilities in these matrices, one can discover whether the state that occurs at $t + 1$ is independent of or dependent upon the state that occurs at time t. By cross-tabulating variable 3 with variable 2 with variable 1, one may create a larger matrix that contains the transition probabilities for variable 1, given variables 2 and 3. Now variable 1 is the state that occurred at $t + 2$; variable 2, at $t + 1$; and variable 3, at t. (This matrix is the one necessary to test for the existence of the tripartite relationship—see Chapter 11.)

It is possible to create different matrices of probabilities based on cross-tabulating different variables, and to discover only the form that the talking assumes. Thus, by cross-tabulating variable 1 by variable 2, one can discover whether utterances at t and $t + 1$ are independent or other-contingent; cross-tabulating variable 1 by variable 3, self-contingent; cross-tabulating variable 1 by variables 2 and 3, self- and other-contingent. Mathematically, a set of different terms is used to designate some of these different contingencies. If what occurs at $t + 1$ is independent of what occurs at t, then mathematicians term this a zero-order process. If what occurs at $t + 1$ is dependent only on what occurs at t, then it is termed a first-order process. The tripartite relationship, ABA or BAB, is one in which the state at $t + 2$ is dependent upon both what occurs at t and $t + 1$. This is termed a second-order process.

Since mathematics is deductive, it is possible to examine the purely logical implications of a mathematical model. This is true of the matrices such as those of transition probabilities that we have created. In examining them for their mathematical properties, we are going well beyond just answering the question of whether interaction displays any particular form of contingency. First, learn what the purely mathematical properties of transition matrices are. Then discover whether the data display these properties. There is no guarantee of any kind that the data will approximate the mathematical predictions. In this way, we make a fascinating and thought-provoking transition from purely mathematical properties—properties that are the pure creation of mind—to the discovery of whether the empirical data manifest these same properties. By some magic it often appears that nature displays an underlying order which accords with that dreamed of previously only in some mathematician's imagination. In testing whether our data fit a particular Markov process, we are going beyond testing only for the form of the contingency. We are testing whether interaction manifests an underlying order similar to the characteristics of a Markov process, a process which is the product of the mathematical imagination applied to matrices of probabilities like that which we created to discover the form of talking.

What are some of these mathematical assumptions and properties? First assume that the transition matrix is the same at all times in the process and under all the different circumstances under which the process might occur. If this is true, then, for example, the probability of the transition from state OQ to a state CA is the same at the beginning, middle, or end of the encounter. It is also the same, though circumstances have changed in real life, from a call to take a report about a burglary to a call about a street robbery in progress. The assumption about time is called the *assumption of stationarity*. The assumption about circumstances is called the *assumption of homogeneity*. If these assumptions that are taken as given, mathematically, are found to be true, empirically, then these transition matrices will display other purely mathematical properties that the data may also possess.

Imagine the beginning of several processes—for instance, several police-civilian encounters. These encounters will start in different states. Since, in our illustrative example, there are six possible states, the total number of starting states may be summed, the count for each particular starting state divided by the sum, and the distribution of starting states thereby converted into a probability vector. The time at which all these starting states occur we shall designate t, and this particular vector, the *state vector*, describing the state of the system at time t. Sometimes the state vector is called the *output vector* (e.g., Hernes, cited earlier in this chapter). In moving from the beginning states of the process to the next state at $t + 1$, the original states "pass through" the matrix of transition probabilities. The processes that started out in the state OQ at time t will, depending upon the magnitude of the transition probabilities, move to state CQ or CA or CC at time $t + 1$. At each step after t: $t + 1$, $t + 2$, $t + 3$, $t + n$, the proportion of each state will change, though, because of the assumption of stationarity, the transition matrix remains the same. At each point in time, the probabilities of each state within the state vector change while the transition matrix remains the same.

In order to discover the exact state vector at $t + 1$, it is necessary to multiply the vector at time t by the transition matrix. In order to discover the state or output vector at time $t + 2$, multiply the output vector at $t + 1$ by the transition matrix. The output vector at any time, $t + n$, can be discovered by multiplying the transition matrix by the output vector at time $t + n - 1$. Because of their mathematical properties, transition matrices of this type possess a property that makes the discovery of an output vector at a particular time, say, $t + 9$, much simpler than multiplying each new output vector through the matrix until the desired state is reached. One can merely raise the transition matrix to the desired power; in this case, to the 8th power, multiply the resulting matrix by the initial state or output vector at time t, and the result will be the same as if one multiplied step-by-step until one reached time $t + 9$.

These output vectors and the transition matrix possess another property. If one knows the initial state or output vector, and the transition matrix, then it is possible, by multiplying through the individual cells of the matrix, to discover how many replications of a state of a specific length there may be. That is, given knowledge of the probability of initial occurrence of the state CQ at time t, one may discover how many occurrences of that state in uninterrupted sequence there may be of various lengths. Each reoccurrence is termed a run. For instance, (t) CQ, $(t + 1)$ CQ, $(t + 2)$ CQ, $(t + 3)$ CQ, $(t + 4)$ CQ, is a five-step run. The predicted distribution of different lengths of runs varies. A few runs may be very long or short; others of medium length. One may test whether the actual distribution of runs is similar to that expected mathematically.

Transition matrices of this type possess another property. Raised to a sufficiently high power, the probabilities in each column become identical, or almost so. This is called the equilibrium distribution. The probabilities in Table 6.3 were approaching such a distribution. It happens that this distribution, or more precisely, the distribution in any row, is equal to the output vector that would have resulted from multiplying each output vector from time t through the transition matrix up to that time $t + n$ at which n is equal to the power to which the matrix has been raised. If one takes this output vector, which is equal to each of the rows in the matrix that has been raised to the power at which the equilibrium distribution has been reached, and multiplies it through the *original* transition matrix, an output vector that is exactly the same will be the product. For instance, if the equilibrium distribution is reached at time $t + 7$, then if one multiplies the output vector at time $t + 8$ through the original transition matrix, then the output vector at time $t + 9$ will equal the vector at time $t + 8$; and this will continue for all remaining steps in the process. While a particular state, say, CQ, may move to another state, some other state will assume the state CQ. Thus, while individual states still move, the probability that a particular state at any particular time after the equilibrium distribution has been reached remains the same.

Equilibrium is reached quickly in some processes, and only after a very long time in others. It is substantively interesting to know how long it takes for the equilibrium to be reached, and what the output vector looks like at equilibrium. For instance, in regard to police and civilians, the equilibrium distribution might be reached quickly, but the equilibrium might consist of high probabilities of categories that constitute confrontation. Equilibrium is not equivalent to peace or lack of change. It is the aggregate probabilities of a set of particular states. The individual states continue to change.

We have been considering the purely mathematical properties of transition matrices and of Markov processes. The question is whether the data gathered on the process of police-civilian interaction display any of the characteristics of these mathematical phenomena. Has imagination anticipated reality?

Much of the analysis in Part 3 of this book focuses on testing not only whether police-civilian interaction manifests a particular contingency form, but also whether it manifests other characteristics similar to the assumptions and properties of a Markov process. Is the transition matrix stationary? Are the transition probabilities calculated from the data the same at the beginning, middle, and end of the process? Do they remain the same under different real-life circumstances? Do the aggregated encounters display distributions of patterns of specific lengths that would be expected were the process Markovian? Is an equilibrium distribution achieved in real life so that the effect of the initial-state vector wears off? If so, how quickly does this occur?

THE STATISTICS OF PROBABILISTIC MATHEMATICAL MODELS

Mathematics is very precise; data (and, by implication, reality) are very messy. Since data will never mirror the perfection of a mathematical derivation, it is necessary to estimate the extent to which the mess approximates the perfection. Statistical tests are needed for this estimate. Log-linear modeling techniques developed during the middle 1970s (Bishop, Fienberg, and Holland, 1975) provide a new statistical method for determining whether or not the data approximate the forms, assumptions, and properties of a Markov process. Log-linear models are very similar to traditional chi-square tests except for two differences. First, log-linear models of multidimensional phenomena may be examined. Observed counts in cells in multidimensional space may be tested against the expected counts. While more than two dimensions may be tested by a traditional chi-square, the actual test is usually made on each two-dimensional table while the other variables are held constant. The entire multidimensional set of counts is not tested simultaneously as in a log-linear model.

Second, social scientists utilizing the chi-square statistic usually look for significant differences between observed and expected frequencies. Log-linear models are utilized in just the opposite way. Modeling means that the investigator hypothesizes what contingency relations are in his data. A log-linear model is a model of what the data would be like if they met the hypothesized criteria. The model is then compared to the data. If there is a significant difference, then the model does not fit the data and is an inappropriate model. Whereas users of chi-square tests often subjectively hope for significant differences, users of log-linear models hope there will be no such differences. Thus, in examining the form, assumptions, and properties of a Markov process, we fitted statistical models to data to discover whether the data approximate the model. If they do, there will be no significant difference between the data and the model.

Log-linear models are fitted one variable at a time. The change in the goodness of fit statistic as each variable is added indicates whether the addition of the variable makes for a significantly better fit. Statistically significant *changes* in goodness of fit, as hypothetically important variables are added to the model, are desired by the investigator. After each of the hypothetically important variables has been entered into the model so that all are included, the investigator hopes that the difference between the data and the model is insignificant. If so, then the hypotheses are not disproven. In our case, then the data may be said to approximate a particular mathematical model. The marvelous transition from the imagination of orderliness to ordered reality has been achieved. We now turn to these tests applied to officer/single-suspect and officer/single-complainant data.

The results of a log-linear analysis of the five-dimensional contingency table for police-suspect dyads are presented in Table 6.1. On the left of this table are a series of hierarchical log-linear models and the G^2 values and degrees of freedom indicating the fit of the model to the data (the larger the G^2, the poorer the fit). On the right side of this table are the changes in G^2, degrees of freedom associated with that change, and the terms which differ between pairs of models. The right side of this table indicates the relative contribution of the terms that differ between pairs of models. Thus, by examining the right side of this table, we can assess the relative contribution of different effects in accounting for the frequency distribution. Specific terms correspond to specific hypotheses; hence this is a means to test several alternative hypotheses directly. For example, a first-order Markov model assumes that current acts depend solely on the immediately preceding act, and the assumption of stability implies that this relationship will be constant over time. Thus, the terms, u_{12}, u_{23}, u_{34} represent the association between acts at t and $t + 1$, acts at $t + 1$ and $t + 2$, and acts at $t + 2$ and $t + 3$, respectively; and, together, these three u-terms estimate the effects of such a first-order Markov process. The middle of Table 6.1 at the top shows that these terms, when added into the model, lead to a

Table 6.1. Tests of order, contingency, and role heterogeneity for officer-suspect encounters

Model	df	G^2	Models	ΔG^2	Δdf	P	Terms Differing between Models
1. $u_1+u_2+u_3+u_4+u_5$	152	3526.3					
2. All 1* $+u_{12}+u_{23}+u_{34}$	140	2999.0	1–2	527.3	12	P < .0001	1st-order other-contingent effects $u_{12}+u_{23}+u_{34}$
3. All 1 $+u_{12}+u_{23}+u_{34}+u_{13}+u_{24}$	132	2003.9	2–3	995.1	8	P < .0001	2nd-order self-contingent effects $u_{13}+u_{24}$
4. All 1 $+u_{12}+u_{23}+u_{34}+u_{13}+u_{24}$ $+u_{14}$	128	1984.0	3–4	16.9	4	.001 < P < .01	3rd-order other-contingent effects u_{14}
5. All 1 $+u_{12}+u_{23}+u_{34}+u_{13}+u_{24}$ $+u_{14}+u_{123}+u_{234}$	112	1878.1	4–5	105.9	16	P < .0001	2nd-order other/self-contingent effects $u_{123}+u_{234}$
6. All 1 $+u_{12}+u_{23}+u_{34}+u_{13}+u_{24}$ $+u_{14}+u_{123}+u_{234}+u_{124}+u_{134}$	96	1846.7	5–6	31.5	16	P > .01	3rd-order other/other + self/other effects $u_{124}+u_{134}$
7. All 1 $+u_{12}+u_{23}+u_{34}+u_{13}+u_{24}$ $+u_{14}+u_{123}+u_{234}+u_{124}+u_{134}$ $+u_{1234}$	80	1821.2	6–7	25.5	16	P > .01	3rd-order other/self/other effects u_{1234}

Table 6.1. continued

Model	df	Tests of Role Heterogeneity				Terms Differing between Models
		G^2	Models	ΔG^2	Δdf	P	
8. All 1, all 2, u_{123}, u_{234}	104	374.3	5–8	1503.8	8	P < .0001	Effects of role on distribution of responses $u_{15} + u_{25} + u_{35} + u_{45}$
9. All 1, all 2, u_{123}, u_{234}, u_{125}, u_{235}, u_{345}	92	338.7	8–9	35.6	12	P < .001	Role × 1st-order other-contingent effects $u_{125} + u_{235} + u_{345}$
10. All 1, all 2, u_{123}, u_{234}, u_{125}, u_{235}, u_{345}, u_{135}, u_{245}	84	221.3	9–10	117.4	8	P < .0001	Role × 2nd-order self-contingent effects $u_{135} + u_{245}$
11. All 1, all 2, u_{123}, u_{234}, u_{125}, u_{235}, u_{345}, u_{135}, u_{245}, u_{1235}, u_{2345}	68	98.0	10–11	123.3	16	P < .0001	Role × 2nd-order other/self-contingent effects $u_{1235} + u_{2345}$

*Where "all 1" means all u's having one subscript (i.e., u_1, u_2, u_3, u_4, and u_5), "all 2" means all u's having 2 subscripts, and so on. Dimensions 1, 2, 3, 4 = acts at times t, $t-1$, $t-2$, $t-3$
Dimension 5 = role or actor

reduction in G^2 of 527.3 while reducing the degrees of freedom by 12. Hence, these terms contribute significantly (at the .001 level) to producing a better fit of the model to the data.

We utilize these data to determine first whether they best fit a first-, second-, or third-order Markov process. Then we examine the effect of role differences on each of the significant relationships determined in our tests of order to see if the parameters of the Markov process are different for civilians and officers. The results indicate that a second-order Markov model provides a substantially better fit to the data than the first-order model and does not differ substantially from a third-order model (the third-order effects, though statistically significant, have considerably smaller contributions than first- and second-order effects). The effects of role on the first- and second-order effects are also highly significant, indicating officers and civilians differ substantially in their behavior. We conclude that police-suspect interaction is best described by a second-order Markov model with heterogeneous roles.

To test the additional assumptions of stationarity and homogeneity, we examine three similar five-dimensional matrices. The first dimension in one matrix is time (i.e., a two-value variable consisting of the aggregated first 10 interactions versus the last 10 interactions of each encounter); in another matrix it is the perceived social class of the civilian (i.e., upper or middle versus lower); and in the last matrix it is the nature of the offense (i.e., traffic versus nontraffic). In all of these matrices, the other four dimensions are those from the second-order, heterogeneous role model (i.e., acts at times t, $t + 1$, and $t + 2$, respectively, and role). The assumption of stationarity is tested by examining the interaction of this time variable with the model effects, and the assumption of homogeneity is tested by examining the interaction of social class and offense with the model effects. The results of these tests are presented in Table 6.2.

The objective of this analysis is not to determine the best fitting log-linear model for these data matrices, but to assess the generalizability of this second-order Markov model with heterogeneous roles by assessing its stationarity and its homogeneity. Our primary interests in Table 6.2 are the effects for each of these three variables on the parameters of the

Table 6.2. Tests of stability and homogeneity for a second-order model of police-suspect interaction

Model		df	G^2	Models	ΔG^2	Δdf	P	Effects
1. 1,2,3,4,5*	X = Time X = Soc class X = Offense	99 99 99	1318.9 1995.1 2424.6					1. Second-order model
2. 1,2,3,4,5,23,24,34,234	X = Time X = Soc class X = Offense	79 79 79	940.3 1266.9 1508.9	1–2 1–2 1–2	378.6 728.2 915.7	20 20 20	P<.0001 P<.0001 P<.0001	2. All role effects on second-order model
3. All 1,23,34,24,234,235,245, 345,2345,25,35,45	X = Time X = Soc class X = Offense	53 53 53	133.9 38.9 86.2	2–3 2–3 2–3	806.4 1228.0 1422.8	26 26 26	P<.0001 P<.0001 P<.0001	3. Effects of X on distribution of responses
4. All 1,23,24,34,25,35,45, 12,13,14,234,235,345,245, 2345	X = Time X = Soc class X = Offense	47 47 47	95.6 33.7 78.3	3–4 3–4 3–4	38.3 5.2 7.9	6 6 6	P<.0001 P>.10 P>.10	4. Effects of X on first- and second-order main effects on distribution of responses
5. All 1,23,34,24,25,35,45,12, 13,14,234,235,345,245,123, 124,135,2345	X = Time X = Soc class X = Offense	35 35 35	79.5 27.7 62.1	4–5 4–5 4–5	16.2 6.0 16.2	12 12 12	P=.1839 P=.9134 P=.1824	5. Interactions of role and x, and interactions of role, x, and distribution of responses
6. All 3,2345	X = Time X = Soc class X = Offense	28 28 28	54.3 25.7 44.6	5–6 5–6 5–6	25.2 2.0 17.5	7 7 7	P<.001 P>.95 P>.10	6. Interaction of role, x, and second-order effects
7. All 4	X = Time X = Soc class X = Offense	8 8 8	11.5 9.7 14.5	6–7 6–7 6–7	42.8 16.0 30.1	20 20 20	P=.001 P=.7194 P=.0676	

*Dimension 1 = time, class, or offense
Dimensions 2,3,4 = acts at times t, $t-1$, and $t-2$
Dimension 5 = actor

Markov model (effects 4 and 6 on the right side of this table). For purposes of comparison we present the effects of the second-order Markov process and the role effects (effects 1 and 2, respectively). Because of the requirement that we consider hierarchical models for this log-linear analysis, we also present effects 3 and 5, which represent the effects of variable X and role on the distribution of responses at different times, and the effects of the interaction of X and role on those distributions, respectively. These last two effects do not represent changes in the interaction model and the interaction model makes no predictions regarding their magnitude, so they are not of concern in this analysis. (If our objective were to fit these particular data optimally, these would require consideration.)

The results indicate that there are no significant effects of social class or the nature of the offense on the parameters of the model. However, the observed data differ significantly (at the .001 level) from the predictions of the second-order Markov process model with heterogeneous roles for the first 10 and last 10 interactions. The sources of this difference are broken down on the right side of Table 6.2 into effects 4, 5, and 6. A substantial portion of this difference is due to effect 3 and 5, which are the effects of time on distribution of responses, and the interactions of role and time, and the interactions of role, time, and distribution of responses at different times, respectively—effects that are of no interest for assessing the stability of the interaction process model. The type-4 effects, which are the effects of time, are insignificant. But the type-6 effects, which are the effects of the interaction of role and time on the transition probabilities, are significant at the .001 level. That is, although time by itself has no significant effects upon the transition probabilities of the interaction process model, time and role together interact to produce significant differences in transition probabilities. In the latter way the interaction process model appears to be nonstationary.

At this point we could modify our model to include nonstationarity of this sort. However, more important than statistical significance is the consideration of the relative importance of these effects compared to the Markov model effects. It is well known that the chi-square statistic increases in proportion to the number of cases. The G^2 statistic employed here has the same property. Hence, while tests of significance based upon these statistics may be appropriate for intermediate numbers of cases, for very large samples, such as we have here, relatively minor effects may be statistically significant. G^2/n is a rough measure of association. For all type-6 effects for time, this coefficient is 42.8/1900 = .0225. In contrast, for combined effects producing the second-order Markov process model with heterogeneous roles, the coefficient is 1185/1900 = .623. Clearly, whatever lack of stationarity there may be in this model is considerably smaller than the order or role effects of the model. The addition of a time dimension also requires a considerable increase in the complexity of the model. For all of these reasons, we argue that although there is some lack of stationarity, it is small relative to the hypothesized effects of the model, and, particularly given the large number of cases, it is judged not to be substantively significant in this case. These results thus support the assumptions of homogeneity and stationarity for the second-order Markov model with heterogeneous roles.

To facilitate this discussion, consider the following example of a sequence of acts, which is consistent with the data employed in this analysis:

$$3, 2, 1, 1, 1, 2, 1, 2, 2, 2, 3, 3,$$

where 1 is a definitional act, 2 is a confirming act, and 3 is a controlling act; and the first act occurs at time t, the second at the time $t + 1$, and so on. There are three possible values that may occur at each time (1, 2, or 3). Because we have determined that this process is best described by a second-order Markov process, we want to think of this series of interactions as a series of each of the two adjacent acts, i.e., 32, 21, 11, 11, 12, 21, 12, 22, 22, 23, 33, where the last act of the first pair is the same as the first act of the second pair, and so on. We are simply redefining the sequence of acts, not as a series of individual acts, but as a series of paired acts occurring in sequence. Each state can now take on nine possible values based on all possible combinations of two acts (i.e., 11, 12, 13, 21, 22, 23, 31, 32, and 33). Because we also know that we have to distinguish between officers and civilians, the interaction sequence now becomes

$$O_3C_2, C_2O_1, O_1C_1, C_1O_1, O_1C_2, C_2O_1,$$
$$O_1C_2, C_2O_2, O_2C_2, C_2O_3, O_3C_3,$$

where O_i indicates a response by an officer and C_i indicates a response by the civilian. Because O_1C_1 is not the same as C_1O_1, we now have 18 possible combinations of acts that define each state of the Markov process:

$$O_1C_1, O_1C_2, O_1C_3, O_2C_1, O_2C_2, O_2C_3, O_3C_1, O_3C_2, O_3C_3$$

and

$$C_1O_1, C_1O_2, C_1O_3, C_2O_1, C_2O_2, C_2O_3, C_3O_1, C_3O_2, C_3O_3.$$

We can represent the Markov process by a transition matrix that includes estimates of the transition probabilities from every possible state at some time t to every possible state at time $t + 1$. For the second-order Markov process with heterogeneous roles, we thus have an 18×18 transition matrix (e.g., see Rausch, 1972).

Not all of the cells in this 18×18 transition matrix represent logically possible transitions. Recall that, because of the way we coded our data, there can be no direct transitions from a state in which the last response was that of the officer to a state in which the first response was one of the civilian (i.e., $P[O_iC_j:O_kC_l] = O$ for all i, j, k, l). In addition, because the last act of one state is the same act as the first act in the next state there can be no direct transitions from states having a last act, j, to states having a first act, k, where $j \neq k$ [i.e., $P(O_iC_j: C_kO_l) = O$ for all $j \neq k$ and $P(C_iO_j:O_kC_l) = O$ for all $j \neq k$].

The parameters of this Markov model may be estimated using the same contingency-table data used to test the assumptions of the model. It has been shown (Anderson and Goodman, 1957; Birch, 1963) that the maximum likelihood estimate of the transition probability, $P(j:i)$ (the probability that event j will occur at time t given that event i occurred at time $t - 1$) is simply

$$P(j:i) = x_{ij}(t)/x_i(t - 1),$$

Mathematical Model of Symbolic Interaction 127

where $x_{ij}(t)$ is simply the number of joint occurrences of event i at time $t - 1$ and event j at time t, and $x_i(t - 1)$ is the number of occurrences of event i at time $t - 1$.

The transition matrix for the second-order Markov model with heterogeneous roles is presented in Table 6.3. Cells that are logically impossible are left blank. In the remaining cells the estimated transition probabilities are presented along with the frequency of occurrence for that particular transition for the data (the latter are in parentheses). This model provides the basis for all of the analysis that follows.

A number of properties of this model should be pointed out here because they have implications for the type of interaction that occurs. Because a single actor does not make two consecutive responses, this model is periodic with a period of 2. That is, the probability of the system's going from state $O_iC_j(t)$ to state $O_iC_j(t + n)$ is zero unless n is a multiple of 2 (Feller, 1968). It should also be pointed out that although the model is a second-order model, it is only second-order in the sense that current acts are contingent upon the most recent past act of the other actor and the most recent past act of the actor. Current actions are not contingent on the second most recent act of either actor. Because the effect of role is incorporated into the matrix as a whole, the process as a whole is Markovian.

The logical rigor of Markov models makes possible many predictions that provide insight into police-civilian interaction. Before exploring these logical properties, we will test three predictions which should yield positive results if the model is valid. These predictions are (1) the distribution of runs, (2) the multistep transition probabilities, and (3) the equilibrium distribution of responses.

A run may be defined as the occurrence of one state repeatedly in a sequence of interactions with no other states intervening between occurrences of that state. There can be no simple runs for periodic models such as this one, because the states alternate between officers and civilians. The related two-step transition matrix generated by finding the second power of the transition matrix in Table 6.3 is aperiodic, and each state may succeed itself directly. The frequency of occurrence of runs of different lengths for each state may be com-

Table 6.3. Transition matrix for the second-order Markov model with heterogeneous positions for officer/single-suspect encounters

Actions of Officers and Civilians at Times $t-2$ and $t-1$ ($t-2, t-1$)	O_1C_1	O_1C_2	O_1C_3	O_2C_1	O_2C_2	O_2C_3	O_3C_1	O_3C_2	O_3C_3	N
O_1C_1	.461 (18)	.462 (18)	.077 (3)							39
O_1C_2				.285 (145)	.530 (270)	.185 (94)				509
O_1C_3							.488 (20)	.171 (7)	.341 (14)	41
O_2C_1	.226 (14)	.629 (39)	.145 (9)							62
O_2C_2				.193 (186)	.657 (634)	.150 (145)				965
O_2C_3							.184 (12)	.508 (33)	.308 (20)	65
O_3C_1	.176 (6)	.500 (17)	.324 (11)							34
O_3C_2				.450 (121)	.256 (69)	.294 (79)				269
O_3C_3							.291 (37)	.276 (35)	.433 (55)	127

Table 6.3. continued

Actions of Officers and Civilians at Times $t-2, t-1$	\multicolumn{9}{c}{Actions of Officers and Civilians at Times $t-1$ and t ($t-1, t$)}	
$t-1$ ($t-2, t-1$)	O_1C_1	O_1C_2	O_1C_3	O_2C_1	O_2C_2	O_2C_3	O_3C_1	O_3C_2	O_3C_3	C_1O_1	C_1O_2	C_1O_3	C_2O_1	C_2O_2	C_2O_3	C_3O_1	C_3O_2	C_3O_3	N
C_1O_1	.143 (5)	.771 (27)	.086 (3)							35
C_1O_2				.329 (25)	.592 (45)	.079 (6)				76
C_1O_3							.148 (4)	.593 (16)	.259 (7)	27
C_2O_1	.064 (29)	.885 (401)	.051 (23)							453
C_2O_2				.034 (33)	.951 (912)	.015 (14)				959
C_2O_3							.061 (19)	.703 (218)	.236 (73)	310
C_3O_1	.087 (6)	.710 (49)	.203 (14)							69
C_3O_2				.053 (4)	.347 (26)	.600 (45)				75
C_3O_3							.115 (10)	.471 (41)	.414 (36)	87

O_1 = officer defining C_1 = civilian defining
O_2 = officer confirming C_2 = civilian confirming
O_3 = officer controlling C_3 = civilian resisting

puted (data not shown). When these are assessed using log-linear models, they do not differ significantly (these were tested separately for officer-first states and for civilian-first states producing a G^2 of 54.4 and 52.5, respectively, each distributed with 50 degrees of freedom).

It is a well-known property of Markov chains that the multistep transition probability (i.e., the probabilities that a particular response will occur on the $(t + n)$th interaction given that some particular response occurred on the tth interaction) is obtained by raising the appropriate coefficient in the one-step transition matrix to the nth power. If this is done, there is a systematic tendency for the predicted transition probabilities to underestimate the frequency of unchanged responses (i.e., the main-diagonal values) and to overestimate the frequency of changed responses (the off-diagonal values). The predicted and observed frequencies for this table as a whole differ significantly beyond the .01 level (log-linear models were used to test the fit separately for the upper left-hand and lower right-hand submatrices producing a G^2 of 145.1 and 160.2, respectively, each distributed with 81 degrees of freedom) (data not shown).

It has been shown in general (Feller, 1968) that for Markov chains which are periodic with period t and in which all states have similar properties, as these do, the states can be divided into t mutually exclusive classes, $G_0, \ldots, G_{t-1}$ such that a one-step transition leads to a state in the right neighboring class of states. Each of these submatrices corresponds to an irreducible closed set. When those states have a finite mean recurrence time, as these do, then, relative to the chain with transition matrix p^t, each class is ergodic and each of these submatrices approaches an equilibrium distribution of responses that is *totally independent of the initial distribution* and is defined solely in terms of the transition matrix.

The equilibrium distribution for such a model may be obtained by raising the transition matrix to some power. There the multistep transition probabilities in each column will approach a stable value that is the same for each row. The equilibrium distribution probability of each response is then

Mathematical Model of Symbolic Interaction

Table 6.4. **Expected and observed equilibrium distribution of states for second-order Markov model with heterogeneous roles**

	Equilibrium Distribution			
	Observed		Predicted	
State*	Frequency	%	Frequency	%
O_1C_1	11	1	9	1
O_1C_2	111	12	108	11
O_1C_3	5	1	9	1
O_2C_1	18	2	14	1
O_2C_2	228	24	226	24
O_2C_3	9	1	14	1
O_3C_1	7	1	7	1
O_3C_2	65	7	63	7
O_3C_3	21	2	26	3
C_1O_1	6	1	9	1
C_1O_2	20	2	17	2
C_1O_3	7	1	5	1
C_2O_1	119	13	103	11
C_2O_2	201	21	221	23
C_2O_3	84	9	72	8
C_3O_1	12	1	15	2
C_3O_2	6	1	16	2
C_3O_3	20	2	19	2

*O_1 = officer defining C_1 = civilian defining
C_2 = officer cooperative C_2 = civilian cooperative
C_3 = officer controlling C_3 = civilian resisting

simply the probability in the column associated with that response. In Table 6.4 the predicted equilibrium distributions are compared with the distributions observed during the last ten interactions in each encounter. Clearly, the observed and predicted response distributions are quite close. In addition, the goodness of fit of these distributions was assessed utilizing log-linear models and the difference between the predicted and observed responses was found not to be statistically significant.

SINGLE-COMPLAINANT ENCOUNTERS

We hypothesize that the second-order Markov model with heterogeneous positions derived from the single-violator analysis will fit the single-complainant sample. We expect differences in the specific parameters of the model that reflect the different role expectations of both the complainant and the officer. We assess the fit of this model in the same way we originally tested the model in the single-violator analysis. In Table 6.5 we report the results of log-linear tests of order of contingency, and position heterogeneity. As before, the data are in the form of a five-dimensional contingency table. The first four dimensions are acts at times t, $t + 1$, $t + 2$, and $t + 3$, and the fifth dimension is the position of the person speaking.

Just as for the single-violator sample, we find that the process of interaction between police and complainants is best fitted by a second-order Markov model. Examining the results in the table, we see that there are substantial first-order effects but only very slight and nonsignificant third-order effects. When we look at the effect of position, we find that it is very small and in many cases nonsignificant. The only significant effect, other than its main effect, is on the second-order transition probabilities.

Differences in behavior between officers and complainants are very small compared to the differences between officers and alleged violators. Even though there are very few differences in the transition probabilities between positions, there is still a substantial main effect of position, indicating that the distribution of acts by civilians and by officers in these encounters is still very different. We will examine these role differences in greater detail shortly.

Although the position differences are very small in this set of encounters, we will continue to use the second-order Markov model with heterogeneous positions as the model of the process of interaction between police and civilians for these data. We retain this model because we know that in certain circumstances there are substantial differences. It is important to have a model that accounts for these differences. Maintaining the distinction allows us to examine several differences between officers and complainants compared to officers and suspects.

Because the analysis just discussed examines the effects of

Table 6.5. Tests of order and role heterogeneity for the single-complainant model

Model	G^2	df	P	Models	ΔG^2	Δdf	P	Effects
1. 1,2,3,4,5	1965.72	152	<.0001					
2. 1,2,3,5,12,23,35	1449.52	140	<.0001	1–2	516.20	12	<.0001	12,23,35 1st-order other-contingent effects
3. 1,2,3,5,12,23,35,13,25	894.36	132	<.0001	2–3	555.16	8	<.0001	13,25 2nd-order self-contingent effects
4. + 15	879.37	128	<.0001	3–4	14.99	7	.036	15 3rd-order other-contingent effects
5. + 123,235	840.10	112	<.0001	4–5	39.27	16	<.0001	123,235 2nd-order other/self-contingent effects
6. + 1235	825.64	80	<.0001	5–6	14.46	32	.997	1235 3rd-order other/self/other effects
7. + 14,24,34,45	86.69	72	.114	6–7	738.95	8	<.0001	14,24,34,45 main effects of role
8. + 124,234,345	70.93	60	.158	7–8	15.76	12	.202	124,234,345 role × 1st-order effects
9. + 134,425	37.46	52	.936	8–9	33.47	8	<.0001	134,425 role × 2nd-order effects
10. + 145	31.93	48	.964	9–10	5.53	4	.237	145 role × 3rd-order effects
11. + 1234,2345	16.12	32	.991	10–11	15.81	16	.466	1234,2345 role × 2nd-order other/self-contingent effects
12. + 12345	0	0		11–12	16.12	16	.445	12345 role × 3rd-order other/self/other effects

order for positions of officers and complainants combined, we also ran an additional analysis, which examined the order of the process separately for officers and complainants. The purpose of the second analysis was to assure that both were engaged in a second-order process rather than some other process. This test confirmed that it is a second-order process. In fact, it is almost a third-order process. But because the third-order effects are so small relative to the first-or second-order effects, and contribute so little to accounting for the distribution of frequencies in the contingency tables, fitting a third-order Markov process would probably be overfitting, and it is likely to produce results that are not generalizable in other settings. There appears to be little difference in the magnitude-of-order effects for each role. There is little difference between the tendency of either actor to respond to himself as contrasted to responding to the other actor. Whereas officers have more influence on both themselves and suspects, officers and complainants have about equal influence on the other and themselves.

The additional Markov assumptions of stationarity and homogeneity are tested and the results reported in Tables 6.6 and 6.7. The stationarity assumption is tested by comparing the first 10 interactions in the encounter with the last 10. The homogeneity assumption is tested by comparing subsamples of encounters differing by gender of the complainant, the education of the officers (less than high school versus high school or more), the severity of the offense (felony versus no felony), the severity of the outcome (report versus no report), and the age of the complainant (adult versus young adult). Although there are a number of significant interaction effects between time and these other variables, there are no significant differences in the transition probabilities as a function of any of these variables alone. Except for these statistical interaction effects, the second-order process is both stationary and homogeneous.

While testing whether the parameters of the interaction process remain the same for these subsamples, we took advantage of the opportunity to test each of the subsamples separately for the order and position heterogeneity effects that are the bases of this interaction model. These subsamples afford

Table 6.6. Tests of stationarity for single-complainant encounters

Model	χ^2	G^2	df	P	Models	χ^2	ΔG^2	Δdf	P	Effects
1. 1,2,3,4,5	18031.6	2146.2	99	<.0001						
2. 1234,5	50.8	51.9	53	.517	1–2	17980.8	2094.3	44	<.0001	1234 Markov model effects
3. 1234,15,25,35	33.9	34.5	47	.912	2–3	16.9	17.4	6	.008	15,25,35 effects of time on distribution of acts
4. 1234,15,25,35,45	33.6	34.2	46	.900	3–4	0.3	0.3	1	.584	45 effects of time on role differences
5. + 125,235	26.2	26.9	38	.911	4–5	7.4	7.3	8	.505	125,235 effects of time on 1st-order effects
6. + 135,1235	22.2	26.7	26	.425	5–6	4.0	0.2	12	.999	135,1235 effects of time on 2nd- & 3rd-order effects
7. + 145,245,345	9.9	10.1	20	.966	6–7	12.3	16.6	6	.011	145,245,345 effects of time and role on distribution of acts
8. + 1245,2345	6.9	7.0	12	.858	7–8	3.0	3.1	8	.928	1245,2345 effects of time and role on 1st-order effects
9. + 1345	5.0	5.1	8	.747	8–9	1.9	1.9	4	.754	1345 effects of time and role on 2nd-order effects

Table 6.7. **Tests of homogeneity for single-complainant encounters**

Partitions	Model	χ^2	G^2	df	P	$\Delta\chi^2$	ΔG^2	Δdf	P	Effects
Sex	1234	91.0	95.5	54	.001	17.0	17.4	1	<.0001	5
Education ($<$HS/$\geq$HS)		81.6	83.3	54	.007	41.4	42.2	1	<.0001	Main effects of partitions
Felony/No Felony		815.3	856.3	54	.000	634.2	695.3	1	<.0001	
Report/No Report		167.7	179.5	54	.000	83.6	86.3	1	<.0001	
Adults/Young Adults		340.1	354.1	54	.000	294.6	302.9	1	<.0001	
Sex	1234,5	74.0	78.1	53	.014	44.3	47.0	7	<.0001	15,25,35,45
Education ($<$HS/$\geq$HS)		40.2	41.1	53	.883	5.1	4.8	7	.684	Effects of partitions on acts and role differences
Felony/No Felony		181.1	161.0	53	.000	135.0	116.2	7	<.0001	
Report/No Report		84.1	93.6	53	.001	35.5	45.4	7	<.0001	
Adults/Young Adults		45.5	51.2	53	.545	7.4	12.4	7	.088	
Sex	+15,25,35,45	29.7	31.1	46	.955	2.4	2.9	8	.940	125,235
Education ($<$HS/$\geq$HS)		35.1	36.3	46	.847	9.8	10.6	8	.225	Effects of partitions on first-order contingencies
Felony/No Felony		46.1	44.8	46	.523	7.4	7.0	8	.537	
Report/No Report		48.6	48.2	46	.385	4.8	5.4	8	.714	
Adults/Young Adults		38.1	38.8	46	.765	14.5	13.9	8	.084	
Sex	+125,235	27.3	28.2	38	.877	1.8	1.5	4	.827	135
Education ($<$HS/$\geq$HS)		25.3	25.7	38	.936	4.3	4.3	4	.367	Effects of partitions on second-order contingencies
Felony/No Felony		38.7	37.8	38	.776	5.4	5.4	4	.249	
Report/No Report		43.8	42.4	38	.287	10.9	11.1	4	.025	
Adults/Young Adults		23.6	24.9	38	.950	2.4	2.0	4	.736	

Table 6.7. continued

Partitions	Model	χ^2	G^2	df	P	$\Delta\chi^2$	ΔG^2	Δdf	P	Effects
Sex	+135	25.5	26.7	34	.809	9.2	9.8	14	.777	1245,2345
Education ($<$HS/$\geq$HS)		21.0	21.4	34	.954	11.7	12.3	14	.582	Effects of partitions and role on first-order contingencies
Felony/No Felony		33.3	32.4	34	.546	17.8	16.8	14	.267	
Report/No Report		32.9	31.3	34	.601	20.1	18.6	14	.181	
Adults/Young Adults		21.2	22.9	34	.926	7.3	9.5	14	.798	
Sex	+1245,2345	16.3	16.9	20	.659	3.6	3.6	4	.463	1345
Education ($<$HS/$\geq$HS)		9.3	9.1	20	.982	0.7	1.1	4	.894	Effects of partitions and role on second-order contingencies
Felony/No Felony		15.5	15.6	20	.741	2.7	2.7	4	.609	
Report/No Report		12.8	12.7	20	.890	0.5	0.8	4	.938	
Adults/Young Adults		13.9	13.4	20	.860	3.4	3.5	4	.478	
Sex	+1345	12.7	13.3	16	.651	12.7	13.3	16	.651	12345
Education ($<$HS/$\geq$HS)		8.6	8.0	16	.949	8.6	8.0	16	.949	Effects of partitions and role on remaining second-order contingencies
Felony/No Felony		12.8	12.9	16	.680	12.8	12.9	16	.680	
Report/No Report		12.3	11.9	16	.751	12.3	11.9	16	.751	
Adults/Young Adults		10.5	9.9	16	.872	10.5	9.9	16	.872	

1,2,3 = acts
4 = role
5 = partitions

Table 6.8. **Transition matrix for the second-order Markov model with heterogeneous positions for officer/single-complainant encounters**

Actions of Officers and Civilians at Times $t-2$ and $t-1$ ($t-2, t-1$)	\multicolumn{12}{c}{Actions of Officers and Civilians at Times $t-1$ and t ($t-1, t$)}											
	O_1C_1	O_1C_2	O_1C_3	O_2C_1	O_2C_2	O_2C_3	O_3C_1	O_3C_2	O_3C_3	C_1O_1	C_1O_2	C_1O_3	C_2O_1	C_2O_2	C_2O_3	C_3O_1	C_3O_2	C_3O_3
O_1C_1										.519 (14)	.444 (12)	.037 (1)						
O_1C_2													.337 (110)	.641 (209)	.021 (7)			
O_1C_3																.333 (2)	.500 (3)	.167 (1)
O_2C_1										.128 (5)	.821 (32)	.051 (2)						
O_2C_2													.167 (195)	.813 (948)	.020 (23)			
O_2C_3																.385 (5)	.538 (7)	.077 (1)
O_3C_1										.143 (1)	.714 (5)	.143 (1)						
O_3C_2													.273 (9)	.394 (13)	.333 (11)			
O_3C_3																.100 (2)	.100 (2)	.800 (16)
C_1O_1	.375 (9)	.625 (15)	.000 (0)															

Table 6.8. continued

Actions of Officers and Civilians at Times $t-2$ and $t-1$ ($t-2, t-1$)	O_1C_1	O_1C_2	O_1C_3	O_2C_1	O_2C_2	O_2C_3	O_3C_1	O_3C_2	O_3C_3	C_1O_1	C_1O_2	C_1O_3	C_2O_1	C_2O_2	C_2O_3	C_3O_1	C_3O_2	C_3O_3
C_1O_2				.138 (8)	.793 (46)	.069 (4)												
C_1O_3							.000 (0)	1.000 (3)	.000 (0)									
C_2O_1	.049 (15)	.938 (287)	.013 (4)															
C_2O_2				.025 (29)	.970 (1128)	.005 (6)												
C_2O_3							.122 (5)	.707 (29)	.098 (7)									
C_3O_1	.222 (2)	.667 (6)	.111 (1)															
C_3O_2				.154 (2)	.615 (8)	.231 (3)												
C_3O_3							.059 (1)	.235 (4)	.706 (12)									

O_1 = officer defining C_1 = civilian defining
O_2 = officer confirming C_2 = civilian confirming
O_3 = officer controlling C_3 = civilian resisting

an opportunity to test the generalizability and pervasiveness of these assumptions across various types of encounters.

Because these results are similar for each subsample, and very much like those for the entire sample, we do not report the breakdowns for each subpopulation here. Each of the transition matrices looks very much like the transition matrix for the entire sample of complainant encounters. Each of these subsamples of encounters displays substantial first-order effects, second-order effects, and substantial effects of position and first-order statistical interactions. The second-order and position statistical interactions remain relatively small, as before. The first-order and position statistical-interaction effects are much stronger in each of these subsamples than they were in the original complete sample. These results provide stronger evidence for the position-heterogeneity hypothesis than the results for the entire sample.

The second-order Markov model with heterogeneous positions for single-complainant encounters is specified in Table 6.8. The structure of this model is identical to the one for the single-violator encounters and the only differences between them are the differences in specific transition probabilities.

Just as we did with the single-violator sample, we may test specific predictions of this model on the single-complainant sample. The three predictions tested are the same as those tested earlier for single violators. They are (1) the equilibrium distribution of responses, (2) the multistep transition probabilities, and (3) the distribution of runs.

The predicted and observed distribution of runs, generated in the same way as for the single-violator analysis, are reported in Table 6.9. There is a striking similarity between these two distributions. A test of the difference between the observed and predicted distributions produces a chi-square of 123.3 with 109 degrees of freedom, which is nonsignificant. The model accurately predicts the distribution of runs.

The predicted and observed multistep transition frequencies are generated in the same manner as they were for the single-violator encounters. Tests comparing the observed and predicted frequencies (data not shown) lead to the following results: for the 4-step prediction a chi-square of 745.8 with 241 degrees of freedom, $p = .001$; for the 20-step prediction a chi-square of 680.0 with 241 degrees of freedom, $p = .0001$. As with the suspect sample, the model does not fit adequately in this regard.

The observed and predicted equilibrium distributions for this model were examined. A test comparing the predicted and observed distributions produces a chi-square of 65.6 with 17 degrees of freedom, which is significant at $p = .0001$ (data not shown). The predicted equilibrium distribution for complainants did not fit the data as well as that for suspects.

For two independent subsamples of police-civilian interaction we have found that a second-order Markov model with heterogeneous positions provides the best fit to the data. In each case we have found the process to be both relatively stationary over time and relatively homogeneous among various subsamples within each set of encounters. In each case the predictions of the model are partially supported. The similarity of the results in these two independent analyses and the extent of support of the model in each case provide compelling evidence that the process of police-civilian interaction approximates a second-order Markov process with heterogeneous positions.

These tests add further support to our distinction between integral and situated roles. The fitting of the model requires the inclusion of the distinction between them.

SOME LIMITATIONS OF THIS AND OTHER STUDIES

The discussion of the full implications of these findings will be reserved for the following chapters. Before pursuing the specifics of that discussion we will outline both some limitations of our findings and the fundamental modifications they necessitate for understanding police-civilian relations.

These data are *estimates* based upon two different groups of police-civilian encounters, both of which are limited to encounters at least 20 utterances long: those with a single sus-

Table 6.9. **Expected and observed distribution of runs for each state of a second-order Markov model with heterogeneous roles (officer-complainant)**

	O_1C_1		O_1C_2		O_1C_3		O_2C_1		O_2C_2		O_2C_3		O_3C_1		O_3C_2		O_3C_3	
	Obs	Pre	Obs	Pre	Obs	Pre	Obs	Pre	Obs	Pre	Obs	Pre	Obs	Pre	Obs	Pre	Obs	Pre
1.	15	(15)	116	(105)	5	(5)	78	(90)	104	(59)	19	(18)	5	(5)	23	(19)	8	(6)
2.	3	(3)	29	(33)			16	(14)	42	(47)	0	(2)			2	(5)	2	(3)
3.	1	(1)	6	(10)			8	(2)	36	(37)	1	(0)			0	(1)	1	(2)
4.			2	(3)			3	(0)	19	(29)							0	(1)
5.				(2)			1	(0)	15	(23)							1	(0)
6.									10	(18)							0	(1)
7.									11	(15)								
8.									7	(11)								
9.									9	(9)								
10.									3	(7)								
11.									5	(5)								
12.									3	(5)								
13.									1	(3)								
14.									0	(3)								
15.									2	(2)								
16.									2	(2)								
17.									0	(1)								
18.									0	(1)								
19.									3	(1)								
20.									3	(1)								
21.									2	(0)								
22.									1	(0)								
23.									0	(1)								
24.									0	(0)								
25.									2	(0)								
26.									0	(0)								
27.										(1)								
28.																		
29.									1	(0)								
TX	19		153		5		106		281		20		5		25		13	

Obs = Observed O_1 = officer defining
Pre = Predicted O_1 = officer confirming
                 O_3 = officer controlling

pect and those with a single complainant. The probabilities are estimated by aggregating all the transitions from these encounters. Any interpreter should beware of making the equivalent of the ecological fallacy. No particular encounter will necessarily display these transition probabilities. Particular encounters will display a range of transition probabilities. The larger the sample, the more closely the transition probabilities should approximate the overall estimate.

Second, the suspect and complainant encounters are alike in

Table 6.9. continued

C₁O₁		C₁O₂		C₁O₃		C₂O₁		C₂O₂		C₂O₃		C₃O₁		C₃O₂		C₃O₃		
Obs	Pre	Obs	Pre	Obs	Pre	Obs	Pre	Obs	Pre	Obs	Pre	Obs	Pre	Obs	Pre	Obs	Pre	
15	(15)	85	(97)	5	(5)	114	(103)	102	(59)	24	(21)	11	(11)	15	(16)	8	(4)	1.
4	(3)	17	(14)			28	(33)	38	(46)	4	(5)			2	(2)	0	(3)	2.
	(1)	6	(3)			7	(10)	39	(37)		(2)			1		1	(1)	3.
		6	(0)			2	(3)	20	(29)							0	(1)	4.
							(2)	13	(23)							1	(0)	5.
								12	(18)								(1)	6.
								11	(14)									7.
								6	(11)									8.
								10	(9)									9.
								1	(7)									10.
								7	(5)									11.
								2	(5)									12.
								1	(3)									13.
								1	(3)									14.
								2	(2)									15.
								2	(2)									16.
								0	(1)									17.
								1	(1)									18.
								2	(1)									19.
								1	(1)									20.
								3	(0)									21.
								2	(0)									22.
								0	(1)									23.
								0	(0)									24.
								2	(0)									25.
								0	(0)									26.
									(1)									27.
																		28.
								1										29.
19		114		5		151		279		28		11		18		10		

C_1 = citizen defining
C_2 = citizen confirming
C_3 = citizen resisting

only one substantively important way—both are second-order. They differ in particular parameter structures and particular output structures. While they are similar in approximating a Markov model in regard to predictions of distributions of runs, and to a lesser extent in the predicted equilibrium distribution, these are only very abstract similarities. Since they approximate Markov models, this suggests that in both cases the effect of the initial distribution of states will wear off and that a relatively stable distribution of states (output structure) will characterize each aggregated set of encounters. This does *not* mean that this will be true of every individual encounter. This does *not* mean that stability or equilibrium is identical to cooperation. It means that over an *aggregated* set of encounters, at some point past the first few utterances, the distributions of defining, confirming, and either controlling or resisting utterances will remain the same. They will be approximately the same at the twentieth utterance as they were at the twelfth, and approximately the same at the twenty-fifth utterance as at the fifteenth. The exact probabilities and proportions *differ* for the suspect and the complainant sets, and these exact probabilities are of primarily substantive import.

What these data mean then is that the estimated transition probabilities for the aggregated encounters provide a guide for making a best bet in any individual encounter, and that the proportion of acts represented by the output structure when it reaches equilibrium is a guide for making a best bet of the state of any encounter at any particular time—for instance, after eight utterances have occurred.

We should further emphasize that the tests of homogeneity are based on variables which were distributed in such a way as to make statistical tests practical. Thus there was not a sufficient number of blacks to test for the effects of race of either suspects or complainants, nor sufficient female suspects to test for the effects of gender on the suspect data. Inferences regarding homogeneity must be made cautiously because of these limitations. Nonetheless, various sources of error and heterogeneity effects can only dilute or weaken the model. This is why we feel there are compelling reasons to accept it as valid. It is sufficiently robust to endure the many possibilities of observer error, and of the multitude of other factors which impinge upon officer/single-civilian interaction.

These findings modify a wide range of previous conclusions about police-civilian relations. They do so because of fundamental flaws in the design, or limitations in the nature of the data of previous studies. Here we will limit our discussion to the finding that police-civilian interaction is a second-order process. This finding is important because it questions the interpretation, if not the validity, of many previous findings. It also will force future investigators to conceptualize much more clearly what *form* police-civilian relations take, and what import the detailed interpersonal behavior taking place in the encounter has in comparison to personal, demographic, and situational factors. These are the first empirical data that make an initial estimate of the relative importance of these variables. Such data are absent in police research and rare in social psychology. In one study by Rausch (1965), acts of a child were found to be mostly attributable to the previous act of another child, and to a much lesser extent due to group membership and situation. We believe our findings confirm, as will future findings of other social psychologists, that this is true not only for police interaction, but for many other instances of interaction.

An example of the limitations of previous data, and of the perilous generalizations that may be made from them, as well as of the failure to conceptualize explicitly the "order" of a process, is found in Black's otherwise excellent chapter, "Dispute Settlement by the Police," in his book *The Manners and Customs of the Police* (1980). There Black utilized a distinction between four basic styles of social control (see also Black, 1976), which he attributed to police: penal, compensatory, therapeutic, and conciliatory. While he did not clearly specify the operational definitions upon which identification of these styles was based (though the structured-observer schedule is included in an appendix), he found that 45% of disputes were settled using a combined conciliatory-penal style, 24% in an entirely conciliatory style, and 22% in an entirely penal style. A penal style involved condemnation and punishment, and a conciliatory style involved an attempt to settle a dispute without regard to who was right or wrong (131). Unfortunately, Black provided no tables for type of style by outcome, so we do not know, for instance, whether an encounter characterized by a conciliatory style resulted in a penal outcome.

Our objection to Black's interpretation of the meaning of his data is more fundamental. First, since no detailed data on the processes of interaction are present in his data, it is impossible to know, specifically, of what kinds of acts, and in what numbers, each style consisted. In fact, we doubt that such styles (nominal categories) exist. Only continua exist (more or less of each).

Second, Black presented numerous bivariate and multivariate distributions in which style was presented as a function of the characteristics of either persons or situations. He related person and situational characteristics to the style "chosen" by the officer. Black concluded that the requests by whites of white police are more often granted than requests by nonwhites (136); that social class is a major predictor of how the police handle disputes (142); and that police are more often conciliatory in their style when disputes are between equals than when between those in some hierarchical relationship (147). In all these cases and in others that he mentioned, Black utterly omitted any consideration of the detailed process of interpersonal behavior that our data show mediate the effects of these other variables. We imagine they have much more indirect effect (through the interaction) than direct effect.

Third, Black never clearly expressed any concept of order. He attributed causal influence to such factors as race, alleged offense, or closeness of relation over the style of control of the officer. He gave almost no attention to the possibility that *civilians* as well as officers have characteristic modes of interacting (though he notes that 9% of suspects and 4% of complainants are either disrespectful or violent [170]). By suggesting that he does not clearly conceptualize order we mean that he does not ask to what extent a civilian's act affects the probabilities of an officer's consequent act.

Might some of the differences he found be due to differences in the interactions of civilians? An officer with a stable predisposition to respond in particular ways to particular acts of civilians will display phenomenologically different acts, and therefore will appear to be treating civilians differently, when there are differences in the distributions of civilian acts directed to him. This is equally true of civilians dealing with officers or other civilians. Underlying stable predispositions to respond result in *different* actual responses depending on the different proportions of the kinds of acts the other externalizes. A small difference in style of social control by, for instance, social class, may merely mean that a small percentage of lower-class suspects direct more resisting acts to the officer. This increases the probability that the officer will use either imperative or coercive regulation, that is, a penal style. This is not directly due to the effect of social class on the officer, who would be affected similarly by any suspect, but due to a difference of interaction style of a small proportion of lower-class suspects *together with* the stable response tendencies of the officer. Support for this alternative interpretation is provided by our data, which show that both process and parameter structures are unaffected by social class. We found that, regardless of the apparent social class of the civilian, the interaction between officers and civilians took the same basic form and was described by essentially the same parameter values. Officers were as likely to respond to particular acts with imperative or coercive regulation for upper- or middle-class civilians as for lower-class civilians.

Finally, Black asserted that police-civilian interaction is, at most, first-order. Such an assumption is implicit in his conclusion that police are more apt to acquiesce to the request of a white, or that they arrest more black juveniles because black complainants request it (Black and Reiss, 1970). These findings take the form: citizen request → officer acquiescence. This form is first order. It manifests the common-sense assumption that police acts affect civilians and vice versa. The discovery that police-civilian interaction is a second-order process falsifies the assumption of simple mutual influence. The officer's response is made not just to the citizen's request, but also to his own response *before* the citizen's request. His response takes both his previous act and the citizen's into account, not just the citizen's. Neither Black nor other police scholars give much implicit recognition, and no explicit recognition, to this possibility. Both officers and civilians take not just the other's previous act, but their own previous act into account. This is a much more subtle set of effects than is implied by the mere assumption that officers and civilians affect each other.

We have chosen to focus on Black because we believe his is among the best empirical work on policing. His omissions are common to almost all police research, because little of that research actually involves the collection of utterance-by-utterance or act-by-act data on police-civilian interaction. Only with such data is an accurate estimate of the direct and indirect effects of personal, demographic, and situational variables possible. The greatest significance of the data in this chapter is that they demonstrate the great importance of the actual acts occurring in the process of interaction as both direct and mediating variables, and that the process of those acts manifests a second-order form.

7

Further Explorations of Police-Civilian Dyads

In the preceding chapter we examined two independent sets of encounters between police officers and civilians. One of those subsamples consisted only of encounters with a single violator and the other with a single complainant. In each case we found that the same model, a second-order Markov model with heterogeneous positions, provided the best fit to the data. We tested the basic assumptions of this model, including order, homogeneity, and stationarity; and also a number of specific predictions, including the equilibrium distribution, multistep transition probabilities, and the distribution of runs. It was clear that the process of interaction between police and civilians could be described best as a second-order process with relatively minor influences from third-order processes. These processes remain stationary over the duration of the encounter, and are remarkably alike for various subsamples. The purpose of this chapter is to explore further the substantive implications of this model.

In the last chapter we distinguished three interaction process components: process structure, parameter structure, and outcome structure (Hernes, 1976). In Chapter 6 the *process structure* was examined. It is the form of the contingencies between aggregated acts. In those data we have shown that this form is a second-order Markov process with heterogeneous positions.

Though the particular form of the relationship remains the same, the *exact magnitude* of the contingencies may vary. Thus, while both officer-civilian, and civilian-officer process structure are second-order, the second-order transition probabilities calculated over the aggregate from one particular act to another may be very different for each. This is termed the *parameter structure*.

Third, given some particular initial distribution of acts, these will "pass through" both the process and parameter structure at each step of the process and be "redistributed" at the next, and redistributed at the step after, and so forth. The distribution of aggregated acts at each particular step is the *outcome structure*.

What, at the aggregate level, we term the parameter structure, at the individual level we term "response propensity." We assume that the parameter structure is the best estimate of how officers, or suspects, or complainants will respond. A "reponse propensity" is a probability of a position responding to some act in a particular way. For example, civilians tend to respond cooperatively to cooperative acts by officers with a probability of .951 when their own past act was also cooperative; hence it is said that in these circumstances they have a propensity to respond cooperatively.

It is very important to maintain the distinction between parameter and outcome structure. The one measures much of the dynamics of the interaction, whereas the other measures states at rest. There has been little opportunity in the social sciences for empirical examination of both.

A convenient way to evaluate the parameter structure is through the use of directed graphs (digraphs) of the transition probabilities for each of the two subsamples of encounters. Digraphs enable us to summarize and interpret the process more easily because of their visual form.

An approach to more precise understanding of the output structure is to treat each transition matrix as a series of equations. The mathematical solution contains the equilibrium distribution predicted for the process, if it is Markovian, as well as information on how quickly it will approach this distribution. The mathematical solution is expressed by what are called eigenvalues and eigenvectors.

DIGRAPH ANALYSIS OF THE PARAMETER STRUCTURE

Because the process is second-order, it is necessary to consider the four possible states in pairs. Each officer performed defining, cooperative, or controlling acts, while each civilian performed defining, cooperative, or resisting acts. Each act is in the contingency form: officer-civilian, officer; or civilian-officer, civilian. It is necessary to interpret the meaning of each of the possible pairs substantively.

Since each actor may externalize one of three acts, when an act of one is combined with the act of another, nine possible combinations result. Each combination suggests a different relationship between the actors. Each relationship is a more specific example of what Simmel (in Simmel, 1950) termed the forms of interaction. We would prefer to reserve the term "form" for the more abstract contingency between antecedent and consequent acts, that is the process structure. Thus we have found that this contingency is second-order, or possesses a second-order *form*. The more specific relationship, the particular combination of these acts by an officer and a civilian we prefer to term, after Mead (1934), a social act, an act that requires the participation of two or more persons if it is to occur. Each social act consists of a pair of acts, one by each actor. The names we give to each of the nine possible social acts are analogous to Simmel's forms. These nine social acts are displayed in Figure 7.1.

A social act labelled *competition* occurs when both officer and civilian attempt to assert definitional regulation. One may ask a question, but the other, instead of answering, responds by asking another question. Alternatively, one may accuse the other, situationally defining the other's identity, but the response of the other may be either another accusation or a question. Both are competing to define the domain of discourse, or the situational identities of the actors.

If the officer defines the situation and the civilian cooperates in the definition, then that social act is one of *agreement*.

Figure 7.1. **Social acts formed from the permutation of officer-civilian and civilian-officer acts**

Civilian Act	Officer Act		
	Defining	Confirming	Controlling
Defining	**Competitive** (−)	**Redirective** (−)	**Evasive** (−)
	Competitive (−)	*Agreeing* (+)	*Sanctioning* (−)
Confirming	**Agreeing** (+)	**Cooperative** (+)	**Dominant** (+)
	Redirective (−)	*Cooperative* (+)	*Dominant* (−)
Resisting	**Noncooperative** (−)	**Reassertive** (−)	**Confrontative** (−)
	Tacking (−)	*Persistent* (−)	*Confrontative* (−)

NOTE: **Boldface** indicates officer-initiated civilian response; *italics* indicate civilian-initiated officer response; (+) indicates positively perceived by the officer; (−) indicates negatively perceived by the officer.

On the other hand, the citizen may refuse to accept the definition, in which case the social act is one of *noncooperation*. If the officer responds to this refusal by asking a question on another subject, then this social act is *tacking*. We borrow this term from sailing, because it suggests that the officer is attempting to approach the civilian "from another angle."

If the officer's last act was a confirming act, that is, an act which simply continued a previously defined line of discourse, and the citizen externalizes a defining act, for example, by asking a question related to a different topic, then this social act is one of *redirection*. The civilian is trying to change the topic of conversation. If the civilian's defining act is followed by an order by an officer, this social act is *sanctioning*.

The officer may have given an order. If the civilian responds to the order by asking a question, or by making an accusation, both defining acts, then this is an *evasive* social act. It is evasive because rather than overtly obey or disobey the order, the citizen has sought simply to redefine the situation, and avoid confrontation.

Social acts known as competition, redirection, and evasion involve an officer externalizing a defining, confirming, or controlling act, in each case followed by a civilian's defining act.

Social acts known as competition, agreement, and noncooperation occur when an officer has externalized a defining act, followed by an act of the civilian which is, respectively, defining, confirming, or resisting. Four possibilities remain.

The officer may externalize a confirming act, followed by a confirming act of a civilian. In this case this combination of acts constitutes the social act of *cooperation*. Both actors are simply continuing a previously defined line of discourse.

The officer may externalize a confirming act, followed by a resisting act of a civilian. This can only occur when some particular line of discourse has been established with the cooperation of both, but then the civilian decides not to cooperate further and refuses to continue it. We term this social act *reassertion*, because a previously cooperative civilian decides to withhold further cooperation, and reasserts his autonomy. If the officer then merely continues the broken line of discourse by another confirming act, this social act is *persistence*.

The officer may externalize a controlling act and the civilian respond by a confirming act. In other words the civilian obeys an order. The social act combining command and obedience is termed *dominance*, whether the civilian's confirming act precedes or follows the officer's controlling act.

Finally, the officer may give an order and the civilian refuse to obey it. This social act is *confrontation*.

These social acts are named more from the perspective of the officer than from the perspective of the civilian. The second act, in Figure 7.1, when it is the act of the civilian, "completes" the officer's act. The officer's act, alone, has no meaning apart from the civilian's response. A command has no meaning in isolation. Its social meaning lies in the response of the civilian. Social acts of evasion, domination, and confrontation can only result from the *pair* of acts. Neither domination nor confrontation can occur unless a command is confirmed or resisted. The pair constitutes domination or confrontation.

The important difference between these social acts and Simmel's forms is not only in terminology. Not only are there more types of acts than forms, but these acts, empirically, are in sets of three, not sets of two. If interaction is second-order, then each *act* is contingent upon the *social* act that preceded it.

Another way to conceptualize this contingency is to assume that the middle act of three acts is the second act completing the first pair, and at the same time the first act of the second pair. The second social act is contingent upon the first in every case. It also means that since the second act is the last act in the first social act and the first act in the second social act, then the second social act is constrained to only those social acts that begin with the same act as completed the previous social act. If the second act of the previous social act was a confirming social act by a civilian, then the next social act can only be one in which the officer completes the pair by a defining, confirming, or controlling act. We may give some but not all of these civilian-officer acts the same names as those given to officer-civilian acts in Figure 7.1. Thus the officer-civilian social act of agreement can only by followed by a civilian-officer social act that is redirecting or cooperative or persistent.

That police-civilian interaction is second-order means that we must continuously think of pairs contingent upon pairs, that is, social acts contingent upon social acts, not acts alone contingent upon acts. Simmel did not anticipate this possibility, though, as we shall demonstrate in Chapter 11, G. H. Mead did.

We must always remember that when we think in terms of a process of social acts such as: competition, agreement, cooperation, etc., each designates a social act, and therefore a pair of acts, and not only are the *acts* contingent, but the *social acts* are also contingent.

It is likewise important to remember that because citizens so seldom gave orders, and officers even less often obeyed them, that these combinations are not represented in these data. We have chosen to ignore, because of their statistical infrequency, such role reversals. Consequently, from inspection of Figure 7.1, it is evident that the social acts known as competition, redirection, agreement, and cooperation may begin with an act by either an officer or a civilian, while the social acts of evasion, domination, and confrontation may only begin by an officer's giving a command, and the social acts of noncooperation and reassertion end only by a resisting act of a civilian. While it is empirically possible for a civilian to give an order and an officer to obey it, such social acts are too infrequent to consider separately. Citizen-defining/officer-controlling, citizen-resisting/officer-defining, and citizen-resisting/officer-confirming social acts are frequent enough to give them the appropriate names of sanctioning, tacking, and persistence, respectively. All these names are given from the officer's perspective and connote a likely interpretation of such social acts by an officer.

As one moves from the upper left corner of Figure 7.1 to the lower right corner one moves from a zone of disagreement over definition, through a zone of agreement, to a zone of more or less overt conflict, and from a zone of general cognitive structuring to one pertaining to specific facts of the case, and thus to one of very direct legal relevance to both actors. *From the officer's point of view*, we assume that only agreement, cooperation, and domination are entirely positive social acts, while the other six combinations represent some measure of civilian assertiveness. One might hypothesize, given the greater power and status of the officer, a movement from the negative to the positive states. This movement is identical to the principle of balance (Heider, 1958). In this case, the balance sought is between civilian's behavior and officer's concept of the proper conduct of civilians toward officers. The negative social acts in Figure 7.1 will be unstable, but the positive social acts will be stable. The probabilities will be high of moving from unstable to stable social acts, but not vice versa.

A digraph of the second-order Markov model with heterogeneous positions for police-suspect interaction is presented in Figure 7.2. In this digraph each possible social act is represented by a circle. Arrows connecting social acts represent the transition probabilities from one to another. Solid arrows

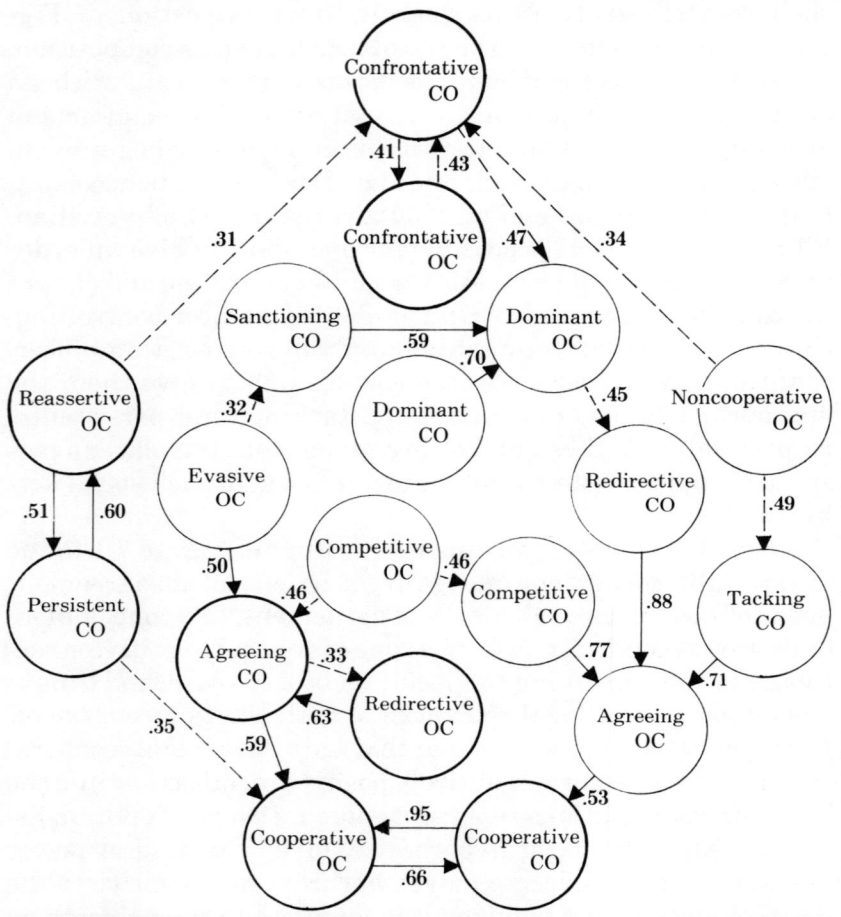

Figure 7.2. **Digraph of a second-order Markov model of social acts of officers and suspects**

represent transition probabilities greater than or equal to .500; dotted arrows represent transition probabilities ranging from .300 to .499.

The digraph shows four recurring cycles of social acts, that is, processes represented by closed loops connecting series of social acts in which all of the arrows are going in the same direction. These four cycles are: confrontation-confrontation, reassertion-persistence, agreement-redirection, and cooperation-cooperation. Of these cycles, two represent combinations of the positive social acts. Confrontation-confrontation represents the refusal of either actor to concede, but even this cycle has a probability of .47 of moving to the positive state of domination. The other, reassertion-persistence, has about the same probability of ending in either cooperation, .347; or confrontation, .308.

The cooperation cycle is the most stable cycle in the digraph. It occupies a unique position indicating that it is very likely to be entered in the course of the encounter. Considering that we are limiting our purview to officers and suspects—those who have a strong potential conflict of interest—it is noteworthy that the cooperation cycle may be entered after defining acts of either officer or suspect with almost the same probability (.592 and .530). From every state some continuous path of arrows leads eventually to the cooperation cycle. Both actors possess a strong predisposition to come to agreement on the definition of the situation, on the situated identity of the civilian actor, and on the prerogatives of the officer.

Paths into the confrontation cycle are likely to issue either from noncooperation, or reassertion, both attempts by the suspect to negate the officer's definition of the situation. Evasion, on the other hand, does not have a high probability of leading to confrontation.

The general flow of the digraph tends to confirm the import of authority and power in the social definition of reality. "Taking charge" occurs less explicitly in the sense of overt physical acts and more in terms of cognitive and symbolic behavior. Ultimately, encounter behavior typically centers upon how actors present themselves and their identity claims. Defining acts are very important. Perhaps, instead of "taking charge," police are really "thinking charge."

In Chapter 3 we demonstrated that officers establish their initial authority over a volatile work group simply by asking a question, and only in less than 20% of encounters by giving an order. Figure 7.2 displays the probabilities of social acts following these initial acts of the officer. If the next act of the suspect after the officer's first defining act is defining, then the first social act of the encounter is competitive; if confirming, then agreeing; and if resisting, then noncooperative.

How does the officer typically respond to each of these acts? If the first act of the encounter is competitive, then the chances are equal (.46) that the next social act will be either *agreeing* or competitive. If an agreeing social act occurs, then there may follow a brief series of agreeing and redirective acts in which the *suspect* takes the initiative, then moving to the cooperative cycle. By initiative we mean that the essential meaning of the act is given by the suspect's *response*. The cooperative cycle is entered by the *officer* agreeing to the suspect's definition of the situation.

If the first social act is competitive and is followed by a second competitive social act taken at the initiative of the officer, then the probabilities are quite high that an agreeing social act will follow, and then the cooperative cycle will be entered. While the suspect takes the initiative in the first sequence (competitive-agreeing-redirective-agreeing-cooperative), the officer takes the initiative in the second sequence (competitive-competitive-agreeing-cooperative). One might interpret the first sequence as one in which the officer is not in control, and thus one which, according to Muir (1977), would be a threat to the officer. Yet it is notable that this sequence is as likely to lead into the cooperative cycle as the other. The probability that it will lead to sanctioning is low (.07) (for probabilities less than .30, see Table 6.3). Though less common than officer-led cooperation, there are police-suspect sequences in which suspect initiatives are accepted by officers and lead to cooperation. It is also notable that because the probability of sanctioning is so low, the probability of confrontation resulting from competition is also very low (.07 × .26). Confrontation is similarly unlikely if the second sequence predominates. The ability of the officer and the suspect to discuss the situation, whether initiative is taken by the civilian or the officer, leads to cooperation.

On the other hand, if the officer's initial act is controlling, followed by a suspect's defining act, the two thus constituting an evasive social act, the probabilities are relatively high (.50) that the next act will be agreeing, again with the suspect taking the initiative. This sequence of social acts is: evasive-agreeing-redirective-agreeing-cooperative. Again, this is a se-

Police-Civilian Dyads

quence essentially controlled by the suspect, this time under even more surprising conditions, for the sequence begins by the civilian evading a controlling act of the officer. If this sequence of social acts does not occur, then the second most likely is a complex series: evasive-sanctioning-dominant-redirective-agreeing-cooperative. The probabilities are still low that evasion will lead to confrontation. The ways to cooperation may be either by a sequence in which the suspect takes the initiative (the most probable), or in which the officer does. The former sequence again appears to contradict the assumption that officers always feel threatened when the suspect takes the initiative.

A second examination of Figure 7.1 will now demonstrate that our hypothesis that police-perceived negative acts (competition, redirection, evasion) appearing in the first row of the figure will transform to the police-perceived positive acts in the second row is correct. Social acts in row one are transients generally giving way to a positive set of social acts dominated by cooperation.

On the other hand, the acts that are most likely to lead to a confrontation cycle are in the third row: reassertion-persistence-reassertion-confrontation and noncooperation-confrontation; though a sequence beginning with noncooperation is somewhat more likely to lead to tacking, on the officer's initiative, and thence to agreeing and cooperation. The cycle of confrontation is preceded by overt verbal resistance on the part of the suspect. Sometimes this leads directly to confrontation, and at other times it will lead to a cycle of reassertion and persistence. This contest of wills has about an equal chance of leading to cooperation or confrontation. No particular social act has a high probability of leading into the reassertive-persistent cycle. Its origins are diffuse, and we do not have sufficient information to suggest which particular conditions, if any, steer it toward confrontation instead of cooperation.

The acts in the first two cells of the third row of Figure 7.1 are those which lead either to the officer-perceived positive acts in row two, or to the mutually perceived negative acts in the third cell of the third row. On the whole these data suggest that officers will tolerate indirect disagreement by suspects, and even briefly tolerate overt verbal resistance, and seek, in both cases through such social acts as agreeing, sanctioning, persisting, and tacking, to elicit agreeing or cooperation on the part of the suspect. Failing this, a cycle of confrontation is likely to occur. There is no one highly probable sequence leading out of this cycle.

Finally we should note that the identification of these particular social acts permits us to describe the process of social action specifically and in detail, retaining its actually probabilistic character, avoiding the vagueness of terms such as "penal" or "conciliatory" (Black, 1980:131).

ANALYSIS OF THE OUTPUT STRUCTURE

Often it is desirable to go beyond specific but limited predictions of a model to get a comprehensive view of the dynamic process represented, (i.e., to look for regularities in the output structure, in Hernes's terms). One method for doing this is to examine the eigenvalues and eigenvectors of the transition matrices. From those we may determine: whether the system approaches any equilibrium points; where those equilibria occur; how stable they are; and how fast the system approaches equilibrium. Such an equilibrium may contain various proportions of each of the three acts.

The transition matrix can be analyzed by determining the eigenvalues and eigenvectors which characterize that matrix. It can be shown (Feller, 1968) that for periodic Markov chains one of the eigenvalues will be -1.0; and for probabilistic matrices in general, when the Markov chain is aperiodic, one of the eigenvalues will be equal to 1.0 and the others will be less than 1.0. In addition, it can be shown that as the number of interactions becomes very large, the actions of the participants aproach the stable equilibrium distribution corresponding to the eigenvector associated with the eigenvalue of 1.0 at a rate which is determined by the second largest eigenvalue.

We already know the interaction is periodic. This periodic character of the interaction means nothing more than that officers and civilians take turns speaking. We pointed out in Chapter 6 that the interaction tends toward an equilibrium distribution. Here we focus on the single-violator results to illustrate this analysis. The single-violator equilibrium distribution is dominated by cooperation and domination (together these responses make up 70% of the responses). Twenty-six percent of the social acts at equilibrium are either noncooperative or sanctioning, and only 4% are confrontational. Police-civilian interaction at equilibrium is rarely characterized by confrontation. Officers and suspects manage to keep such acts to a minimum. These results replicate the common finding in studies of police that most police-civilian encounters are routine and involve infrequent confrontation (Reiss, 1971).

By computing eigenvalues for the irreducible subsets of the matrix for the Markov chain based on the two-step transition matrix, it is possible to determine the rate at which interaction approaches this equilibrium (Feller, 1968). As anticipated for aperiodic ergodic submatrices, the largest eigenvalue is 1.00 and the remaining eigenvalues are less than 1.00. The rate of approach to the equilibrium solution is given by the second highest eigenvalue, which is .404. This means that whenever the interaction continues two more steps (i.e., one act by the officer and one act by the civilian), the contribution of the other eigenvectors to the distribution of responses diminishes to only .404 times its prior contribution. This is relatively fast. Within very few cycles the equilibrium distribution should predominate and be closely approximated by the data. The remaining eigenvalues are considerably smaller (i.e., the largest is $.201 + .015i$), hence there is no need to consider them here and their values will not be reported. The approach of the system to equilibrium is affected primarily by the second largest eigenvalue and its associated eigenvector. These eigenvalues suggest relatively simple dynamic behavior of police-civilian interaction. The interaction process is aperiodic, highly stable, and quick to approach equilibrium.

One might predict, on the basis of these data, that however an encounter begins, it is likely to become either cooperative or dominating quickly.

Comparisons of Processual and Static Models

This analysis of police-civilian interaction may appear to some readers an overly complex solution to a relatively simple problem. In this section we address this issue by explicitly comparing the predictions of the second-order Markov model with heterogeneous positions to predictions from a static model.

The static-model predictions are obtained by taking the equilibrium distribution of acts and computing the probability of occurrence of specific chains of three successive acts using only the probabilities in the equilibrium distribution (i.e., the successive acts are statistically independent of one another and unaffected by the transition probabilities). The static model does a very poor job of predicting the observed transition frequencies ($X^2 = 1085$, $df = 53$, $p < .0001$) (data not shown). Generally, the static-independence model greatly overestimates the frequency of the most common events and greatly underestimates the frequency of less common events. This is significant because the static model makes confrontative and resisting acts appear much *less* likely than they are. The processual model is more faithful in reflecting the potential for such acts to occur.

Both the static and the processual models account rather accurately for the observed aggregate interactions, but only the processual model adequately explains the parameter structure. This indicates that *the observed aggregate structure of interactions is a product of underlying interaction processes.* The importance of the processual aspect of interaction in accounting for the parameter structure is also supported by additional analyses that we conducted. Although those findings are limited by the relatively few cases available to estimate some of the higher order process parameters (i.e., two-step transition probabilities), the results indicate *the underlying processes characterizing the encounter are more stable throughout the course of the encounter than is the output structure which describes the state of the interaction at any one point in time.* By inference, the response propensities of the actors remain stable throughout the encounter, despite momentary perturbations in the behavior of each. This suggests that aggregated frequencies alone are an inadequate measure of police-civilian behavior. Data on the process and parameter structures help explain outcomes that are mistakenly attributed to personal, situational, and demographic factors.

Relationship of Process to Structure

As we discussed earlier, one may think of social interaction as involving several interlocking levels of structure and process. The order of the process determines the number of levels. For a second-order process we may distinguish three levels: *response propensities, opportunity structures,* and *situation.* The *response propensities* correspond to the second-order transition parameters of the Markov model. Response propensities are tendencies of actors to respond in particular ways. *Opportunity structures* (a term borrowed from Coleman, 1973) correspond to the first-order probabilities of a particular response by the one actor given some action by the other actor. Opportunity structure is used here because this is an indication of the opportunity facing each of the actors. Though both officers and civilians may emit the same range of behaviors, the likely *consequences* of those actions *differ* considerably as a function of their different positions. Officers or civilians may accuse one another, but with different consequences. First-order transition probabilities give an indication of what an experienced actor might estimate would be the likely response to his act.

The opportunity structure is an aggregate construct analogous to Mead's concept of "role-taking" at the individual level (Mead, 1934). Each actor chooses his act in anticipation of the likely response of the other. A first-order matrix reflects not just the actual probability of responses to an act, but may also

Table 7.1. **Opportunity structures of officers and suspects based on the probability of a particular act by one at time *t*, given the act of the other at time *t*−1**

Action by Actor 1 at Time *t*−1		Probable Response at Time *t* by Actor 2					
		Officer			Suspect		
		Defining	Confirming	Controlling	Defining	Confirming	Resisting
Officer	Defining				.087	.874	.039
	Confirming				.071	.894	.035
	Controlling				.075	.699	.226
Suspect	Defining	.182	.606	.212			
	Confirming	.295	.498	.208			
	Resisting	.316	.167	.556			

Table 7.2. **Situations for officers and suspects**

Role	Defining	Confirming	Controlling/Resisting
Officers	27	53	20
Alleged violators	7	83	10

estimate the anticipations of those responses by the first actors. It operationalizes in aggregate form the construct "role-taking."

Situations are the *aggregate* state of the encounter at any one point in time based upon the interactions that have occurred so far in the encounter. They summarize what the actor will have experienced up to that time. Here we will estimate what the situation might be, based upon all observed acts in the suspect and in the complainant groups of encounters. This should be representative of the situations the actors experienced in typical encounters.

In Tables 7.1 and 7.2 we report the opportunity structures and situations for officers and suspects. In Tables 7.3 and 7.4 are displayed the estimated opportunity structures and estimated situations for officers and complainants. Thus we may compare the differences between officers, on the one hand, and complainants or suspects, on the other; or compare with officers interacting with suspects to officers interacting with complainants.

It is clear from Table 7.1 that officers can anticipate that the citizen will respond with a confirming act no matter what their own act is. The citizen's response is likely to make their mutual social act agreeing, cooperative or dominant. The only other probability greater than .09 is .226 for a resisting act by a suspect in response to a controlling act by an officer. Thus, while the probabilities of agreeing, cooperative, or dominant social acts are .874, .894, and .699, respectively, the probability of confrontation is .226. Suspect behavior is predictable.

Suspects, on the other hand, are much less able to predict officer behavior. Only one social act, agreeing, has a proba-

Table 7.3. Opportunity structures for officers and complainants based on the probability of a particular act by one at time t, given the act of the other at time $t-1$

Action by Actor 1 at Time $t-1$		Probable Response at Time t by Actor 2					
		Officer			Complainant		
		Defining	Confirming	Controlling	Defining	Confirming	Resisting
Officer	Defining				.05	.93	.02
	Confirming				.03	.96	.01
	Controlling				.20	.59	.20
Complainant	Defining	.25	.75	.00			
	Confirming	.22	.72	.05			
	Resisting	.19	.31	.50			

Table 7.4. **Situations for officers and complainants**

	Responses (%)		
Role	Defining	Confirming	Controlling/Resisting
Officers	22	71	6
Complainant	5	93	2

bility greater than .5 when it is the officer who is responding, and that probability is only .606. It is not certain why officers are so unpredictable. In Chapter 3 we suggested that one way higher status is maintained is by retaining freedom of response and thereby, by implication, being unpredictable. On the other hand, officers have far more experience dealing with suspects than the average suspect has dealing with officers. For this reason, officers may be better at taking the role of the suspect and therefore eliciting the desired response. Their ability to anticipate the response of the suspect means they are in greater control of the resulting social act than appears on the surface. They can get suspects to do what they (the officers) want. At the present time we are unable to devise a test of which, if either, of these hypotheses is true.

Turning to an estimate of the situation, summarized in Table 7.2, it is evident that by the end of a typical encounter an officer will have experienced mostly confirming acts from the suspect (.826). Resisting acts are a distant second in probability (.103). Nonetheless, a typical encounter with a suspect will have included a mix of all three types of acts. The suspect, on the other hand, will typically have experienced many defining and controlling acts of the officer. Only about half the officer's acts will have been confirming. Thus the suspect is likely to emerge from an encounter not only with a feeling that the officer's acts are unpredictable, but also having experienced significant amounts of definitional and imperative supervision and regulation.

From the points of view of both officers and *complainants*, cooperative and agreeing social acts are the norm. These social acts will be due to the responses of the complainant more than those of the officer. Complainants are more likely to be evasive than suspects. Officers are more likely to use tacking behavior and less likely to use sanctioning behavior. Interestingly, officers are more likely to be reassertive with complainants than with suspects. Confrontation is about equally likely with both suspects and complainants, once either actor has initiated a controlling or a resisting act. Nevertheless, an estimate of the situation of the complainant, Table 7.4, shows that such acts are less likely to occur in the first place when police and complainants are interacting. This is an example of the importance of distinguishing between the opportunity structure and the situation. If a complainant is resisting, then the probability is about the same as with a suspect that the officer will respond with a controlling act, and thus a confronting social act will occur. While this can be anticipated as the likely response to such an act, the actual likelihood of either the complainant resisting or the officer controlling is much less than half what it is with suspects. Thus, a response propensity may remain the same, but the likelihood of its being elicited changes dramatically.

These same figures and tables permit the other comparisons not explored earlier. In Table 7.5 are reported the results of log-linear tests comparing officers in the two types of encounters with one another; and civilians in the two types of encounters with one another. The last three results on the right-hand side of each of these tables are of relevance to our analysis here. Those results indicate whether there are significant differences in situation, opportunity structures, and response propensities. The results indicate that officers interacting with alleged violators differ from officers interacting with complainants in situation, opportunity structure, and response propensities. Civilians on the other hand, differ in situation and opportunity structure but not in their response propensities.

Since the interaction response propensities (as measured by the second-order transition probabilities) for civilians were not significantly different in the two subsamples of encounters, we may focus upon the differences in the officers' response propensities under the two circumstances. Comparing

Table 7.5. Officers compared, whether interacting with suspects or with violators (dimension 4, top model); and civilians compared, whether officers think they are suspects or complainants (dimension 4, bottom model)

Model	χ^2	G^2	df	P	$\Delta\chi^2$	ΔG^2	Δdf	P	Effects	
							Officers			
1,2,3,4	2347.9	1446.5	46	.000						
+12,23	1030.5	952.8	38	.000	1317.4	493.7	8	.001	12,23	1st-order effects
+13	599.7	646.3	34	.000	430.8	306.5	4	.001	13	2nd-order effects
+14,24,34	202.4	141.8	28	.000	397.3	504.5	6	.001	14,24,34	Diffs. in situation as a function of position of other
+124,234	90.0	77.6	20	.000	112.4	64.2	8	.001	124,234	Diffs. in opportunity structure as a function of position of other
+134	42.0	42.7	16	.000	48.0	34.9	4	.001	134	Diffs. in transition as a function of position of other
							Civilians			
1,2,3,4	2290.4	1323.4	46	.000						
+12,23	1825.5	872.8	38	.000	464.9	450.6	8	.001	12,23	1st-order effects
+13	572.3	548.6	34	.000	1253.2	324.2	4	.001	13	2nd-order effects
+14,24,34	196.1	169.3	28	.000	376.2	379.3	6	.001	14,24,34	Diffs. in situation as a function of position defined by other
+124,234	120.6	115.4	20	.000	75.5	53.9	8	.001	124,234	Diffs. in opportunity structure as a function of position defined by other
+134	112.2	109.8	16	.000	8.4	5.6	4	.250	134	Diffs. in transition as a function of position defined by other

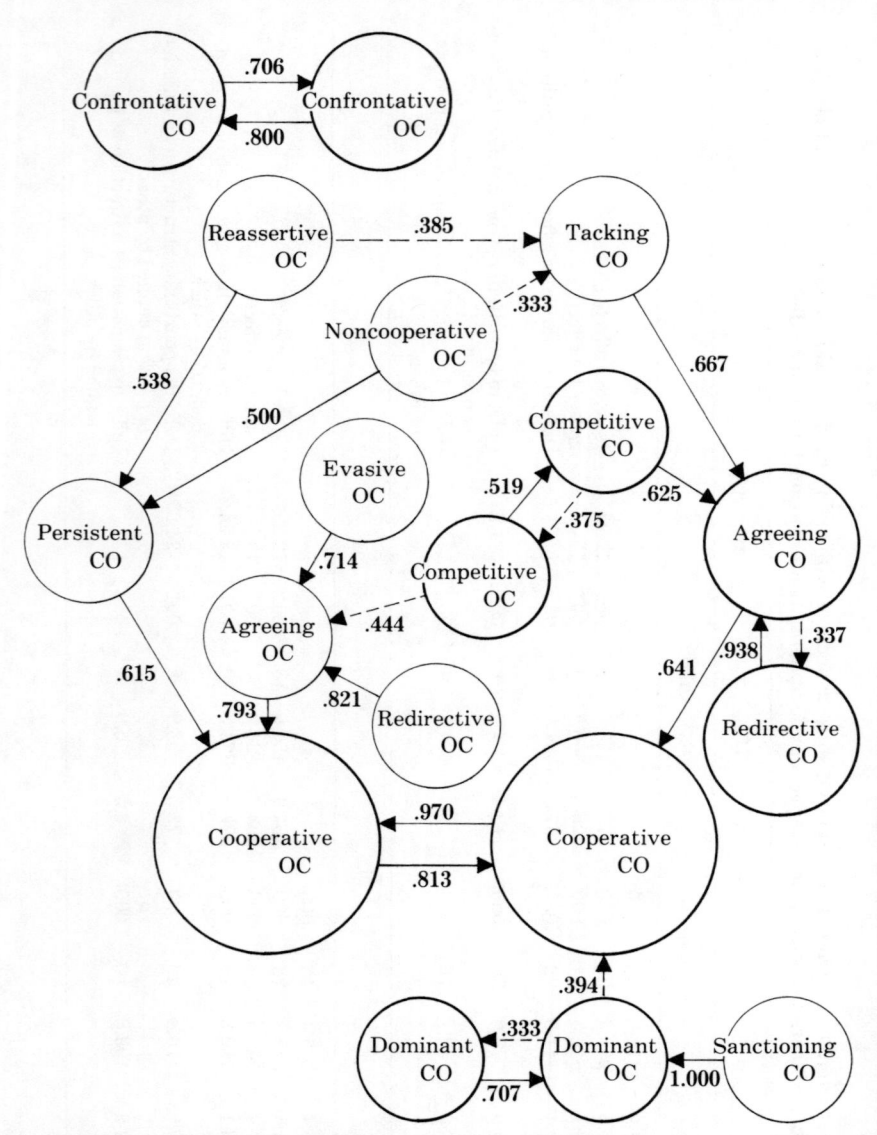

Figure 7.3. **Digraph of a second-order Markov model of social acts of officers and complainants**

the transition probabilities of officers with single complainants in Figure 7.3 to those of officers with single violators in Figure 7.2 we see a number of interesting differences: (1) officers are more likely to continue the mutually cooperative cycle with complainants than with alleged violators (.970 versus .657); (2) officers are more likely to enter the cooperative cycle in the first place with complainants than with alleged violators; (3) officers are considerably more likely to continue the confrontation cycle with complainants than with alleged violators (.800 compared to .433).

In short, it appears that, when interacting with complainants, officers are more likely to enter and stay in the cooperative cycle or to remain in a confrontation cycle if it should arise than when officers interact with alleged violators. Officers appear less eager to avoid (or perhaps less able to overcome) confrontation with complainants than with alleged violators, but also more eager to work cooperatively with them.

The net result of these differences in the officer response propensities for complainants relative to alleged violators and the accompanying, but generally insignificant changes of the civilian response propensities is a dynamic pattern of interaction with complainants which is very similar to that with alleged violators. It still approaches an equilibrium dominated by confirming acts. Every state leads along some path to the cooperative cycle, but it approaches that equilibrium even faster with complainants than with alleged violators. Surprisingly, the actors have more trouble extricating themselves from the confrontation cycle should it occur. Perhaps this is because officers have less authority over complainants than over suspects.

It is clear there are substantial role differences between police and civilians. These differences persist whether the civilians are suspects or violators. There are also differences due to situation, but these differences are not nearly so striking as those based on position.

Another way to assess role differences between officers and civilians is to examine how they differ in initiating and closing encounters. We examine these differences in the final sections of this chapter.

Table 7.6. **Who has the last word in encounters?**

	Officers (28%)		Civilians (72%)	
Who has the last word?	N	%	N	%
What is the last word?				
Defining (Def.)	7	26	2	3
Confirming (Conf.)	16	59	64	94
Resisting/Controlling				
(Res./Cont.)	4	15	2	3
Total	27	100	68	100

Beginnings and Closings of Encounters

The utterance that initiates an encounter between an officer and a civilian is important because it sets the tone for the entire encounter. It is indicative of the relationship that will be established between them. Examining the first utterance in each of the encounters for the single-violator sample, we find that 90% are made by officers and only 10% are made by civilians. Officers are 9 times more likely to initiate an encounter than are civilians. When officers do initiate encounters, 65% of their initial utterances are defining acts, whereas 35% of their initial utterances are controlling acts. When civilians initiated, all of their initial utterances were defining acts and none of them were resisting acts (data not shown). Recall that, because the "resisting" acts of civilians and the "controlling" acts of officers actually include the same acts, it is theoretically just as possible for civilians to initiate encounters with resisting acts as it is for officers to initiate encounters with controlling acts. By definition, the very first act in an encounter cannot be cooperative, because for that first act there is no prior act with which to cooperate.

The closing utterances in encounters, like the beginnings of encounters, offer another insight into the relationship between civilians and officers. The sample of single violators illustrates the ways in which officers and civilians end the encounter. The results of this analysis are evident from Table 7.6.

Police-Civilian Dyads

Table 7.7. **Last social acts of encounters**

	Officer Last Word			Civilian Last Word	
	%	N		%	N
Competitive	11	3	Competitive	3	2
Agreeing	7	2	Agreeing	31	21
Sanctioning	0	0	Noncooperative	1	1
Redirective	15	4	Redirective	0	0
Cooperative	48	13	Cooperative	29	20
Dominant	7	2	Reassertive	0	0
Tacking	0	0	Evasive	0	0
Persistent	4	1	Dominant	34	23
Confrontative	7	2	Confrontative	1	1
Total	100	27		100	68

At first glance, it appears that more civilians than officers have the last word. Seventy-two percent of the observed encounters were ended by civilians, whereas only 28% of the encounters were ended by officers.

On closer examination, officers may have had more influence over the last *social* act than first appears. Though civilians had the final "word" in 72% of the encounters, Table 7.7 shows that the last act was *confirming* in all but four cases. Thirty-one percent of these last social acts were agreeing; 29% cooperative, and 34% dominant. Officers appear to be able either to take the role of the suspect, or altercast the suspect (Weinstein and Deutschberger, 1963), or establish their supervision so completely, that while the suspect emits the last utterance, 94% of these social acts end with the suspect's confirming act.

In contrast, when officers have the last word they seldom confirm the citizen's prior utterance if it is either defining or resisting. Even if the suspect's utterance is confirming, the officer may conclude the encounter with a defining or controlling utterance. Consequently, when officers have the last word, the final social act is likely to be competitive, redirective, dominant, or confrontative.

A BRIDGE FROM AGGREGATED DATA TO INDIVIDUALS

The most important concepts in this chapter were response propensity, opportunity structure, and situation. These concepts are the bridge between the aggregated data and the interaction processes of officers, suspects, and complainants in particular encounters.

Response propensities are the individual equivalent of aggregated second-order transition probabilities. They constitute a best bet of how each actor will respond, given his own previous act and that of the other. This second-order process is most basic. Other processes derive from it.

We suggested that just as one could look at a *response* contingent upon the two previous acts, by looking at the first-order matrices implicit in the second-order matrix, we could discern for each actor his opportunity structure, an estimate of how the other actor would respond to him. Response propensities look back. Opportunity structures looked forward. We suggested that the first-order opportunity structure constitutes an operationalization of the concept of role taking. It is an estimate of the probabilities of particular responses one actor may expect from another. We operationalized a second important Meadean concept, social act, by suggesting that the combination of two acts, one by each actor, constitutes a social act, the meaning of which is dependent upon the second act of the pair.

We then asked what measure of situations is possible. Our conclusion was that a situation is essentially the sum of all that has happened to an actor up to any particular point in an encounter. We then estimated the typical situation by calculating the zero-order probabilities, i.e., the absolute proportions of various acts.

Digraphs of social acts were convenient devices for examining the response propensities. Concerning ourselves exclusively with the interaction process and not with the outcomes of encounters, e.g., arrest (which will be dealt with in the last chapter) we showed that surprisingly many sequences of officer-suspect social acts involved not only suspect initiative over the meaning of the social act, but suspect control of that meaning. Despite this, these sequences ended in cooperative cycles. Police do not always have to be in control of the process. We also showed that by persistent or tacking social acts, police are able to direct the encounter toward the cooperative cycle in many cases. Reassertive and noncooperative acts by suspects may lead to the confrontation cycle. There were no highly probable sequences out of confrontation.

Police are less predictable than either suspects or complainants. This may be because of their higher status; because civilians are less able to take the role of the officer, and therefore less able to elicit the desired response; or because officers may have more influence over themselves in the sense that they are more influenced by their own preceding act. We were unable to determine which, if any, was the correct explanation.

Finally we showed that officers exerted considerable influence over both the first and last social act of the encounters.

In Chapter 1 we hypothesized that the primary task of the police officer is talking. These two chapters describe how officers go about their tasks in dyads with single suspects or complainants. It is clear that in most cases officers are able to go about their tasks without resorting to overt force. It is clear from these data that their work possesses a process, a parameter, and output structure that can be described mathematically. It is also clear that while the average situation includes resisting acts by both suspects and complainants, in most cases officers can talk their way to cooperation and avoid confrontation. The concept of opportunity structure permits us to speculate that this may be because the officer is better at taking the role of the civilian than vice versa.

Although we do not have enough data to test the hypotheses suggested by these data because of an insufficient number of, among others, ethnic minority civilians in our data, we wish to note the potential of such tests. One of the most interesting questions is whether officers are less predictable when interacting with minorities (relative to their own ethnicity) than with either members of the majority or with their own group. Such increased unpredictability would suggest either that officers perceive themselves superior to such groups or that they are less able to take the role of the other when interacting with members of such groups. Such data would also help us trace the microprocesses that lead to confrontation.

8

The Model and Multiple-Position Interaction

We have analyzed dyadic relationships between three positions: an officer and either a suspect or complainant. Most encounters are not as simple. Officers settle fights, domestic disputes, quarrels between neighbors, and disagreements over money. Two or more civilian positions, often in conflict with one another, engage the officer. It is necessary to conceptualize a model that can accommodate these complex relationships. Of the several possible models, we have chosen one that is simply a more complex version of the dyadic model. Multiple-position interaction is broken down into subsets of successive dyadic interactions among different pairs of interactants. Two interlocking interaction processes result: (1) interaction within each dyad; (2) a metaprocess of transitions from one dyad to another.

Police-civilian interaction consists of a series of dyadic interactions occurring within a larger process of dyad formation and dissolution. Officers first exchange several utterances with one civilian; then with another civilian; consult with each other; and, finally, speak again to each civilian in turn, imposing upon them a resolution to the problem.

We shall first analyze the metaprocess, that is, who speaks to whom; and then examine the dyads themselves.

In the who-to-whom analysis, we shall distinguish three positions: (1) officer(s) (O); (2) "old" civilian(s)—civilians who participated, either by speaking or by being spoken to, in the last utterance or interaction (Co); and (3) "new" civilian(s)—civilians who were not participants, either speaking or being spoken to, in the last utterance (Cn). Nine who-whom combinations result:

O-O, O-Cn, O-Co, Cn-O, Cn-Cn, Cn-Co, Co-O, Co-Cn, Co-Co.

Because civilian-civilian interaction occurs so infrequently in these observations, we combine all of the civilian-civilian interactions into one category, C-C, leaving six categories:

1. O-O   officer-officer
2. O-Cn   officer-new civilian
3. O-Co   officer-old civilian
4. Cn-O   new civilian−officer
5. Co-O   old civilian−officer
6. C-C   civilian-civilian

By distinguishing "old" from "new" civilians we can identify when new civilians enter the interactions, or old ones cease to participate. Data on initiators of new dyads permit us to infer which positions control the interaction. Interactions between civilians or officers may be important in themselves.

Any logically possible who-to-whom combination may follow any other. Hence, for a series of two such utterances, there are $6 \times 6 = 36$ possible combinations. For a series of three, there are $6 \times 6 \times 6 = 216$ possible combinations.

In this subsample were 467 encounters. All included at least one suspect and in 30% of them there were two or more. These encounters averaged 29 utterances in length and included 13,185 transitions between utterances. The breakdown of the number of particular who-to-whom transitions is displayed in Table 8.1.

In one-third of the cases at least one violator had been drinking. They were mostly working class (approximately 61%). Eighty-five percent were white. Eighty percent were male. Suspects were likely to be either young adults or teenagers.

In 33% of the encounters, in addition to the violators, there was one or more complainant. Only 7% of the complainants were under the influence of alcohol. Most were adults. Complainants were distributed among social classes in the same proportion as violators. Half of the complainants were female,

Table 8.1. **Substantive significance and frequency of speaker-subject pair sequences**

Speaker-Subject Pair Sequence	Substantive Significance	Number of Sequences Observed
Co-O,Co-O	When civilians say more than one thing at a time, what is the second thing they say?	1,191
O-Co,O-Co	When officers say more than one thing at a time, what is the second thing they say?	1,204
O-Cn	How do officers initiate interaction with another civilian?	819
Cn-O	How do civilians initiate interaction with an officer?	321
Co-O,O-Co,Co-O O-Co,Co-O,O-Co	How do officers and the same civilian interact over a prolonged period?	8,335
O-O,O-O,O-O	How do officers interact among themselves over a prolonged period?	994
C-C,C-C,C-C	How do civilians interact among themselves over a prolonged period?	321

whereas most suspects were male. Compared to the violators, complainants tended to be sober, older, and female.

WHO-TO-WHOM ANALYSIS

In encounters with multiple actors, who first speaks to whom has practical import, since initiation is related to achieving control (Chapple, 1940, 1953) and eliminating conflict. In the earlier analysis of the single-suspect and the single-complainant subsamples, we showed that officers maintained control in a number of ways. Do they also control who speaks to whom?

In Table 8.2 are reported the results of log-linear tests of the order of the who-to-whom transition matrix for "old" civilians

Table 8.2. Tests of the order for transitions within "old" civilian-officer dyads

Model	χ^2	G^2	df	P	$\Delta\chi^2$	ΔG^2	Δdf	P		Effects
Co-O,O-Co,Co-O										
1,2,3	3125.5	2296.2	20	.000						
+12,23	2739.7	1462.9	12	.000	385.8	833.3	8	.000	12,23	1st-order
+13	315.1	309.6	8	.000	2424.6	1153.3	4	.000	13	2nd-order
					315.1	309.6	8	.000	123	2nd-order
O-Co,Co-O,O-Co										
1,2,3	2046.5	1590.7	20	.000						
+12,23	737.2	725.6	12	.000	1309.3	865.1	8	.000	12,23	1st-order
+13	107.1	105.6	8	.000	630.1	620.0	4	.000	13	2nd-order
					107.1	105.6	8	.000	123	2nd-order

and officers. The process is at least second-order and may be an even higher order. There are too few observations to test reliably for a higher order.

In Figure 8.1 we summarize in graphical form the second-order transition probabilities. There is a pattern of transitions between who-to-whom pairs that is much like the transition matrix of acts of single civilians. Officers control who speaks to whom in ways analogous to their direction of the form and symbolic content of that interaction.

This is evident from the transition probabilities in Figure 8.1. The interaction among multiple actors is dominated by sequences of dyadic interaction between officers and "old" civilians (O-Co, Co-O, and Co-O, O-Co). The two states together represent 64% of the interactions observed. There are large transition probabilities from virtually every other state to these, and small transition probabilities from these to any other. Instances within the context of the established pairs Co-O, Co-O, and O-Co, O-Co in which the same actor emits two utterances in succession account for roughly 10% of the interaction. Pairs also occur between officers or civilians (O-O, O-O) (C-C, C-C). In Figure 8.1 there are no transition arrows to those states because of their infrequent occurrence. Once either of these pairs is initiated, it persists (e.g., the probability of O-O, O-O interaction continuing once it begins is .664 and the comparable probability for C-C, C-C interaction is .582).

There are differences in the ways these pairs begin and end. The states that mark the beginning of officer-officer interaction (O-Co, O-O, and Co-O, O-O) frequently lead to continued officer-officer interaction (the probabilities are .831 and .888, respectively). In contrast, the states that mark the beginning of civilian-civilian interaction (O-Co, C-C, and Co-O, C-C) lead to continued civilian-civilian interaction with considerably lower probabilities (.497 and .472, respectively) and lead almost as often to the C-C, O-Co state (the probabilities are .325 and .317, respectively), which leads back to the officer-civilian interaction. When one civilian begins talking to another civilian, officers interject themselves into the conversation before the other civilian has a chance to respond. Interaction is forced back to the officer-civilian modality. This is in

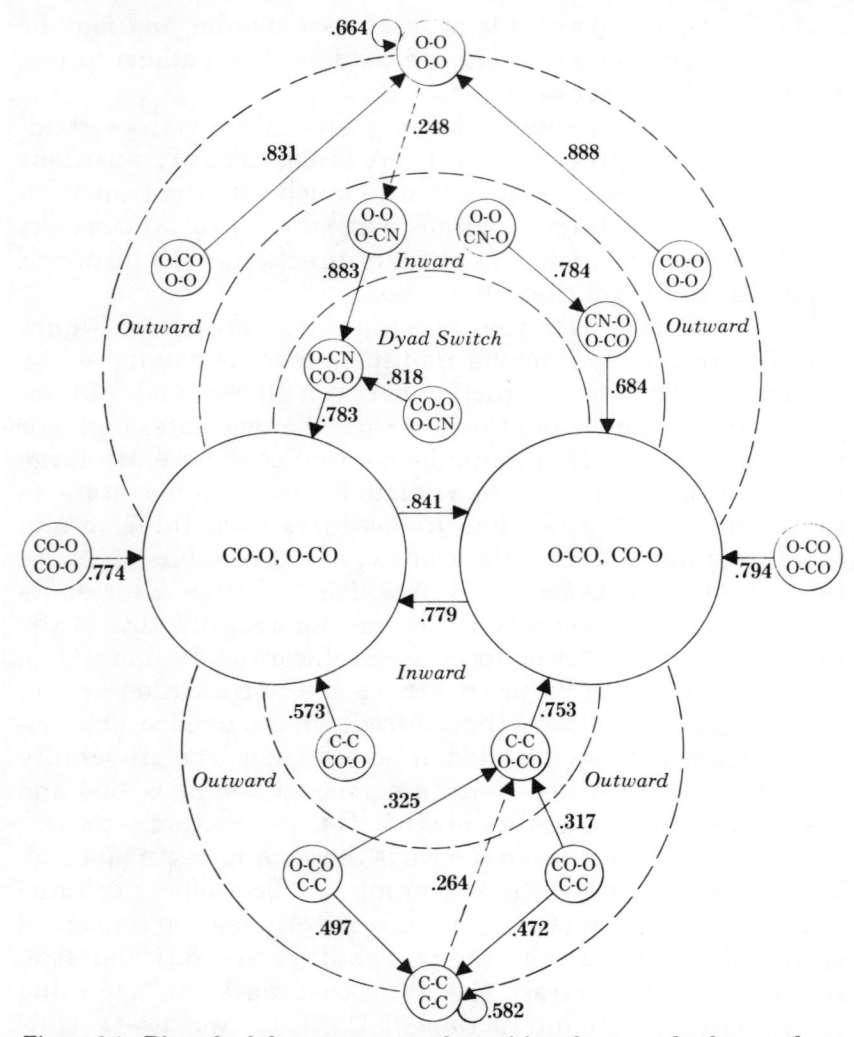

Figure 8.1. **Digraph of the metaprocess of transitions from one dyad to another**

marked contrast to the officer-officer communication, which civilians avoid interrupting. Officers regulate both their own and civilians' interaction.

The ways officer-officer and civilian-civilian pair-sequences end display the control officers maintain over the interaction. The most likely way for officer-officer sequences to end is

Table 8.3. Tests of the order of officer-civilian interaction in officer/multiple-civilian encounters

Model	χ^2	G^2	df	P	$\Delta\chi^2$	ΔG^2	Δdf	P	Effects
1,2,3,4	8731.2	7857.2	46	.000					
+12,23	6911.2	6587.7	38	.000	1820.0	1269.5	8	.000	1st-order model
+13	4133.2	4534.7	34	.000	2778.0	2053.0	4	.000	2nd-order model
+14,24,34	926.9	803.7	28	.000	3206.3	3731.0	6	.000	Effect of position on zero order
+124,234	735.1	669.8	20	.000	191.8	133.9	8	.000	Effect of position on 1st order
+134	422.2	415.3	16	.000	312.9	254.5	4	.000	Effect of position on 2nd order

for one of the officers to initiate interaction with a civilian. Civilian-civilian sequences are more apt to end at the initiation of an officer. Here, too, officers regulate who speaks to whom.

The switching of the dyadic pairs indicated by state Co-O, O-Cn, an officer beginning to interact with a civilian not currently communicating with any officers or civilians, occurs when the officer resolves, or fails to resolve, a problem. He turns to the other either for additional information or to regulate him. This switching is uneventful and indicative of the supervision officers exercise over the conduct of conversation.

Tests of the order of the symbolic interaction between officers and civilians using log-linear models show that the interaction is second order. These results displayed in Table 8.3 suggest that dyadic interaction in multiple-position encounters is like that found earlier in single-violator and complainant encounters. There are differences in the transition parameters for officers and civilians, as is evident from the effect of dimension 4 in Table 8.3. The specific transition parameters are summarized in the digraph, Figure 8.2. As before, the interaction is dominated by the cooperative cycle. A direct path leads to this cycle from almost all other states. The officers continue to exert more regulation than the civilians over how the cooperative cycle is entered and left. The officers use definitional and imperative supervision and regulation in the usual manner.

To examine the differences in the way officers interact with one another and civilians interact with one another, we examine the transition probabilities of sequences of three consecutive interactions among civilians (C-C, C-C, C-C) and compare them to the probabilities of three consecutive interactions among officers (O-O, O-O, O-O). There were 321 instances of the former sequence and 994 instances of the latter.

Perhaps the first step in comparing the interactions between officers to those between civilians is to determine whether they are of the same order. In Table 8.4 are reported the results of log-linear tests that assess the order of each. Officer-officer interaction and the civilian-civilian interaction are both at least second-order. When we compare the transition matrices di-

Model and Multiple-Position Interaction 185

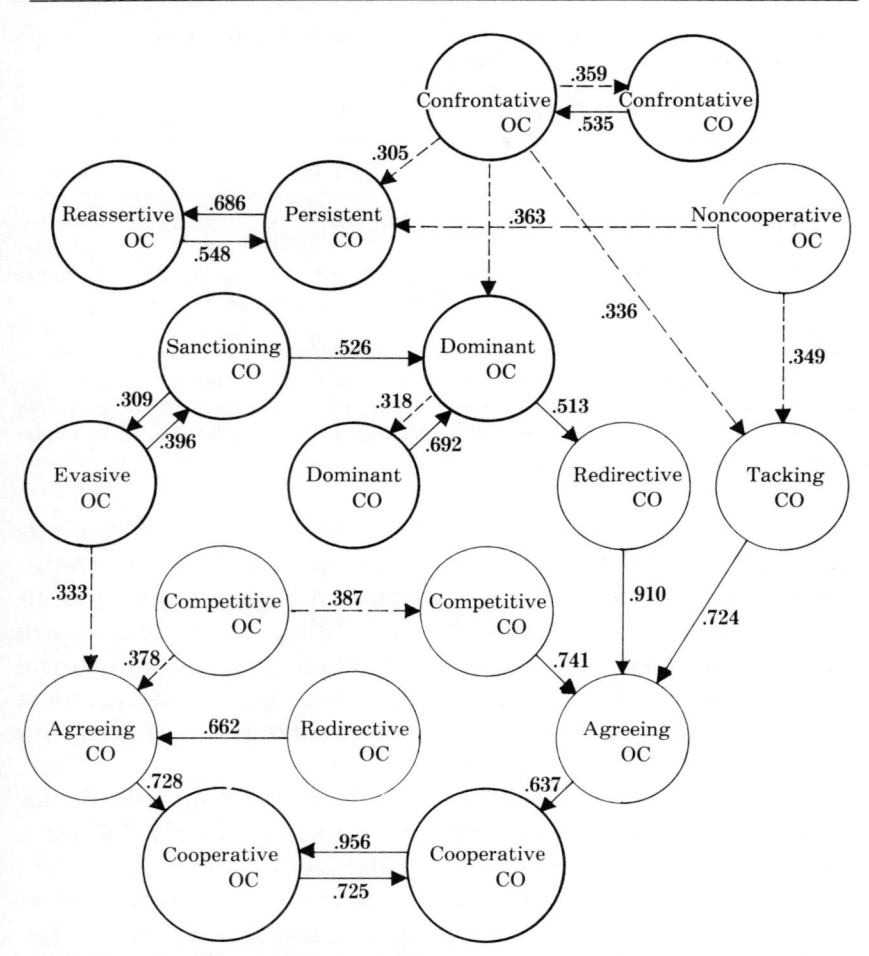

Figure 8.2. **Digraph of a second-order Markov model of social acts of officers and civilians in multiple-position encounters**

rectly we find significant differences in interaction between civilians and between officers. It is evident from Table 8.5 that officer-only and civilian-only interactions differ significantly in the distribution of acts, i.e., in the "situations" that develop. In addition, they display less strong, but significant differences in first-order transition probabilities. There are differences in the second-order transition probabilities, but they are not statistically significant for this reduced subsample size.

Table 8.4. **Tests of the order of officer-officer and civilian-civilian interaction in multiple-position encounters**

Model	χ^2	G^2	df	P	$\Delta\chi^2$	ΔG^2	Δdf	P		Effects
C-C,C-C,C-C										
1,2,3	179.5	162.2	20	.000	92.0	81.8	8	.000	12,23	1st-order
+12,23	83.9	80.4	12	.000	74.9	71.6	4	.000	13	2nd-order
+13	9.0	8.8	8	.362	9.0	8.8	8	.362	123	2nd-order
O-O,O-O,O-O										
1,2,3	202.5	170.9	20	.000	173.1	146.6	8	.000	12,23	1st-order
+12,23	29.4	24.3	12	.018	22.1	17.5	4	.001	13	2nd-order
+13	7.3	6.8	8	.500	7.3	6.8	8	.500	123	2nd-order

The transition probabilities for officers compared to civilians are displayed in Figures 8.3 and 8.4. Solid arrows represent probabilities of .50 or greater, and dotted arrows probabilities of between .49 and .20. Probabilities less than .20 are not represented. The size of the circle is proportional to the relative probability of that type of interaction (interactions with a probability of less than 5% are excluded). These diagrams dramatize the differences.

The distribution of events (i.e., the situations) that develops between officers and between civilians is clearly different. Officers interacting with officers are very cooperative. Most officer-officer interaction takes place in the cooperative cycle. The remainder involves defining and confirming states. Resisting or controlling acts are very rare.

Civilian-civilian interaction is in marked contrast. The distribution of states is different. Civilians behave in either of two almost unconnected subsystems of possible states. Either the civilian who initiates determines the topic and the process settles into the cooperative cycle, or else a cycle of confrontation between civilians occurs. Citizen-citizen conflicts tend toward either one of two possible equilibria: confrontation or reassertion (the cycle in which a resisting act by one civilian is followed by a confirming act by the other civilian). There is little hope of these civilians resolving the conflict themselves.

Table 8.5. **Comparison of the transition probabilities of officer-officer and civilian-civilian encounters**

Model	χ^2	G^2	df	P	$\Delta\chi^2$	ΔG^2	Δdf	P	Effects
1,2,3,4	6201.9	1022.4	46	.000					Independence model
+12,23	1400.9	591.1	38	.000	4801.0	431.3	8	.000	1st-order transition probabilities
+13	545.8	449.4	34	.000	855.1	141.7	4	.000	2nd-order transition probabilities
+14,24,34	55.3	45.1	28	.022	490.5	404.3	6	.000	Diffs. in distributions of acts by position
+124,234	18.2	17.1	20	.500	37.1	28.0	8	.001	Diffs. in 1st-order transition probabilities
+134	16.3	15.6	16	.485	1.9	1.5	4	.867	Diffs. in 2nd-order transition probabilities

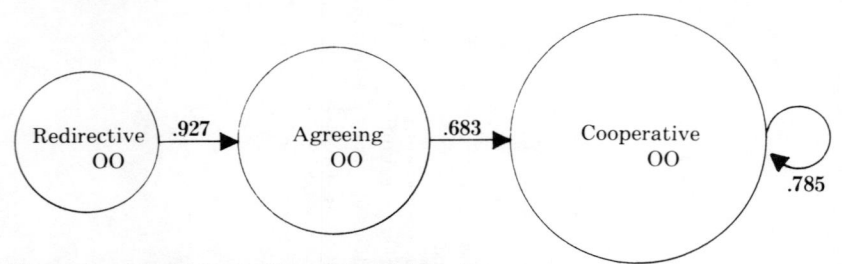

Figure 8.3. **Digraph of officer-officer interaction**

There is a probability of only .265, of entering the cooperative cycle as a result of a confirming act in this context. These civilians are unable to limit their conflict and come to some resolution. Police intervention seems necessary.

These two subsystems represent different types of encounters; one in which civilians have a conflict of interests—e.g., one alleged violator and one complainant—and another in which civilians agree—e.g., when there are several alleged violators.

INITIATING NEW PHASES OF INTERACTION

Officers initiate dyadic interaction more than civilians. Do officers initiate new dyads differently from civilians? To discover the answer to this question we examine those sequences of three acts for which the third act is either O-Cn (i.e., an officer-initiated, new dyadic pair) or Cn-O (a civilian-initiated new dyadic pair). That is, we examine the series of three acts: ———, ———, O-Cn, and ———, ———, Cn-O (where the blanks could be any acts). Table 8.6 displays results of log-linear tests of the order of the interaction in such three-act sequences. When interaction is initiated by a new civilian, Cn (one who did not participate in the most recent prior act and who probably did not participate in the second most recent act), there is a second-order interaction effect. The act, Cn, is a function of the two most recent prior acts. Even though this

Model and Multiple-Position Interaction 189

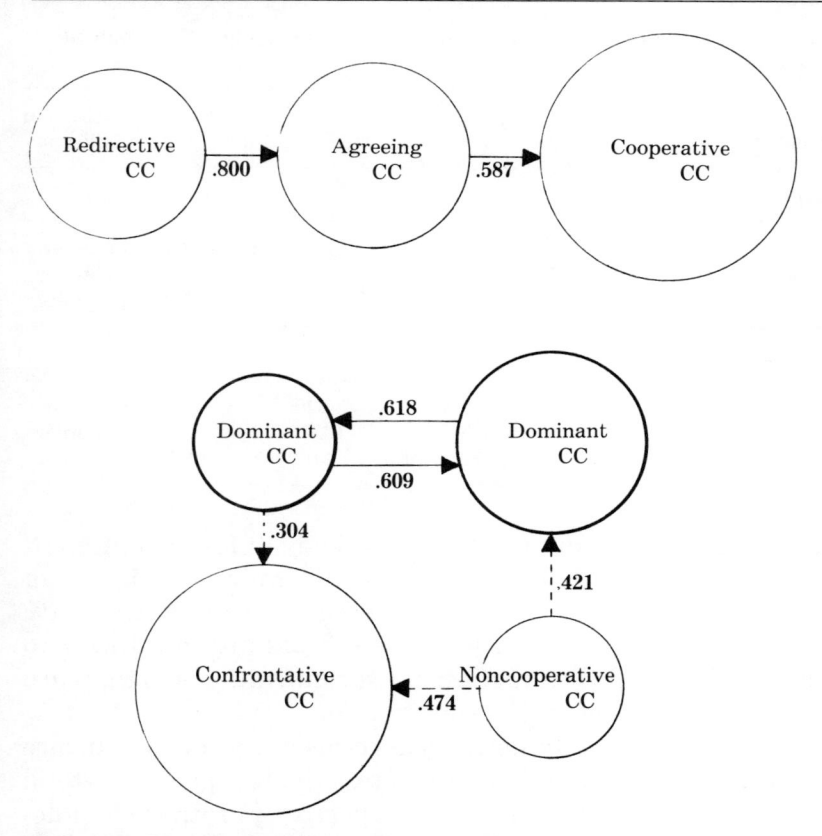

Figure 8.4. **Digraph of civilian-civilian interaction**

civilian did not participate in the prior interaction, he "jumps in" in a way that reflects the processual development of that interaction. One common way civilians interject themselves into the interaction is by answering questions asked of other civilians.

The transition probabilities for initiation of interaction with new dyads by officers are summarized in Figure 8.5. The transition probabilities might be thought of as "filters" that determine how interaction will shift from one dyad to another. These two "filters" are similar in many respects.

Actors initiate most dyads with defining acts. Such acts account for 64% of the civilian initiations and 68% of the officer

Table 8.6. **Tests of order for initiations by new civilians in officer/multiple-civilian interaction**

Model	χ^2	G^2	df	P	$\Delta\chi^2$	ΔG^2	Δdf	P	Interaction Effects
All O-Cn									
1,2,3	100.8	92.0	20	.000	81.8	72.7	8	.000	1st-order
+12,23	19.0	19.3	12	.082	11.6	11.7	4	.02	2nd-order
+13	7.4	7.6	8	.470	7.4	7.6	8	.470	2nd-order
All Cn-O									
1,2,3	63.6	52.8	20	.000	49.9	39.2	8	.000	1st-order
+12,23	13.7	13.6	12	.323	12.1	12.0	4	.01	2nd-order
+13	1.6	1.6	8	.991	1.6	1.6	8	.991	2nd-order

initiations (civilian data not shown). They differ in that civilians are less likely to initiate new dyadic interaction by using resisting acts than officers are by using controlling acts (11% versus 26%, respectively), whereas officers are less likely to initiate new dyadic interaction using confirming acts than are civilians (6% versus 25%, respectively).

There is also a systematic pattern of last prior acts before the shift to a new dyad. For both actors the last prior acts tend to be confirming (77% and 69%, respectively) rather than defining, resisting, or controlling. Interaction with new dyads is initiated only after the prior topic is resolved. In the final chapter we shall suggest that there is a tendency for the "forces" which hold a series of utterances together to weaken. When the forces reach a low threshold, a new dyad is initiated. For example, we might find a second civilian initiating a new dyad by replying to a question asked by an officer after the first civilian addressed by the officer has answered the same question. Officers, on the other hand, are more likely to initiate new interaction by controlling acts such as an order to "shut up," or "stand over there."

To determine whether the transition probabilities differ significantly between officers and civilians, a log-linear model was used to compare officer initiation of new dyads to civilian

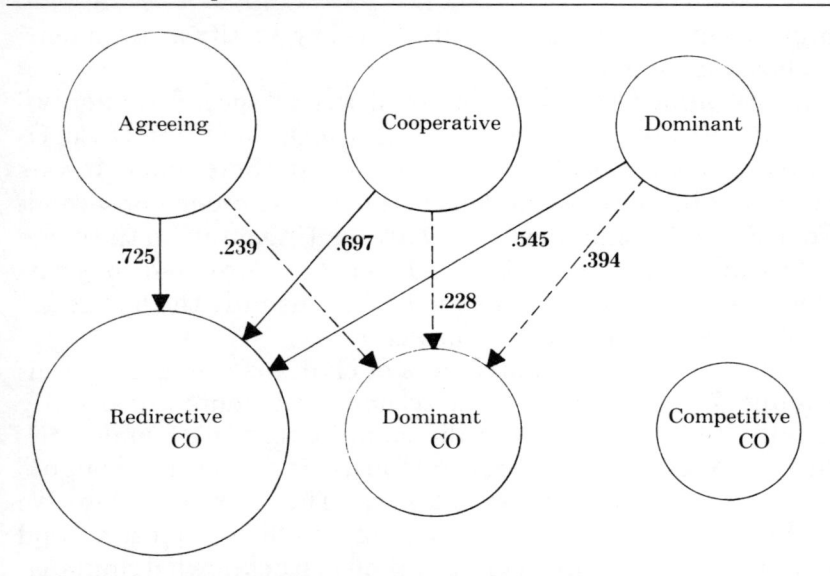

Figure 8.5. **Initiation of new dyadic interactions by officers**

initiation of new dyads (data not shown). Neither first-order nor second-order transitions to new dyads are significantly different given this sample size. Officers and civilians initiate new dyads the same way and under the same circumstances. However, we should not forget that officers initiate new dyads more than twice as often as civilians.

Second Thoughts— or Second Utterances

An interesting sidelight of interaction between police and civilians is the common occurrence (in roughly 10% of the interactions) of an officer or civilian "emitting" two or more utterances adjacent to one another. For example, the officer may say something to the civilian and, before he has replied, say something else to the same individual. This is common in interaction generally, not just that between officers and civilians. The officer might want to clarify a statement, add force to a command, or elaborate an order. Similarly, a civilian might want to moderate a refusal to obey, justify a statement, or clarify a comment.

We examined the occurrences of these "second thoughts," both directed to the same other role: Co-O, Co-O, and O-Co, O-Co. Log-linear models were used to test their order. It was found that in this case the interaction is first-order, not second-order. Second thoughts at time t are contingent upon the same actor's first thoughts at time t-1, but are unrelated to whatever acts preceded them at time t-2 (i.e., usually the last statement by the other actor to this actor).

It is clear that first statements of civilians are usually confirming (73%), whereas their second statements are usually defining (66%). For officers the same is true (51% and 48%). This suggests that the most common use for a "second thought" is to switch to a new content area. This is reasonable. We might imagine a civilian answering an officer's question and then asking one of his own; or an officer acknowledging a civilian's response to his question, and then beginning a new line of inquiry.

The transition probabilities are similar. For civilians, there are high probabilities of a defining "second" act after the first act regardless of what the first act was. For civilians, probabilities are higher that the second act will be like the first (e.g., second acts following confirming first acts are more likely to be confirming and second acts following resisting first acts are more likely to be resisting). Officers show a high probability of a defining second act regardless of what the first act was. Following defining and controlling first acts we find a relatively high probability of a controlling second act. Officers exert control more with their second statement than with their first. The tendency toward continuity is also found (e.g., second acts following confirming first acts are more likely to be confirming and second acts following controlling first acts are more likely to be controlling).

Two facts stand out from our analysis of these data. Except for "second thoughts," not only is dyadic interaction *second-order*

Model and Multiple-Position Interaction

in form, but even the metaprocess of transition between dyad pairs is second-order. Actors take into account *who* was speaking and *to whom* before entering a conversation. Despite the fact that each takes himself and the other into account there is no doubt that *officers dominate* both the metaprocess and the dyadic interaction.

9

Exploring Model Implications through Simulation

An advantage of the models we have fitted is their utility for answering the question, What would happen if . . . ? Markov models are suited for this purpose because their mathematical properties have been studied extensively. They may be used to generate a great many predictions regarding the behavior of a system. To explore events, one need only modify the parameters or form of the model to reflect the hypothetical situation and observe the system's behavior.

There are many reasons why simulation is useful. We do not want to create riots; yet it would be useful to study the circumstances that lead to such confrontations. It would be unethical to allow disputes between civilians to escalate without intervening, but important to know the effect of intervention. Other events warrant investigation for substantive reasons, but cannot be studied directly.

There are sound methodological reasons for simulating the model under different values of the parameters. Such simulations permit us to examine its sensitivity to change. By changing a specific parameter we can better understand the interaction process and the extent it can change as a function of parameter values. If it changes with minor alterations in the parameters, then we should be careful about generalizing. If the process is insensitive to such changes, then it may be generalized more safely. Simulation is important for both substantive and methodological reasons.

There are a number of ways in which we could determine

values to assign to parameters for purposes of simulation. One method we tried was to calculate the standard deviation of the parameters so they could be kept within a realistic range. Because there are so many parameters to estimate and because there is a small number of utterances per encounter, there were too few cases to provide reasonable estimates of the distribution of these parameters. We often found such large standard deviations that there was virtually no reasonable limit to the parameter values.

Another way to select the values is to assign some of those that were observed. We can simulate the interaction between civilians using the parameter values of the sample of violators. The simulation demonstrates what would happen if such persons continued to interact and the officers did not intervene. This method has the great advantage of using parameter estimates that are realistic. It has the disadvantage of limiting simulation to observed parameters.

A third way to establish realistic values is to examine police literature that describes those situations to be studied through simulation. There have been a number of studies of confrontations in which police brutality was alleged, studies of racial conflict, and studies of mass demonstrations. It may be possible to develop estimates of realistic parameter values from those studies. When empirical studies are not available, we may choose values that appear to represent parameters of hypothetical situations. The observed distribution of parameter values will aid in keeping a "guesstimate" in realistic bounds. We will employ the last two techniques in determining parameter values in the simulations that follow.

There is no reason to restrict simulations to changes in parameter values. It is possible to simulate changes in the structure of the process itself. We can simulate only first-order interactions rather than second-order interactions. We can simulate interactions that are not a process at all, or in which there is no position heterogeneity. Or we can simulate situations in which the underlying process breaks down or in which an alternative process takes place. For example, we can simulate communication problems in which the officers' interpretations of their own specific acts and the civilians' are different from the civilian's. Acts that have one meaning for the person emitting them may have a very different meaning for the person observing them. This last example is interesting because it illustrates the variety of problems and differences we could explore.

From these alternatives we have chosen the following simulations: (1) confrontations in which the legitimacy of the officers' intervention is questioned; (2) civilian-civilian conflict in the absence of police intervention; and (3) communication problems that might be caused by differences in social class, language, or other background differences between officers and civilians.

THE INTERACTIONAL BASES OF POLICE-CIVILIAN CONFRONTATION

Our examination of the processes underlying police-civilian interaction clearly indicates that encounters are likely to be cooperative regardless of how they begin. Cooperation will predominate as long as the same response propensities and processual structures remain. How, then, can we explain the frequent violent confrontation characterizing many mass demonstrations? Confrontation appears likely only if there are changes in the structure of the process (e.g., if officers or civilians no longer act in response to the other actor), or if there are changes in the parameter values characterizing their response propensities. The latter seems much more likely than the former. The way an actor responds to another actor seems less fundamental than whether the actor responds at all.

The interpretation of the process parameters as response propensities makes it much easier to conceptualize circumstances in which those might change and to predict the types of changes that might occur. Specifically, consider the demonstrations of the 1960s and 1970s in the United States. Civilians participating in those demonstrations might be expected to have had response propensities different from those of civilians in more routine encounters. They saw their actions as legitimate—even noble—taken to address an important social cause; and they saw officers as enforcers of unjust laws. In contrast, in most of the encounters examined in this study the weight of legitimacy was clearly on the side of the officer. Civilians appeared to grant this legitimacy and did not make claims regarding their own (as reflected in their tendency to be deferent and allow the officers to control the encounter).

Civilians participating in demonstrations may have strong value conflicts with officers. Rather than minimizing those conflicts, the demonstration is itself an attempt to articulate those differences and to draw attention to them. Demonstrators are often from different segments of society than suspected offenders. They have greater education, are more articulate, come from more favored social classes than officers, and are used to being treated with deference and respect themselves. For all of these reasons we might expect them to be less deferent to officers, less likely to be distracted from pursuing important goals, and more likely to compete for supervision over the encounter.

A number of authors have suggested that so long as other participants and observers are present, civilians are less likely to be cooperative if such cooperation might be interpreted as loss of face by other civilians. Toch (1977:22) wrote that "officers may take insufficient cognizance of threats they pose to the suspect's reputation or 'position of authority.'" This point was made over a decade ago by Bittner (1970:98), who reported that one patrolman explained to him that "the most important trick" in police work was not to make people obey but to make it possible for them to obey by helping them to avoid losing face.

Earlier, we argued that police normally exercise legitimate authority rather than violence. The important role of authority becomes particularly obvious when civilians do not accept the officer's actions as legitimate. In one study of incidents alleging police brutality, the author found that in most incidents the civilians failed to grant the police the legitimacy to intervene and the officers failed to communicate to the civilians any justification for their actions (Hudson, 1970).

For example, Richardson (1974:196) noted that police "have very strong occupational concern for respect and deference from the civilian population." Toch (1977:19) wrote that "persons who treat the officer with disdain become classed as 'wise guys.'"

In an intensive study of cases of alleged police violence, Paul Chevigny (1969:70) found that "complaints . . . bear out the hypothesis that most such acts arise out of defiance of authority, or what the police take to be such defiance." He added later, "everybody knows that when you defy the law, you go to jail" (139). Together, these considerations suggest that if a crowd is present and civilians reject the authority of the police, then there is a greater likelihood of violent confrontation.

From our earlier analyses it appears that the response propensities of officers are habitual. Although most interaction is cooperative, there may be no need for them to change their response propensities for confrontations to result. This stability of the officers is based on our finding that officers respond in the same way to alleged violators and complainants. For this reason we plan to change only the response propensities of the civilians. We modify them to reflect less deference to the officers, a greater tendency to define and pursue their own topics of conversation rather than limiting them to those topics determined by the officers, and a greater tendency to resist when they view the officers' actions as illegitimate.

The Markov model of police-civilian interaction provides a means to examine the potential consequences of such changes. By adjusting the parameters of the civilians to reflect those we expect of demonstrators, we can predict the patterns of interaction that would result. In Table 9.1 are summarized specific changes in parameter values corresponding to the differences just discussed. In Table 9.2 is the equilibrium distribution predicted for the interaction based upon these changes in civilian response propensities.

The simulation shows that a quite different pattern of interaction would occur. In the simulated interaction with demonstrators, approximately 50% of all paired responses of officers and civilians include at least one negative act (resisting or controlling); approximately 15% are mutually negative; and only

Table 9.1. **Hypothetical response propensities of demonstrators interacting with officers**

Social Acts of Officers and Civilians at Times $t-2$ and $t-1$	\multicolumn{9}{c}{Action of Civilians at Time t and Officers at Time $t-1$}
	O_1C_1	O_1C_2	O_1C_3	O_2C_1	O_2C_2	O_2C_3	O_3C_1	O_3C_2	O_3C_3
Competitive	.393	.371	.236						
Agreeing				.329	.592	.079			
Sanctioning							.298	.193	.509
Redirective	.264	.485	.251						
Cooperative				.284	.551	.165			
Dominant							.161	.403	.536
Tacking	.237	.310	.453						
Persistent				.053	.347	.600			
Confrontative							.215	.071	.714

Table 9.2. **Predicted equilibrium distribution for aggregated encounters between demonstrators and officers**

Social Act (OC)	Freq.	%	Social Act (CO)	Freq.	%
Competitive	38	8	Competitive	38	8
Agreeing	57	12	Agreeing	66	14
Noncooperative	48	10	Sanctioning	19	4
Redirective	57	12	Redirective	52	11
Cooperative	124	26	Cooperative	119	25
Reassertive	62	13	Dominant	38	8
Evasive	28	6	Tacking	57	12
Dominant	24	5	Persistent	62	13
Confrontative	76	16	Confrontative	66	14

26% of all acts are mutually compliant. In contrast, in the observed interactions only 28% of all pairs contained at least one negative act, only 5% were mutually negative, and 47% were mutually positive (agreeing, cooperative, or dominant).

These results suggest that changes in the response propensities of civilians are sufficient to shift the interaction from a cooperative equilibrium to a confrontational equilibrium. When confronted with these novel situations in the 1960s and early 1970s, police may have failed to adapt to them. By pursuing their standard mode of interaction as if the demonstrators were ordinary suspects, they were unable to supervise or regulate such encounters or may even have increased the likelihood of confrontation. The seeds of the confrontations lay at least partly in the routine response propensities of the officers, although these normally lead to cooperation. This irony has never been fully explicated or appreciated by either the police or police scholars.

CIVILIAN-CIVILIAN CONFRONTATION

Our earlier analysis of confrontation between civilians provides us with parameter estimates to use to examine hypothetically what would happen if a police officer did not intervene. Because of the presence of police, civilians likely had already modified their behaviors. There still was much hostile activity between civilians. What might have happened if the officers had not arrived?

We use the civilian-civilian interaction matrix in Chapter 8 to generate the predicted equilibrium distribution and the dynamic behavior of that system as it approaches equilibrium. Those predictions are summarized in Tables 9.3 and 9.4. In Table 9.3 we compare the predicted probability distribution at equilibrium for this civilian-civilian interaction with the equivalent distributions for police interaction with a single violator and with a single complainant. Undisturbed civilian-civilian interaction leads to an equilibrium distribution in which 12% of the social acts are confrontative, twice that observed between police and suspects and 12 times that observed between police and complainants. Thirty-six percent of the two-act states include at least one resisting act. Civilian-civilian interaction would lead to more confrontation if officers did not intervene. It is not clear that Black and Baumgartner (1980:193–208), in their advocacy of self-regulation by civilians, have considered this possibility.

The difference between the civilian-civilian and officer-civilian interaction is even greater when the eigenvalues

Table 9.3. **Predicted equilibrium distribution for civilian-civilian interaction compared to equilibrium distributions for officer-suspect and officer-complainant interactions (by percentage)**

Social Act	Civilian-Civilian Interaction	Officer-Suspect Interaction*	Officer-Complainant Interaction*
Competitive	2	2	1
Agreeing	9	22	21
Sanctioning	3	2	0
Redirective	9	2	2
Cooperative	43	48	68
Dominant	9	2	1
Tacking	3	2	1
Persistent	9	14	4
Confrontative	12	6	1

*Predicted percentage of occurrence of such acts for officers at time $t+1$.

Table 9.4. **Civilian-civilian confrontation compared to officer-suspect and officer-complainant interactions (eigenvalues)**

Civilian-Civilian	Officer-Suspect*	Officer-Complainant
1.00	1.00	1.00
.81	.40	.58
.62	$.20+.02i$	.26
.44	$.20-.02i$	.22
.30	$.07+.01i$	.17
.30	$.07-.01i$	.12
.06	.02	.05
$.02+.09i$	.01	$-.02$
$.12-.09i$	.01	.00

*These are the eigenvalues for the civilian-civilian subset of the two-step transition probabilities matrix for these encounters. Since these eigenvalues refer to a two-step transition matrix, the one-step eigenvalues for civilian-civilian confrontation must be squared to be comparable to these (i.e., $.81^2=.66$ is comparable to .40).

reported in Table 9.4 are examined. Recall that the second largest eigenvalue determines the rate at which the system approaches equilibrium. For the civilian-civilian confrontation the one-step eigenvalue is .81. The same process examined every second step would have an eigenvalue of .66 ($.81^2$). The comparable two-step eigenvalue for the police-suspect interaction is .40. The civilian-civilian interaction is slower approaching equilibrium than the police-violator interaction. When civilian-civilian interaction begins with confrontation, it takes longer to reach a cooperative state than it does if police intervene. Not only is civilian-civilian interaction likely to manifest more confrontation at equilibrium, but it is likely to approach that equilibrium more slowly than when police intervene.

COMMUNICATION PROBLEMS

Implicit in the analysis to this point, is the assumption that officers, civilians, and the observers are attributing to acts the same meanings. This may not always be the case. In a number of circumstances it is likely that the meaning which officers attribute to an act is different from the meaning which civilians attribute to that same act. Such problems may arise from language differences. English is not the native language of some civilians, who may speak it very poorly. Communication problems may arise when officers and civilians come from different subcultures. Problems may also arise if the civilian is incapacitated by drink or drugs and misinterprets the officer or gives ambiguous signals to the officer. Even a disability such as deafness, muteness, or poor eyesight may lead (and often has led) to communication problems.

We have stimulated communication failure by presuming a greater percentage of acts are interpreted negatively by civilians and officers than either intended. For example, suppose 20% of the acts meant to be confirming by civilians are presumed by the officers to be resisting, and 20% of confirming acts of officers are perceived by civilians to be controlling. We could have assumed that the misinterpretations were positive. Then there would be less, not more, of a problem. Such cases are of less concern because they resolve the problem rather than making it more severe. We also regard it as unlikely. It is safer to assume that when people from different groups interact, negative rather than positive misunderstanding is more likely.

A hypothetical communication problem is illustrated by the following sequence of social acts initiated by the officer: agreeing-dominant-dominant (to review the meaning of these social acts see Figure 7.1). Where there is no communication problem these acts would be interpreted the same way by both officers and civilians.

When communication problems occur, two different versions of this sequence of events—one for the officer and one for the civilian—result. For instance:

Officers' Version: noncooperative-tacking-agreeing
Civilians' Version: agreeing-redirective-agreeing

This misunderstanding would lead to a variation in the interaction because the officer would respond the way that he interpreted the act and his response propensity would have a different value. Similarly, the civilian would be confused because he would develop a different notion of the response propensities of the officer. The civilian might conclude the officer was negative even when the civilian was really cooperative; and the officer might believe the civilian was negative when that was not the case. Here we only simulate the direct consequences of such communicative problems; we do not simulate what might be an increase in hostility on the part of both officer and civilian due to this misinterpretation and the corresponding misinterpretation of the other actor's reaction to the misinterpreted acts.

These communication problems are indirectly reflected by the transition probabilities of the officers and civilians in the transition matrix. This is illustrated by the following example. Consider the case where the last social act is agreeing. For the case of police-civilian interaction between officers and a single violator (e.g., see Figure 7.2) the probability of a defining act following such a state was .285. When the hypothetical communication problem is present this transition probability characterizes 80% of the interactions in which the confirming

Table 9.5. **Transition matrix for hypothetical police-civilian interaction with communication problems (officer-suspect)***

		OC Competitive	OC Agreeing	OC Noncooperative	OC Redirective	OC Cooperative	OC Reassertive	OC Evasive	OC Dominant	OC Confrontative	CO Competitive	CO Agreeing	CO Sanctioning	CO Redirective	CO Cooperative	CO Dominant	CO Tacking	CO Persistent	CO Confrontative
OC	Competitive										.143	.771	.086						
	Agreeing											**.293**	**.592**	**.115**					
	Noncooperative										.064	.885	.051						
	Redirective													**.039**	**.901**	**.059**			
	Cooperative															.148	.593	.259	
	Reassertive										.087	.710	.203						
	Evasive													**.065**	**.372**	**.563**			
	Dominant															.061	.703	.236	
	Confrontative															.115	.471	.414	
CO	Competitive	.461	.462	.077															
	Agreeing				**.326**	**.458**	**.216**												
	Sanctioning	.226	.629	.145															
	Redirective				**.191**	**.627**	**.182**												
	Cooperative							.488	.171	.341									
	Dominant	.176	.500	.324															
	Tacking							.184	.508	.308									
	Persistent				**.418**	**.260**	**.322**												
	Confrontative							.291	.276	.433									

*Transition probabilities in bold print are those influenced by hypothetical communication problems.

Table 9.6. **Predicted equilibrium distribution of states for simulated encounters in which both officers and civilians misunderstand each other**

Social Act	Predicted for Civilian Communication Problems	Predicted for Police and Civilian Communication Problems	Observed for Single-Violator Subsample
OC			
Competitive	1	1	1
Agreeing	12	12	12
Noncooperative	1	1	1
Redirective	2	2	2
Cooperative	22	19	24
Reassertive	3	3	1
Evasive	1	1	1
Dominant	7	8	7
Confrontative	3	3	2
CO			
Competitive	1	1	1
Agreeing	2	2	2
Sanctioning	1	1	1
Redirective	10	11	13
Cooperative	22	20	21
Dominant	7	9	9
Tacking	2	2	1
Persistent	2	2	1
Confrontative	2	3	2

acts by the civilian were correctly interpreted by the officer. The remaining 20% are misinterpreted as resisting acts. The transition probability for these acts is that following the noncooperative social act, which was .488. Thus, the effective transition probability for such states would be a weighted average of these two:

effective transition = (.80) (.285) + (.20) (.488) = .326

A similar calculation can be made for cooperative social acts. The net result is the transition matrix in Table 9.5 in which the transition probabilities are adjusted from those in Figure 7.2 to reflect these hypothetical communication problems.

Model Implications through Simulation

Table 9.7. **Predicted eigenvalues for simulated communication problems involving only civilians, involving civilians and officers, and of observed interaction between police and suspects**

Communication Problems, Civilians Only	Communication Problems, Civilians and Officers	Single-Violator Interaction
−1.00	−1.00	−1.00
1.00	1.00	1.00
−.59	−.59	−.40
.59	.59	.40
−.44	−.46	−.20+.02i
−.44	.46	−.20−.02i
.44	−.44	.20+.02i
.44	.44	−.20−.02i
−.26+.01i	−.28+.01i	−.07+.01i
−.26−.01i	−.28−.01i	−.07−.01i
.26+.01i	.28+.01i	.07+.01i
.26−.01i	.28−.01i	.07−.01i
−.13	−.12+.01i	−.02
.13	−.12−.01i	.02
−.10+.01i	.12+.01i	−.01
−.10−.01i	.12−.01i	.01
.10+.01i	−.13	−.01
.10−.01i	.13	.01

To assess the implications of these changes in the transition probabilities we examined the predicted equilibrium distribution of this interaction and the eigenvalues that describe the approach of the system to equilibrium. Those results are reported in Tables 9.6 and 9.7. The predicted equilibrium distribution for these simulated communication problems is very similar to that actually observed between police and a single alleged violator. Approximately the same proportions of social acts characterize each of the equilibrium distributions. When we examine the eigenvalues associated with these different circumstances, we find that the second highest eigenvalue for the simulated communication problem is .59 compared to .40 for the observed interaction. The interaction takes longer to reach equilibrium when subject to misunderstanding than does the observed interaction. Communication problems introduce an element of uncertainty, which results in more noncooperation and requires more time to resolve.

We found that confrontation can occur when police behave *normally*. Response propensities that contribute to the routine and cooperative process of most encounters can also contribute to confrontation if civilians change their behavior. This might be said to prove, in the deductive sense, that changes in the probabilities of acts by civilians, completely independent of personality or demographic characteristics of those civilians, and completely independent of situation, can lead to confrontation. Response propensities of the officers need not change at all.

10

Using Structural Equation Models to Predict Outcomes

Although the previous analyses have elaborated a complex picture of social interaction between police and civilians, it remains to be determined whether this interaction has any influence on the outcomes of the encounters. Until now we have elaborated one complex variable, interaction, but we have yet to show how that variable is related to other variables, both those that affect it and those it affects.

Several studies (e.g., Piliavin and Briar, 1964; Reiss, 1971; Sykes, Clark, and Fox, 1976) found that interaction affects the outcomes of encounters with suspects. Noncooperation, hostility, and disrespect affected report-taking from complainants (Black, 1970).

These studies did not consider the process itself. We must consider the subtleties of the processes between police and civilians in order to assess the impact of interaction upon outcome. We also must recognize that factors extraneous to the interaction probably affect the outcome—the nature of the offense itself, the prior history of the offender, or the presence of onlookers. Any adequate analysis of the effects of interaction on outcome must control for effects of these other variables.

Though interaction may be highly associated with the outcomes, it may be only an intervening variable. It may merely be correlated with some other factor that directly affects outcomes. Hostility, disrespect, or conflict may occur often in encounters with suspects who committed serious offenses and have a prior criminal record. Officers may have little discretion in disposing of such cases (though Black, 1980:101–103, provides evidence of discretion even for serious offenses).

Though such encounters may have more serious outcomes for the offenders, this may have been determined before the encounter began. Like a "B" movie in which the basically good person is connected to some crime and inevitably and inexorably suffers the awful consequences of the act, such interactions may represent almost ritualistic playing out of largely inevitable events as the violators are confronted by the consequences of their alleged indiscretions.

With subtleties such as these in mind we answer in this analysis three questions regarding the effect of interaction processes upon outcomes. *First*, is there a direct effect of interaction on the outcomes of the encounter independent of the effects of other variables? Four possibilities must be considered: (1) interaction has virtually nothing to do with the outcome, the "no effects" model; (2) interaction is spuriously related to outcome, both interaction and outcome being strongly affected by participant characteristics and the situation, the "spurious effect" model; (3) interaction is an intervening variable mediating the effect of participant characteristics and the situation on outcome but having virtually no independent effect of its own, the "intervening variable" model; or (4) interaction has a strong effect on outcome independent of the effects of the situation and participant characteristics, the "independent effects" model. We hypothesize that the latter is true.

Second, if interaction has a strong independent effect, what is the nature of this effect on the outcome? There are two possibilities: (1) Interactions in which the officer sanctions or exerts control over the alleged violator may serve as substitutes for more severe formal outcomes. The officers might "bawl out" an offender during the encounter instead of arresting him. There may be a negative relationship between some kinds of interactions and outcome severity. We term this the "substitution hypothesis." (2) Interactions may be positively related to outcome. Encounters that are civil and cooperative should have more favorable outcomes for the alleged violator. The interactions constitute a context within which outcomes are consistent. This we term the "context hypothesis." We hypothesize that the context hypothesis will prove true for the

Structural Equation Models and Outcomes

violator's contribution to the interaction and the substitution hypothesis, for the officer's contribution to the interaction. Confrontation or resistance by the alleged violator will lead to a more severe outcome, while confrontation and controlling acts by the officers will tend to substitute for severe outcomes. We make no specific hypothesis about the relationship between the complainant's interaction and outcome.

A *third* question is raised by the identification of the varying levels of process and structure in the model of police-civilian interaction developed in earlier chapters. These included first-order transition probabilities, zero-order probabilities, and evolving interaction structures (i.e., the number of times specific acts occur during the encounter). These levels may have independent effects on the outcomes. Alternatively, higher-order processes may be mediated by lower-order processes and evolving structures and may have no direct effect. We hypothesize that the higher-order process effects are mediated through lower-order processes and evolving structures because our prior analyses have shown higher-order transition probabilities to be relatively stable across different populations. Hence, because they do not vary either greatly and/or systematically they will not affect the outcomes directly. Lower-order processes and evolving structures may magnify the effects of slight variations in higher-order processes and also may be influenced by other variables which, through them, affect outcomes. We test these hypotheses in this chapter by using structural equation models to estimate the causal relationships among these variables.

SPECIFICATION OF THE MODEL

The variables included in the model are listed in the causal order predicted, beginning with the variables least likely to be affected by others (i.e., exogenous variables) and progressing to those deemed most likely to be affected by the others: (1) characteristics of the participants and the situation of the encounter; (2) interaction indices including

(a) first-order transition probabilities, (b) zero-order probabilities, and (c) evolving structures; (3) the outcome of the encounter. Characteristics of participants and the situation are determined before the encounter begins and are therefore unlikely to be affected by either the outcome of the encounter or the interaction during the encounter (it is possible to imagine an arrest affecting the violator's future socioeconomic status (SES); but such longer-term changes are not the focus of this study). Interaction could conceivably be affected by the situation and/or participant characteristics, but it occurs before the outcome and hence is unlikely to be affected by it. Within the interaction we posit a causal order with higher-order processes able to affect the lower-order processes and evolving structures, but not vice versa. This is consistent with our view of these latter indices as the consequences of the basic and fundamental processes characterizing the interaction. The outcome of the encounter for the violator could conceivably be affected by all of the above variables. Specific empirical measures of these concepts are described below.

We must also consider other variables that may affect outcomes. There is a limit to the number of variables which may be realistically measured by observing an encounter between police and civilians without asking questions or interfering in the encounter. We were able to measure a number of variables that describe the situation, characteristics of the violator(s), characteristics of the complainants, and characteristics of the police officers. From the variables that were measurable we selected for this analysis all of those which were distributed adequately in the population for this analysis. We were not, for example, able to consider ethnicity in this analysis, because the population of encounters that form our data base contained few minority-group members. It was more than 90% white. The variables included in the analysis are: suspect age, sex, socioeconomic class, and extent of impairment by alcohol; whether the encounter was proactive, reactive, or a traffic stop; whether or not the officers had the power to arrest the suspect; and the age, years of education, and experience of the officers themselves.

Any attempt to analyze the effects of interaction on the out-

Structural Equation Models and Outcomes 213

comes of police-civilian encounters must first address the problem of which indices to use. Brief reflection on the number of parameters used to describe interaction in earlier chapters illustrates the extent of the problem. A second-order Markov model with heterogeneous roles described dyadic interaction between police and civilians. That model had twenty-seven second-order transition probabilities for the civilian and twenty-seven additional second-order transition probabilities for the officers. To describe the evolving structures that result from those processes, eighteen first-order transition probabilities (nine for each role) and six zero-order probabilities (three for each role) must be added, totaling seventy-eight possible parameters characterizing the interaction between officers and a single civilian.

When more than one civilian is present (e.g., officers, alleged violator, and complainant), there are twenty-seven second-order transition probabilities, nine first-order transition probabilities, and three zero-order transition probabilities for each possible dyad (i.e., officer to officer, officer to violator, officer to complainant, complainant to officer, violator to officer, civilian to civilian) or 6 × 39 = 234 parameters. An analysis of triadic interaction must also include the who-to-whom parameters. Not only are there many interaction parameters, but some particular combinations of acts occur infrequently. For these reasons, we include only a few more easily estimated parameters.

The indices of interaction chosen were: (1) the first-order transition probabilities for each of the three possible dyads in multiparticipant interaction; (2) probabilities for each of the three possible acts for each of the three possible dyads; (3) the number of times each of the three possible acts occurred for each of the three possible dyads; (4) the proportion of acts by each of the three actors; and (5) five indices of dyadic change. These indices are summarized in Table 10.1.

It is distressing to exclude the second-order transition probabilities when the second-order Markov model was found to provide the best fit to the data. In this causal analysis we found that the first-order effects were the strongest. There are significant second-order effects but they are not nearly as

Table 10.1. **Interaction indices included in the analysis of outcomes**

2nd-Order Transition Probabilities[1]		1st-Order Transition Probabilities[2]		Number of Times Each Act Occurred for Each Dyad[3]	
Officer-Violator Dyad					
P(OdVd)	P(VdOd)	P(OVd)	P(VOd)	NOVd	NVOd
P(OdVc)	P(VdOc)	P(OVc)	P(VOc)	NOVc	NVOc
P(OdVr)	P(VdOr)	P(OVr)	P(VOr)	NOVr	NVOr
P(OcVd)	P(VcOd)				
P(OcVc)	P(VcOc)				
P(OcVr)	P(VcOr)				
P(OrVd)	P(VrOd)				
P(OrVc)	P(VrOc)				
P(OrVr)	P(VrOr)				
Officer-Complainant Dyad					
P(OdCd)	P(CdOd)	P(OCd)	P(COd)	NOCd	NCOd
P(OdCc)	P(CdOc)	P(OCc)	P(COc)	NOCc	NCOc
P(OdCr)	P(CdOr)	P(OCr)	P(COr)	NOCr	NCOr
P(OcCd)	P(CcOd)				
P(OcCc)	P(CcOc)				
P(OcCr)	P(CcOr)				
P(OrCd)	P(CrOd)				
P(OrCc)	P(CrOc)				
P(OrCr)	P(CrOr)				

Proportion of acts by each actor	PO (proportion of acts by officer)
	PV (proportion of acts by alleged violator)
	PC (proportion of acts by complainant)

Indices of dyadic change	POO (prob. officer-officer interaction)
	PNCV (prob. compl. initiating int'n with violator)
	PNVC (prob. violator initiating int'n with compl.)
	PVNO (prob. vio. initiating int'n with officer)
	PCNO (prob. compl. initiating int'n with officer)

[1] Pabcd—conditional probability of actor c emitting act d at time $t+1$ following actor a emitting act b at time t
a = actor at time t (O=officer, V=violator, C=complainant)
c = actor at time $t+1$ (O=officer, V=violator, C=complainant)
b = act at time t (d=defining, c=confirming, r=resisting or controlling)
d = act at time $t+1$ (d=defining, c=confirming, r=resisting or controlling)

[2] Pefg = probability of actor e emitting act g directed toward actor f

strong as the first-order effects. Our examination of the first-order probabilities should at least capture the grosser aspects of the interaction though not all its subtlety.

The number of the interaction parameters considered in this analysis was reduced from hundreds to sixty-eight. Even sixty-eight parameters are too many. Such a variety poses problems for structural equations analysis. If they were highly correlated it would be difficult to separate their effects. The sheer number might result in the appearance of significant effects when actually due to chance. So many variables in a structural equation model would greatly complicate the model, making it more difficult to interpret the results. For these reasons, we used factor analysis to simplify and summarize the sixty-eight parameters to identify a small number of factors representing the underlying dimensions of the processes.

Factor analysis was chosen over other scaling and classification techniques such as nonmetric multidimensional scaling and cluster analysis because factor analysis and structural equations are both based upon the general linear model. Both make similar assumptions about the data. The factors that result constitute unidimensional scales along which the interaction may be scored. Each of the summary variables is both conceptually and statistically compatible with the approach of structural equation models.

This factor analysis was performed for the entire sample of 521 encounters in which at least one violator was present. A correlation matrix among these variables was first computed using pairwise deletion of missing data. That correlation matrix was then factored using principal components analysis with varimax rotation. Resulting factors were examined us-

---

e=actor speaking (O=officer, V=violator, C=complainant)
f=actor spoken to (O=officer, V=violator, C=complainant)
g=act (d=defining, c=confirming, r=resisting or controlling)

[3]Nefg=number of times actor e emits act g directed toward actor f; e, f, g same as n. 2

ing Cronbach's alpha as a measure of their internal consistency reliability. Items that reduced Cronbach's alpha substantially were dropped from the factors. Factor scores for the resulting factors were computed by including only those items loading highly on the items, excluding all other items, and weighting each item the same in its contribution to the overall summary index. This factor scoring procedure maximizes the Cronbach's alpha of the resulting index (Armor, 1974).

It would be wrong to infer that there are few underlying dimensions of these processes—there are many. Twenty-one factors were found to account for 90% of the variation among the original 68 indicators. The finding that there are twenty-one separate factors clearly indicates that these variables measure many diverse aspects of interaction. Further evidence of this diversity is evident from the amount of variance explained by the first principal component extracted. Principal-components factor analysis extracts first the single dimensional component that explains the most variance possible in the data. If there were few components to the processes the first factor should account for a large proportion of the variance. It accounts for only 11.3%. After rotating the factors, the variance is even more evenly distributed. These twenty-one factors are used as the summary indices of interaction in our structural equation models.

Those civilians usually affected most by contact with police are suspects. Alleged violators may be arrested, given a ticket or summons, warned, or "sent" (ordered to leave the scene). We chose the relative severity of the outcome for the suspect as the dependent variable. This was ranked as follows:

9—arrest for felony
8—arrest for misdemeanor
7—punitive ticket
6—imposed alternative to arrest when arrest was possible
5—negotiated alternative to arrest when arrest was possible
4—problem resolved through the interaction itself
3—official police report
2—no resolution
1—event of no interest to police

Structural Equation Models and Outcomes 217

There were 541 encounters with at least one violator present. That includes encounters with only violators present and encounters with both a violator and a complainant. The interaction in these two conditions may differ in significant ways (see Black, 1980:92) and affect the outcome for the violator differently. For this reason, we partition these data: one subsample includes 140 encounters in which both a violator and a complainant were present; the other, the "violator only" subsample, includes 314 encounters with violators only (the remaining 67 encounters fit into neither of these subsamples). We analyze each subsample separately. The analyses are similar except that the "violator and complainant" subsample includes indices of complainant interaction. Separate analyses are useful because they permit the examination of differences. They also provide an opportunity to "replicate," and thus better assess the stability and generalizability of the results.

VIOLATORS AND COMPLAINANTS: EFFECTS ON OUTCOME

Figure 10.1 is a path diagram of the variables included in the model. Only those paths are included that are significant at or beyond the .05 level. The variables account for 46.4% of the variance in the severity of outcome. The largest single effect is length of officer-violator interaction. More severe outcomes are associated with longer interaction. The only other interaction variable having a direct effect is the first-order probability of officers responding to a resisting act with a defining act (the social act of tacking). The *higher* the probability of this tacking, the more severe the outcome is likely to be for the violator.

Noninteraction variables also have direct effects. Male suspects are treated more severely. Traffic violators are less likely to be let off. Officers with the power to arrest are likely to impose more severe outcomes. The higher their median education and the longer their service, the more likely officers are to impose severe sanctions.

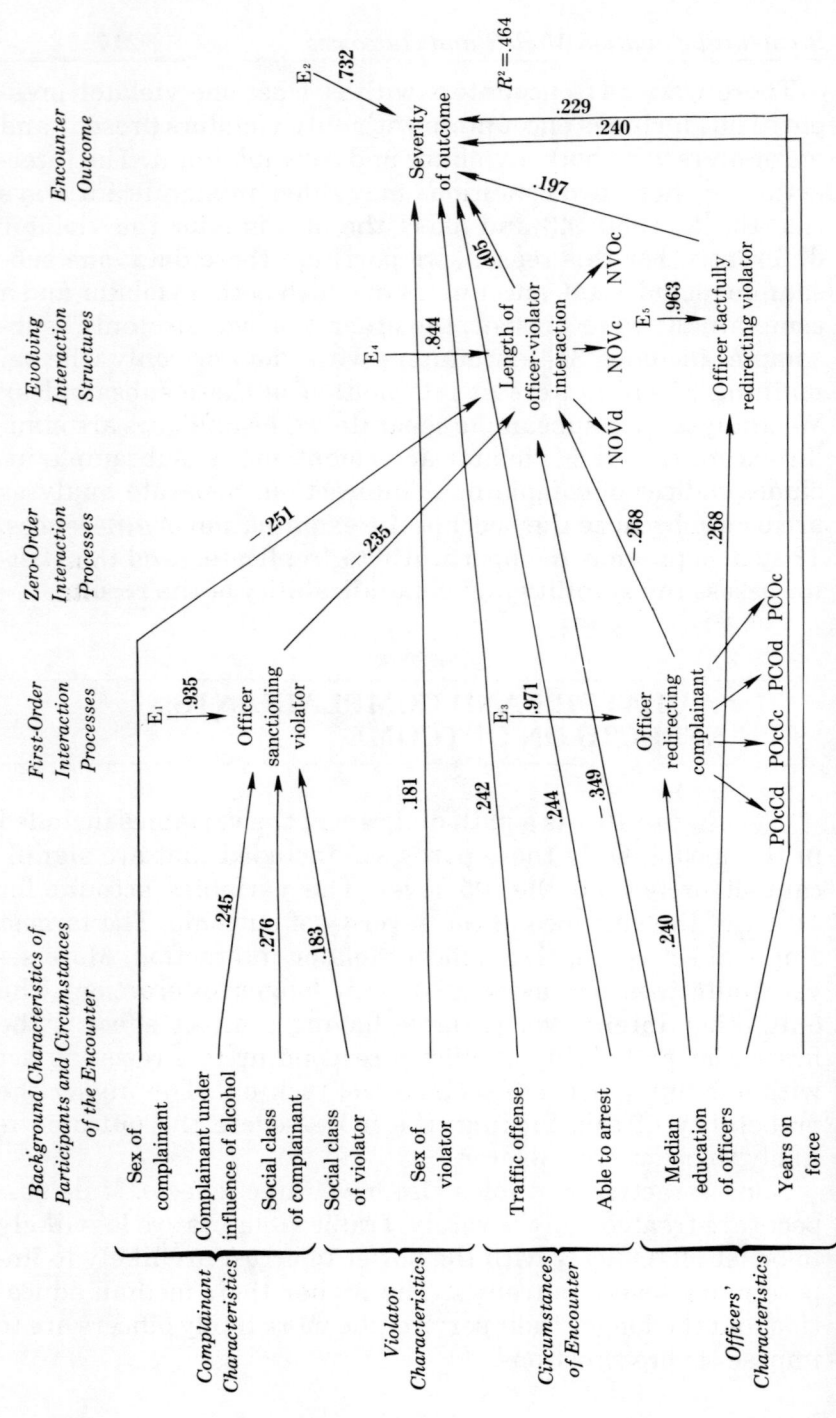

Figure 10.1. Effects of interaction on severity of outcome where both violators and complainants are present

These findings support our hypothesis that the effects of interaction on outcome severity are independent of structural variables. Those effects tend to be strongest for lower-level evolving structures rather than for direct high-level effects. They also support the hypothesis that interaction plays a substitutive role. More confrontational, more controlling interactions are associated with less severe outcomes for the violators. The independence of the effects of interaction on outcome is supported by the finding that both of the interaction variables have direct effects on severity of outcome. Though affected by two structural variables—the median education of the officers and the sex of the complainant—they are by no means determined by those variables, and the indirect effects of those two variables mediated by these two interaction variables are insignificant. These results suggest that interaction processes are something more than intervening variables. Interaction processes are independent and influence the severity of the outcome in addition to structural variables. These factors account for only 28.7% of the variance in this variable.

Interaction processes that affect the outcome of the suspect are those of the officers. The effects of complainant interactions on the severity of the outcome are less and only indirect. The officers' interactions are more likely to affect the severity of the outcome than the violator's. The control the officer exerts is evident.

Violator Only: Effects on Outcome

The analysis was also conducted for the subsample of 314 encounters in which there were present only the officers and the violator. The results are displayed in Figure 10.2. Only those paths are included which are significant at or beyond the .05 level.

The amount of variance accounted for in the dependent variable by these variables (41.9%) is comparable to the 46.4% for the violator and complainant sample. There is a decrease in

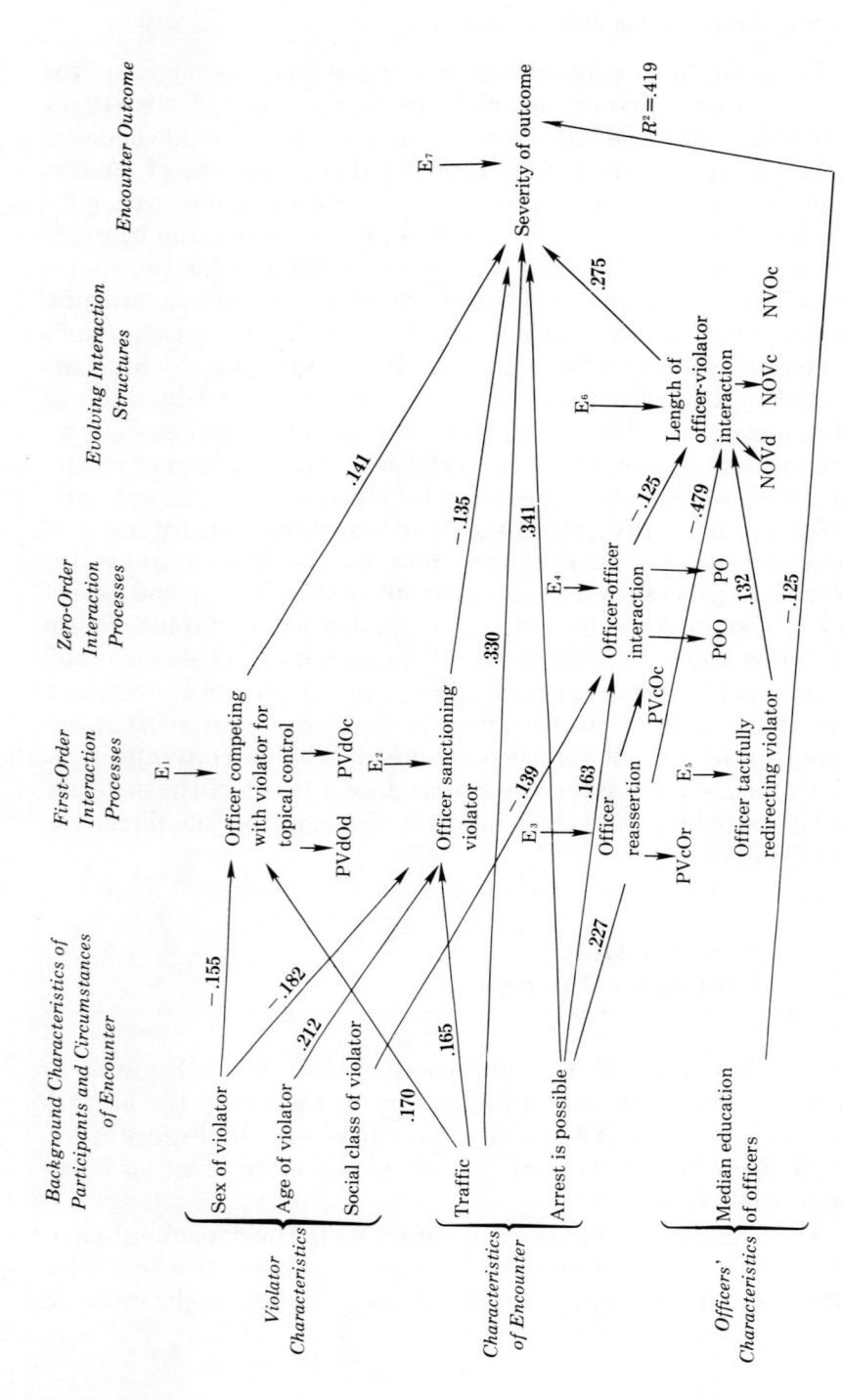

Figure 10.2. **Effects of interaction on severity of outcome where only violators are present**

the total variance accounted for by interaction variables and an increase in the variance accounted for by the structural variables. Traffic offenses are likely to result in more severe outcomes than nontraffic offenses, and possession of the power of arrest influences severity. Possession of the power should not be identified with its actual use, only with a more severe outcome. The effect of officers' median education has reversed from a slight tendency for increased education to increase the severity of the outcome to an even slighter tendency for increased education to decrease the severity of the outcome when complainants are not present.

The strongest interaction variable effect on outcome is once again the length of interaction between officers and violators, with lengthier interactions resulting in more severe outcomes. There are direct effects on the severity from competitive and sanctioning social acts (see Figure 7.1). The more likely the officer is to sanction defining utterances by the violator, the less severe the outcome tends to be. The more likely the officer is to compete with the violator for topical control by answering a defining utterance with another defining utterance, the more severe the outcome is likely to be. This last finding supports the substitution hypothesis. Here is a clear case where the officers have two possible responses to the same utterance by the violator. The more likely the officers are to choose the controlling response (the more negative of the two), the less severe the outcome tends to be; the more likely the officers are to choose the defining response (the more restrained response of the two), the more severe the outcome tends to be.

In this subsample the effects of interaction variables upon the severity of outcome are largely independent of the effects of structural variables on outcome. The interaction variables affecting outcome are parameters describing the officers' rather than the violator's interaction. Though there are some variations in these two analyses, the findings regarding violators and complainants are similar to those with violators alone.

THE EFFECT OF INTERACTION ON OUTCOMES IN POLICE-CIVILIAN ENCOUNTERS

We must regard this analysis as preliminary. We examined only linear additive relationships and did not consider nonlinear relations nor interactions among these variables. We would not be surprised if interactions and nonlinear relations occur. Of necessity too we excluded second-order transition probabilities where we have shown the interaction to be second-order. We limited this analysis to interaction processes and did not consider, for instance, phases of problem solving. We regard this analysis as a relatively crude early attempt to assess the importance of interaction processes on the outcomes. A Markov model utilizing absorbing states might have been attempted.

With respect to the importance of interaction in determining outcomes, we argue that the results clearly support the conclusion that interaction processes are an important determinant of outcomes and clearly merit further investigation. In these analyses, structural and interaction variables already explain 50% of the variance in outcomes. With more sophisticated conceptualizations of the ways interaction might affect outcomes and more sophisticated studies, we think it is reasonable to anticipate further increases in the predictability of outcomes.

The precise ways in which interactions affect outcomes are a bit less clear than the finding that they do affect outcomes. Our results are more suggestive than conclusive. We suggest the following tentative conclusions:

1. Lower-order interaction processes and evolving structures have the strongest effects on outcomes of the interaction variables, and those lower-order processes and evolving structures are a result of higher-order processes, structural constraints, and other variables as yet unidentified.
2. The effects of interaction on outcome are largely indepen-

dent of structural constraints. Events that occur during the interaction have a substantial impact on the outcomes of police-civilian encounters.
3. The acts of officers have more impact on outcomes than those of civilians, though there is evidence that the acts of both have some effect. Officers have considerably greater control over the encounter and its outcomes than do the civilians.
4. Our most tentative conclusion is that interactions may substitute for outcomes. Both tacking and competition are associated with more serious outcomes, while sanctioning is associated with less serious outcomes. Very tentatively we would suggest that this is a function of role-taking by the police. They sanction when they anticipate the suspect is amenable to immediate regulation. They tack and compete in situations in which they assess the suspect as less amenable to direct regulation and therefore more deserving of punishment. Tacking and competition are used when officers perceive the need to temporize or placate to avoid open confrontation. Once they have passed this point, and sense they are fully in charge, they feel free to impose a more severe outcome.

PART FOUR

Theoretical and Substantive Conclusions

In the first of these last two chapters we show that the basic order we have found in interaction was anticipated by George Herbert Mead. We show that the systems and mathematical modeling approach used in Part 3 can be translated into the terms of Meadean neo-social behaviorism. We redefine three basic Meadean processes—tripartite relations, role-taking, and social act—and show how these three processes may be empirically examined using quantitative interaction data and mathematical models. In the final chapter we summarize what we believe are our most substantive findings about policing.

11

Neo-Social Behaviorism

The most fundamental purpose of science is to discover order beneath the unique-appearing, variegated, phenomenological level of reality, in this case, beneath the phenomenological level of communication. The actors themselves may be unaware of lawlike processes which underlie their talk. It is vitally important that these processes, if they exist, be expressed in terms of a general, social-psychological theory.

In doing this analysis we discovered a connection between our systems and mathematical orientation and the thought of George Herbert Mead. We developed a reinterpretation of Mead's ideas amenable to empirical examination, but different from traditional interpretations. First we must discuss what we believe are deficiencies of orthodox symbolic-interaction theory.

Herbert Blumer is among the most widely respected and influential symbolic-interaction theorists. In reviewing the assumptions of contemporary theory we shall draw primarily upon his work. He lists three simple premises of symbolic interaction (1969). (1) "Human beings act towards things on the basis of the meanings that the things have for them"; (2) "The meaning of such things is derived from, or arises out of, the social interaction that one has with one's fellows"; (3) "These meanings are handled in, and modified through, an interpretative process used by the person in dealing with the things he encounters" (2). Blumer asserts both that meaning arises out of interaction, and that interaction is carried out through the exchange and interpretation of meaning.

He then advocates a methodology consistent with his premises, one that requires the investigator to gain an intimate familiarity with the area of life under study, both by experiencing it himself, and by interviewing "native" informants. "The empirical social world consists of ongoing group life and one has to get close to this life to know what is going on in it" (38). The two modes of inquiry he recommends are exploration and inspection. His approach is similar to the approach of those who develop what Deising (1971) termed pattern models. Such models embody a painstaking analysis of that facet of the real world the scientist has chosen to study, and an intimate familiarity with that world. The methodology he advocates is skillfully externalized by Glaser and Strauss in *The Discovery of Grounded Theory* (1967).

Blumer resummarizes his view as follows:

> Human group life consists of the fitting to each other of the lines of action of the participants; such aligning of actions takes place predominantly by the participants indicating to one another what to do and in turn interpreting such indications made by the others; out of such interaction people form the objects that constitute their worlds; people are prepared to act toward their objects on the basis of the meaning these objects have for them; human beings face their world as organisms with selves, thus allowing each to make indications to himself; human action is constructed by the actor on the basis of what he notes, interprets and assesses; and the interlinking of such ongoing action constitutes organizations, institutions, and vast complexes of interdependent relationships. (49)

There is an irony to the history of Mead's ideas. Most of his work was edited and published by others after his death. The intellectual movement that honors him as its herald adopted a name of which he had never heard, and interpreted his ideas in a way that was probably contrary to what he had intended (McPhail and Rexroat, 1979). Since social behaviorism is quite clearly the label he used himself, the reason for the change is not self-evident.

That such changes occurred would be of no surprise to Mead, for one of his most fascinating ideas was that there was no objective past, only a past interpreted from the perspectives of the present (Mead, 1932). As the present changes, so does the interpretation of the past. This notable exception to the usual chronology of causal sequences is one with which only social scientists must deal, for although nearly two centuries ago scientists recognized the import of the "personal equation" in observation, and whereas astronomers study the past every time they peer at a star (recently, they identified four giant elliptical galaxies 10 billion light-years from Earth), they still consider their observations to refer to a reality with an objective status.

We do not claim that our ideas are identical to Mead's. We find many of his ideas helpful to our own thinking about human interaction. We doubt that our systems or mathematical applications of his ideas ever occurred to him. The only claim we make is that it is quite as consistent for us to reinterpret his past ideas in terms of our present, as it is for others in terms of their present.

When we reviewed the world of symbolic interactionists we were puzzled. We agreed with their emphasis on the import of mind, meaning, and symbolic systems in studying human beings. On the other hand, we could never understand where the "interaction" was in most of their studies. It was certainly present in the work of scholars such as Schegloff (1968), but most work seemed long on meaning and short on interaction. Even that which did address interaction, as Goffman's sometimes does (1961b), was exploratory and impressionistically theoretical, not empirical. The best work of symbolic interactionists is in books by participant observers which are, in effect, externalizations of the experience of thoughtful and sensitive scholars. These scholars greatly increased our understanding of particular groups and their experiences.

A relevant example is Jonathan Rubinstein's *City Police* (1973). This book holds a special place in the police literature because of its detailed and sensitive depiction of the world of Philadelphia police officers. Other observers made important contributions to the police literature, notably Skolnick (1966) and Westley (1970), but Rubinstein's is the most comprehensive ethnography of uniformed patrolmen. Yet all these studies suffer from the defects of their genre.

First, despite a theoretical emphasis on process, the portraits they paint tend to be static. They depict a system of meanings of the group in question; they often depict how these meanings relate to each other; but seldom do they deal either with the fate of these meanings when confronted with those of others, or with change in them over time. One gets the sense of closed worlds, though obviously some of these worlds, especially of labeled deviants, may be under siege.

An adequate theory must be able to deal not only with one world of meaning but with the process of interaction, and with the unique emergences from such processes when two worlds meet. Two worlds converge when a lower-class black and a police officer interact, but a knowledge of the meanings of either or both worlds is insufficient. What emerges from their interaction is likely to be different from what either would prefer, and to constitute an emergent from their particular combination. This is true whether at the level of the individual, the position, or the group. For example, whatever an American president's program, much of it must be approved by the Congress. Neither an understanding of the president, nor the presidency, nor the Congress is sufficient, because what will emerge from their relation will be different from what either thought or intended originally. From Rubinstein's book one gets little sense either of those with whom police interact, or of the unique products of their interaction.

Second, most such studies present the worlds of such groups as if they were homogeneous, using the deviant case to make the rule more than for any other reason. Is there really any such thing as *the* world of either the Philadelphia police or big city police? Are Wambaugh's (1972), Serpico's (Maas, 1973), Skolnick's (1966), and Rubinstein's *their* own worlds, or ideal types? Just as we agree with Blumer's critique of much variable analysis, especially his assertion that "there is a process of definition intervening between the events of experience presupposed by the independent variable and the formal behavior represented by the dependent variable," we believe the same is true in regard to those police officers described by Rubinstein and Skolnick. That process may *not* involve the meanings described by these authors, and may result in an outcome unforeseen by either officers, citizens, or observers. There is a tendency to confuse the ordered world of the observer who has completely analyzed his data, with the much more confused and ambivalent world of police and civilians.

Novelists are often more faithful to their subjects than social scientists, because novelists can preserve diversity through the device of portraying different characters. Quantitative studies which are, after all, based on frequency distributions, in fact preserve diversity, even if the diverse elements are each more structured. Through the use of various coefficients of concomitant variation they also acknowledge imperfect, even contrary or contradictory relations that are apt to be reconciled, omitted, or ignored in qualitative studies.

Third, perhaps the most serious defect of many studies by symbolic interactionists is that their emphasis on illuminating shared meaning has resulted in the studies' being written at a degree of abstraction far removed from actual interpersonal interaction. They are of little help in interpreting the interaction. Their focus of interest is the shared culture of the group, or relatively stable aspects of persons, such as their concepts of self, or their reference groups, rather than the very specific act-by-act, utterance-by-utterance process by which persons interact. We are making the same criticism of symbolic interactionists that they have made of other viewpoints. They have too macro a focus. They do not get down to the behavior process. They do not hesitate to make generalizations about this process, but few collect microlevel data about it.

Fourth, Blumer's analysis somewhat downplays social habit, much more adequately dealt with by Dewey in *Human Nature and Conduct* (1922). The emphasis on meaning has resulted not just in an oversocialized, but an overintellectualized interpretation of human beings. Between an utterance by one and a reply by the other, does either really have time to think of all the things implied by such terms as "fitting to each other," "indicating to one another," "constructing," and so forth? Does the average actor have time to spend much effort in roletaking? Do actors really give *continuous* attention to their presentations of self? Is this a case of sociology affecting popular culture so that some reflective people have come to look upon themselves as sociological objects? Their evident self-consciousness has then either been observed or actually projected onto them by other sociologists.

Perhaps sociologists have merely come to observe subjects externalizing their own theories, as casual observation of the many ordinary civilians who appear on television quiz shows and news programs might suggest. Is it not possible that much interaction is either habitual, routine, and scripted, or else unreflective and spontaneous, more or less carried on by trial and error? Possibly the actors are not using what economists would term a maximizing standard in presentation of self and role-taking, but what Simon (1955) termed a "satisficing" standard. They opt for the first seemingly satisfactory alternative that occurs to them, and they do not engage in an exhaustive consideration of alternative behaviors or possible outcomes. Interaction in real life, except on ritual occasions, is much more haphazard and less reflective than we have hitherto been willing to believe.

Fifth, there remains the problem of generalization. Case studies are important to social science, and investigators should conduct them more frequently. They are the exploratory phase in the act of research. Ultimately, what scientists seek to create are valid generalizations. This requires many cases. Since it is unlikely that all cases will turn out as predicted, it requires quantification—certainly counting—and either statistical or mathematical analysis.

The long fruitless argument between sociologists over qualitative versus quantitative research represents wasted effort. Qualitative research is necessary to discover meanings and behavior of hypothetical import to the group members under study, but quantification is necessary to verify personal insight, to go beyond a case to a generalization.

The ultimate goal is a generalization that takes the form of a theoretical proposition or of a law. While the former purports to be an explanation, the latter merely states in mathematical terms those variable values which when calculated properly equal some other variable value. Thus, Einstein's famous equation, $E = mc^2$. There is no effort to explain why this is true, merely an assertion that it is. All that is required of such an assertion is that it be empirically testable.

The current vogue of theory construction tends to be biased against the search for law, and in favor of explanation (for instance, Reynolds, 1971). We take the position that the discovery of an underlying order which may be expressed as law is just as valid as theory building. In fact, in the long run it may be more productive.

In this study we did not seek theory, but law, and to this end our hypothesis testing was rather indifferent to theoretical explanation. Physicists never demanded as a condition of its publication an explanation of the law of gravity. What we seek is the implicit order of human interaction. We are fascinated by the various possible explanations of such an order, but do not require one. What we have found is that the order we discovered was anticipated by G. H. Mead.

We take our departure from Mead's most frequently cited work, *Mind, Self, and Society from the Standpoint of a Social Behaviorist* (1934). "Behaviorism," wrote Mead, "is simply an approach to the study of the experience of the individual from the point of view of his conduct, *particularly*, but not exclusively, the conduct as it is observable by others" (Mead, 1934:2, italics added). Social behaviorism focuses on the process of interpersonal conduct, of actors responding to one another and to themselves. Mead even went so far as to assert that the behaviorist is preoccupied with the "actual reaction itself, and it is only in so far as we can translate the content of introspection over into the *response* that we can get any satisfactory psychological doctrine" (Mead, 1934:105, italics added).

Human behavior differs from that of other animals because of language, the use of the "significant gesture" or "significant symbol." A human being emitting a word either to himself or to another responds to the word itself as a stimulus. If the word means the same to the other, then his response is likely to be similar. In principle, this permits the anticipation of the effects of conduct and therefore its modification prior to its manifestation. Since the subject responds to his own communicative acts much like his auditor he can anticipate the auditor's response. Language (dialogue with oneself) permits analysis of alternate courses of conduct and choice from among them.

Because of his recognition of the import of language Mead's behaviorism is ultimately very different from either Watson's or Skinner's. Mead thought the construct "mind" was necessary to explain human behavior. Mind emerged from and manifested itself in a tripartite relationship: (1) the conduct of actor A; (2) actor A's response to his own conduct; (3) actor B's response to actor A's conduct. Unlike simple reflexive behavior, and unlike conditioned behavior, in both of which the response is essentially one of a set of unmediated acts distinct from the act that sets it off, human behavior involves *both* actors normally responding similarly to the same act. This response is not mechanical, but mediated by the similar meaning that both actors give to the act. This meaning is embodied in the language that both share, and use to classify the act. Since both actors usually classify and evaluate the act in the same way, and since both actors can utilize language to reflect about the act prior to displaying it, each can not only anticipate the other's reaction (since it is usually much like his own), but also select the act that is appropriate to the reaction which he wishes to achieve. Two persons coordinate their behavior, not as automatons, but as minded, imaginative human beings.

Mead's interactionism was the social psychological application of the common pragmatist assumption that "truth" evolved from the continuous testing of behavior within a particular environment. Truth was not a property of an idea, or a person, or the environment itself, but a relation between them. James (1907:202) wrote that "possession of true thoughts means everywhere the possession of invaluable *instruments of action*" (italics added). "Conduct," wrote Dewey (1922:18), "is always shared. . . . Some activity proceeds from a man; then it sets up reactions in the surroundings." While the pragmatist doctrine of truth is difficult to defend as a general philosophic position, its relevance to social psychology is more evident. It implies that only those entities and relations important to the adaptation of a species come to have "existence" for that species. In

Neo-Social Behaviorism

terms of interpersonal conduct, it means that only those behaviors which are mutually meaningful will play a significant part in human interaction. Truth is agreement between actors over the meaning and evaluation of behaviors. How may this view be tested empirically?

The tripartite relationship consisted of the conduct of actor A, actor A's response to his own conduct, and actor B's response to actor A's conduct (Mead, 1934:76). All "minded interaction" consists of such tripartite relationships, but our focus will be on the interaction process, not the emergence of mind.

If the relationship includes A's act, A's response to his own act, and B's response to A's act, then it also includes B's act, B's response to his own act, and A's response to B's act. If this is true then, given a sequence of acts

(1) A_1 (2) B_1 (3) A_2 (4) B_2
A's act—B's act—A's act—B's act . . .

the question may be asked, Where in the above series is B's response to A's act and A's response to his own act? The most common answer to this question might be diagrammed as follows:

(1)
    B's idea of A's act
A's act
    A's idea of his own act

(2)
    B's idea of his own act
B's act
    A's idea of B's act

This model suggests that the act is always mediated by the idea. This is precisely Blumer's position. Acts are contingent not upon acts (there is no relationship between A's act and B's act) but upon ideas, the interpretations which each actor makes.

One may interpret Mead's thought quite differently. Rather than initially concentrating on an idea state, it is possible at the beginning of an analysis to omit it completely (except when such a hypothetical construct is necessary to achieve a satisfactory fit of a model to data). Then B's act, (2) above, is the response of B to A's act; and A's act, (3) A_2 above, is both A's response to B *and* A's response to himself. These three steps constitute, in social behaviorial terms, the tripartite relationship of which Mead spoke.

We do not wish, by these means, to suggest that the actors do not possess ideas, feelings, and evaluations, subjectively, of their own and the other's acts, but rather to suggest that in the study of detailed interaction their inclusion in the model is redundant unless required to explain the data. It is redundant because each actor displays in his behavior that particular act which is habitual or which he has decided he prefers among those he has considered. That is, a study of the ideas themselves would be useful only to discover those ideas that pertained to behavioral options the actor did *not* externalize.

The actor is not a puppet compelled by others to behave despite his ideas of how he should behave. Even where duress exists, an actor is not a puppet, but says to himself, "I had better act in such and such a way, or I will be punished." His act is therefore both a response to his own idea and expresses that idea and an anticipatory response to a potential act of the other, a potential that may never be evoked because the actor's choice of his response is calculated to avoid its evocation. The behaviors actually enacted will be a response to both other and self, and contingent upon them, just as they would have been if the alternative were chosen.

Behaviors express the choices of the actors, and express a set of expectations that can be inferred from the behaviors themselves. The behaviors not chosen were presumably not chosen because the likelihood was that they would lead to undesirable consequences. If, on the other hand, the behavior displayed leads to a response different from that expected, then the act may be modified by another act. It could not be modified only by another idea, since the other actor would have no notion of that idea except as it was expressed behaviorally (we include talk in behavior, action, or conduct). It follows that all the information necessary to study conduct *may* be contained in behavior (except for future behavior, e.g., the actor says to himself, "I will act such and such a way in the future," and this future is not part of the data, or for conduct that imperfectly externalizes the actor's intentions).

There is nothing unscientific about studying thought about conduct or the meanings actors give to objects, but our interest is conduct, not thought, and such an interest is entirely consistent with a Meadean perspective.

When A acts A responds to his own act. Commonly we say, "A responds to himself," but this is an imprecise statement. A does not respond to himself. A's *self* responds to his act. The "reflexive" responds to the externalization or the thought of the externalization.

What is the timing of this response? Among the possibilities are that it occurs simultaneously with B's response or else simultaneously with the original act. In either case it would be only a mental response made while attending to something else. If it occurs during the original act, then it suggests a double consciousness, one that simultaneously attends to acting and responding to acting. But if this is true (and there is no doubt that we monitor and correct our performances), then it can only be either in terms of its concordance with a preconceived idea (for instance, a pianist monitors whether he plays according to the music), or in terms of the concurrent responses of B (e.g., A judges whether his behavior is having the desired effect on B). But in the latter instance A is not responding to himself, but to B's response to A. Not only this, but often it is not possible for A to monitor B's response while A is acting because B inhibits his response until after A has stopped acting.

A's response to his own act will only make a difference to B if A modifies his behavior as a result of his own self- or other-monitoring. Here "modify" includes continuing the same behavior, stopping the behavior, or changing the behavior. The modifying of behavior is, then, an externalization of an internal response. It is all of that response which becomes public. If this is true, then either the concurrent modification by A of his own act, or his subsequent act, if his first act is already complete, may be considered evidence of A's response to his own act. *Such a response might be inferred if A's consequent act is contingent upon his antecedent act.*

There appear to be two foci of contingency (each A,B pair of acts), and the total contingency may be apportioned to two sources (each act may be contingent on the two previous). If A has acted, then his act may elicit a response both from himself and from B. If B's response is not concurrently self-evident, then it must be consequent to A's own act. B's consequential act is, in part, the meaning of A's act because only from the relations between the two does A learn what his act "means" to the other. That is, whatever A's act meant to himself before, during, or after his own act, that meaning was never interpersonally guaranteed. Its social meaning was subject to confirmation by the other, whatever A's intention. At the same time that B is completing the meaning of A's antecedent act, A is responding to his own act and comparing his response, and that of B, to his "intention." A may say to himself: "I did not quite mean to say it in that way," which recognizes (a) some original intention; (b) embodied in a completed behavior; (c) which did not quite fulfill the intention as A had hoped it would. Simultaneously, A observes B to interpret what B's response is. A then acts again. A's second act is both a response to his own previous act, as well as to B. A's second act gives meaning not only to B's act now, but to his own previous act. A may reaffirm his previous act by continuing it; or may respond primarily to B, in this way completing B's act; or may initiate a new act ignoring both his own previous act and that of B. *Such a relation might be inferred if A's consequent act is contingent upon not only his antecedent act, but B's antecedent act as well.* Thus

$$PA_2 = P(A_2/A_1B_1) \qquad (1)$$

Therefore

$$PA_2 = P(A_1)P(B_1/A_1) \qquad (2)$$

But what is the substantive meaning of this hypothetical relationship? Normally A_2 would be said to be statistically conditioned by or contingent on A_1 and B_1. But substantive and statistical import may be quite different. In this case, B_1 and A_2 have retrospective import in that they give meaning to A_1, at least in the sense that they may continue or modify A_1. On the other hand, it is possible that A_2 may lack any such dependence. If the latter is true, then the meaning of A_1B_1 must be complete (noting, however, that except for the first two behaviors of any sequence, all behaviors exist in hypothetical $A_1B_1A_2$ sets). Many of these contingencies are substantively, if not statistically, symmetrical, because the meaning of A_1 is dependent upon consequent interpretation just as much as B_1 and A_2 are response to and therefore dependent upon A_1.

An examination of a sequence of utterances demonstrates two intrinsic sources of contingency: *structural contingency* and *semantic contingency*. Structural contingency is based on the function of the utterance, e.g., declarative, imperative, or interrogative. There can be no answer without a question. Disobedience is impossible unless an order has been given. Not only this, but one cannot respond to an answer unless one knows a question has been asked. Thus

A_1	B_1	A_2
Question	Answer	Response to Answer in Terms of Question

Semantic contingency is based on the meaning that particular utterances have. They are related because they are oriented to a common topic, theme, or object. Not just any answer is appropriate to a particular question. The answer (B_1) and the response to the answer (A_2) are *indexical* in terms of A_1.

Both structural and semantic contingency may themselves be differentially contingent upon factors external to the process itself, especially the location of the behavior in the group. Behavior may be of position incumbents who are normatively guided. Some will be more likely to give orders and others to obey them by virtue of the positions each occupies. This third contingency is substantively a function of the "appropriateness" of the utterance to the position externalizing it. If this is true, then A_2 is a function not simply of A_1 and B_1, but of both their understandings of the appropriateness of A_1 and A_2 to A, and of B_1 to B. If A_1 is inappropriate, then B_1 and A_2 may be different quite apart from the structural or semantic properties in themselves. Under the guise of "appropriateness," society (or what Mead termed "the generalized-other") enters the dyad as an internalized guest more or less guiding the interaction process. It would appear that such a guest is especially likely to be present in socially important situations when strangers such as officers and civilians gather, since few such encounters last long enough for norms to emerge from the particular encounter itself. *If this is true, then an examination of the distribution of responses should find different probability functions based on position, and these functions should provide a clue to the normative and to the deviant.*

Group Manifestations in Interaction. In traditional interaction research, actors are uniquely identified in the sense that, for instance, an identifying number is used analogous to a proper name. The social behaviorist perspective suggests that although such usage is appropriate in informal groups, it is not when studying persons occupying positions, when the positions are the primary focus of interest. If traditional scientific wisdom is correct, then a single position shares a repertoire of behaviors termed *role behaviors*. These express expectations of the position, not the person. Therefore, social psychology that approaches its subject matter from a social-behaviorist perspective is justified in identifying actors in terms, not of their individual identity, but of their position. Behavior is then interpreted as role behavior. It is also interpreted as having its origin in the position, or ultimately the group, more than in the individual.

If our interpretation of Mead's ideas is correct, then it may be easily tested. It is only necessary to collect data on the series of acts of individuals in units of three and test whether the predicted contingencies exist. It is necessary to test whether these differ by position as well as by situation. But it is possible in doing so to specify even more particularly two other important concepts of Mead, "role-taking" and "social act" (Mead, 1934:254).

Because of the complexity of natural language, we have chosen to classify police-civilian interaction using a category system that is essentially functional (Bales, 1950, describes the prototype of most such category systems). From a pragmatist position its functional basis is not a defect. In being functional it is similar to all languages, but is more abstract. For our analysis the utterances of police were categorized as defining, confirming, or controlling. The utterances of civilians were categorized as defining, confirming, or resistant.

Neo-Social Behaviorism

Defining acts were either questions or accusations, that is, they either established a domain of interest to the interrogator or imposed an identity upon someone. Confirming acts either continued a line of discourse, maintained semantic contingency, or were positive responses to questions, accusations, or commands. Controlling acts were commands. Resisting acts were refusals to answer questions, admit to an accusation, or obey orders.

Let us signify the actors in the tripartite relationship by O, for officer, and C for civilian. Each may make one of three utterances. Officers may define (DEF), cooperate (COOP), or order (ORD). Civilians may define (DEF), cooperate (COOP), or resist (RES). Each act in the tripartite relationship may be one of these three states (e.g., $O_{def} C_{coop} O_{coop}$). The simplest way to represent the tripartite relationship is in the form of a matrix. If there are two separate tripartite sets: OCO and COC, then, since each actor may externalize one of three types of utterance, the full matrix must have eighteen rows and eighteen columns (see Table 6.3). The rows and columns will be:

	Rows	Columns
1.	$C_{def}O_{def}$	$(O_{def})C_{def}$
2.	$C_{def}O_{coop}$	$(O_{coop})C_{def}$
3.	$C_{def}O_{ord}$	$(O_{ord})C_{def}$
4.	$C_{coop}O_{def}$	$(O_{def})C_{coop}$
5.	$C_{coop}O_{coop}$	$(O_{coop})C_{coop}$
6.	$C_{coop}O_{ord}$	$(O_{ord})C_{coop}$
7.	$C_{res}O_{def}$	$(O_{def})C_{res}$
8.	$C_{res}O_{coop}$	$(O_{coop})C_{res}$
9.	$C_{res}O_{ord}$	$(O_{ord})C_{res}$
10.	$O_{def}C_{def}$	$(C_{def})O_{def}$
11.	$O_{def}C_{coop}$	$(C_{coop})O_{def}$
12.	$O_{def}C_{res}$	$(C_{res})O_{def}$
13.	$O_{coop}C_{def}$	$(C_{def})O_{coop}$
14.	$O_{coop}C_{coop}$	$(C_{coop})O_{coop}$
15.	$O_{coop}C_{res}$	$(C_{res})O_{coop}$
16.	$O_{ord}C_{def}$	$(C_{def})O_{ord}$
17.	$O_{ord}C_{coop}$	$(C_{coop})O_{ord}$
18.	$O_{ord}C_{res}$	$(C_{res})O_{ord}$

The upper left quadrant and lower right quadrant of the matrix will be empty, because for purposes of most data analyses it is assumed that officers do not speak twice in succession without a civilian's intervening, and that civilians do not speak twice in a row without an officer's intervening.

If one collects many COC and OCO combinations, then it is possible to place in each cell of the matrix the actual number of observed combinations of each particular type (e.g., the number of $D_{def} O_{def} C_{def}$, etc.). From these counts one may then calculate the probabilities of each type. Such probabilities, calculated from data on police-suspect interaction, were displayed in Table 6.3.

This large matrix contains many smaller ones, which can be calculated by merely rearranging and collapsing the rows. If, for instance, one believes that the response (the columns) is dependent only upon the immediately preceding act, rather than the two immediately preceding acts, then one may merely collapse certain rows and columns. Then the rows and columns are:

Rows	Columns
O_{def}	C_{def}
O_{coop}	C_{coop}
O_{ord}	C_{res}
C_{def}	O_{def}
C_{coop}	O_{coop}
C_{res}	O_{ord}

These different contingencies may be calculated and differences between them compared to discover whether in combinations $O_1 C_1 O_2$, O_2 is dependent only on C_1, only on O_1, or on both O_1 and C_1. A similar comparison can be made for the $C_1 O_1 C_2$ combinations.

Now let us consider a two-state contingency: $O_1 C_1$, e.g., $O_{def} C_{coop}$. This contingency is calculated in the form of a probability. This probability is the answer to the question: if the officer externalizes a defining act, what are the chances that the citizen will respond with a cooperative act? This probability would seem to be a measure of role-taking (Mead, 1934:254). While it does not provide an answer to the question of whether the individual is actually, self-consciously anticipating what the response of the other to his contemplated act will be, it does provide a measure of what the actual response may be.

It is important to note that since the probabilities are never 1.00, as persons are never completely predictable, role-taking necessarily involves some measure of chance. We must modify Mead's view somewhat.

If an officer asks a citizen a question he can ask himself, How would I, myself, in this situation, respond to such a question or to the fact of my asking it? Taking the role of the other, despite a shared language and culture, nonetheless, involves making a bet. By examination of such a matrix we are able to say what act O "should" externalize if he wants to maximize the chances of C's responding in a particular way.

Based on our distinction between integral and situated identities, the former with long experience and the latter usually with little, it would seem reasonable to hypothesize that the officer is in a better position to role-take than the civilian. We would hypothesize that as a result of experience in a particular position, incumbents gradually develop more accurate approximations, essentially intuitive judgments of a probability distribution, of how others will respond to their acts. Civilians may be more predictable than officers merely because, from long experience, officers "know how to handle" civilians, but civilians, lacking such experiences, do not know how to handle officers. Thus officers *seem* less predictable. This suggests that role-taking should not be thought of in absolute terms, but rather as an ability which must be measured along a continuum. The tripartite matrix may be decomposed into two smaller matrices, CO and OC, which are measures of the role-taking abilities of C and O, respectively. This measure, like that of the tripartite relationship, is based entirely on the observable conduct of individuals.

Mead (1934) wrote: "Social psychology is behaviorist in the sense of starting off with an observable activity—the dynamic, on-going social process, and the social acts which are its component elements." More specifically he defined "social act" as a member of "the class of acts which involve the cooperation of more than one individual, and whose object as defined by the act . . . is a social object." He goes on to say that the "objective of the acts is then found in the life-process of the group, not in those of the separate individuals alone."

Social acts range from a unit as small as two brief utterances to the realization of a life's ambition made possible because of the cooperation of others. It is clear that an utterance by one person is, like the unheard noise of the proverbial tree falling in a forest, usually incomplete. The meaning of one utterance is found in its *response* (Mead, 1934:105). From our perspective a social act is a pair of acts. The antecedent act is not only a cue for the consequent act, but the consequent act gives the social act its meaning.

If this is true, then a first-order matrix may be viewed from two perspectives. From the point of view of the first speaker, it is an estimate of the probability distribution of responses to his antecedent act. From the scientist's point of view it is a count of the various social acts which have occurred. It is also the actual completed meanings to the acts the individual manifested, but which were completed and given their meaning by the response of the other. Thus the police officer may: (1) anticipate the probable response of a civilian to an order (role-taking); but (2) be described as dominant only if the civilian obeys (be described in terms of a particular social act). It takes two, not only to tango, but to be dominant, cooperative, reassertive, or confrontative.

Each of the matrices we have been discussing is a square matrix. Each has an equal number of rows and columns. Summing the counts in all the cells of a row, it is possible to divide the count in each cell by the total. The resultant row is a probability vector. A matrix of such vectors is a regular stochastic matrix. Such matrices possess a number of properties that can be deduced. Certain of these matrices display characteristics of what is termed a Markov process. Again, these may be deduced mathematically.

Mead's tripartite relation is identical, in part, to what is known as a second-order Markov process. Thus it is possible to think of Mead's theory in terms of a mathematical model. The model is more complex, and possesses more specific implications, than Mead's original theory. If human interaction "fits" the mathematical model, we can say not only that interaction is Meadean, but that it is lawlike. It displays an underlying probabilistic mathematical order, which permits us to understand it much more than before. It permits us to do so solely on the basis of observed conduct. We gradually build a model of police-civilian interaction, and ultimately, in a simple way, simulate it. Through exploring the model we learn a great deal more about the nitty gritty details of the communication process between police and civilians. Thus we make a transition from systems theory and mathematics to a social psychological position a half-century old. We believe that in the long run each of these approaches will have much to contribute to the other. We have sought to initiate that process in this book.

12

A Social Psychology of Policing

Despite the complaints of some policy makers and college freshmen, social scientists have, if anything, been precipitously "applied" in their research. By "applied" we do not mean that they have always been preoccupied with applications, but with collecting "social intelligence," that is, information of current popular interest rather than the kind of data necessary for understanding basic social processes.

This has been especially true of the studies of police and policing. After years of almost total neglect, police became popular subjects of study in the mid-1960s. Because of the civil rights movement, the Vietnam crisis, and possibly because of the expansion of the so-called drug culture to the youth of the middle and upper classes, combined with vivid televised accounts of confrontations, policing came to be perceived as "a social problem." To some, the problem was their inability to handle riots and dissenters. To others it was their seeming brutality and the violation of individual rights. To most it was a problem.

In view of these events, it is no wonder that scholars responded by collecting social intelligence about police, data that policy makers, scholars, or citizens considered important social variables for political, moral, or personal reasons at that particular time. In the sixties, data on poverty, race, and violence were important, as well as data pertaining to the controversial decisions of the Warren Court, which had extended to the state, through the Fourteenth Amendment, constitutional protections of citizens accused of criminal violations.

Much of Skolnick's (1966), Chevigny's (1969), and Reiss's (1971) work was focused on police and policing as a social problem.

Other scholars such as Wilson (1968) and Goldstein (1977) were concerned with policing from not only a social-problems but also a public-administration point of view. Were police effective? If so, why? If not, why not? The *Journal of Police Science and Administration* focused on such issues. Many psychologists concerned themselves with selecting and training police personnel. Sherman (in Niederhoffer and Blumberg, 1976:242) noted that "major 'pure' research on the American police . . . has virtually stopped." Nonetheless, he concluded that pure and applied studies of police "should complement, not contradict, each other." This may have been a kind of "Freudian" slip since studies may not complement each other and still not be contradictory.

This monograph summarizes more than a decade of data collection and analysis. In 1969 we proposed research on the possible application of Markov models of police-civilian interaction to the Center for Studies of Crime and Delinquency. We hope we have contributed to the understanding of the processes of social control by following through on that proposal. Despite the many controversies of the decade, we tried to keep our scientific goals primary, notwithstanding the preoccupation of some scholars and police to label us as political or administrative reformers.

If a science of human transactions, and one of police-civilian interaction is to develop, it must start with a very complex phenomenon—human person-to-person verbal and nonverbal behavior—and dramatically simplify it for the purpose of both data collection and analysis. As the reader now must realize, the analysis of an interaction process that is limited to three acts per position is an extremely complex problem. It is sufficiently complex to give some the illusion that we are preoccupied with methodology when in fact we are only using the necessary analytic tools.

We have tried to relate our findings to current debates and previous findings about police. We have taken the position that, at least in cultures derived from the English, the main task of the police is to exercise legitimate authority in enforcing the law, settling disputes, keeping order, and providing for the public health and safety. We believe they do this mainly by talking. Talking, together with "just being there," is an officer's main job. The better he or she is at it, the less she or he will need to resort to physical violence.

We then set out to (1) describe the groups within which police do their work, volatile working groups, which we see as a basic type of work group, not one involving only civilians and police. Like all work groups these need supervisors and they need to get their work (mostly talking) done. (2) We described the process, parameter, and output structure that characterize police-civilian communication. Again, in studying police, we were seeking to find out about human interaction and to describe it.

From such descriptive data it is possible to discover order. Fancy theories are unnecessary and premature. What is necessary is replication in order to make sure the same order is found in different independent samples. As particular, quantifiable instances of different kinds of order are found, these may gradually be related to one another. These relations are more likely to take the form of laws than of theories. We seriously doubt whether it is even sensible to seek *a* theory of police-civilian interaction. Such a theory, at this time, would be at least premature, and is likely impossible. The best that is possible is a "theory" of some particular police behavior, e.g., brutality, report-taking, giving a traffic ticket. We are not sure there is one social-scientific study of sanctioning moving-automobile violations that includes data on how much, precisely, the alleged violator was exceeding the speed limit. Without such data the alleged effect of personal or demographic or situational variables is virtually meaningless unless it is assumed, for instance, that all women exceed the speed limit exactly the same number of miles per hour under exactly the same safety conditions. It is failure to include such data which makes most theory suspect.

We have tried to relate our findings to other studies. Certainly our data collection was designed to include *some* of the same variables as other studies, e.g., Reiss's (1971). But our true interest has *not* been in doing this, because doing so perpetuates a polite fiction. The fact is, no one else has published (and very few have collected) utterance-by-utterance data on police-civilian interaction. The fact is, social psychologists, to say nothing of police scientists, have collected almost no data encompassing personal, demographic, and situational variables in such a way that they can be combined with interaction data so that the amount of indirect and direct effect on the interaction itself, or on other outcomes can be apportioned to these different variables (Sampson, 1976).

If we have made contributions to social sychology and to the study of police-civilian interaction we believe, so far as this monograph is concerned, that they are as follows:

1. For the first time we have gathered data on, analyzed, and described the process of utterance-by-utterance interaction between police officers and civilians. We have estimated the actual probabilities of certain kinds of acts and responses to these acts by police, suspects, and complainants. Transactions (Miller and Steinberg, 1975:37) turn out to be the basic units of their relationships. It was necessary to simplify this description so that it included only classifications of defining, controlling, resisting, and confirming utterances (many of the latter would be, in Bales's terms, statements of opinion or information). We believe these simple categories are useful for describing interaction in many work settings. We believe these are important dimensions of symbolic interaction. Establishing a topic of discourse or an identity, regulating others, resisting definitions and regulation, or accepting and expanding definitions or regulation are important dimensions of the interactional tasks involved in supervising and being supervised. We do not agree with those who "put down" descriptive studies. Theory preceding descriptive knowledge of a field is more akin to theology.

2. We have found that the utterance-by-utterance process of interaction approximates a second-order Markov model. We have tested this model on three different, independent sets of data. We do not know whether the fact that the fit is only approximate is due to systematic or random error in the data, or to only partial homogeneity or stability. Until we are able to

examine these possibilities much more carefully, we doubt whether it will be possible for police scholars to come to any final conclusions about the effects of personal, demographic, or situational variables since these may be either neutralized or amplified by the interaction itself. This finding means that interaction is much more complex than the common-sense assumption that actors merely have a direct influence on each other.

3. We have shown that a change by *only* one actor in an interaction can make the *other* actor seem like a different person. We have proven the paradox that habitual modes of response which usually lead to cooperation, and which make the actor appear cooperative under the one set of conditions, can lead to confrontation under another set of conditions. Differences in the probability distribution of acts from one civilian to another may account for differences in officer behavior without even considering any variables external to the interaction itself.

4. We have described how officers take charge, supervise, regulate, and solve problems in encounters by talking, and how civilians aid in this task. We have shown that discretion is exercised at many phases of the encounter, not just in deciding outcomes.

5. We have shown that officers do not always have to control interaction for cooperation to develop between them and civilians.

6. We have shown that officers do dominate interaction by initiating encounters, regulating when new speakers enter the conversation, interrupting civilians talking to each other, often defining the cognitive domain, using overtly controlling statements when necessary, and influencing the last social act of the encounter.

7. We have shown that response propensities are unaffected by several demographic variables, but are strongly affected by the position of the actor, that is officer, suspect, or complainant. This suggests caution in interpreting demographic effects in the absence of interaction data.

8. We have shown that officers may be better than civilians at role-taking.

9. We have shown that officers and civilians in the same encounter experience quite different situations.

10. We have shown that the dispatcher's definition of the situation has little effect on initial interaction.

11. We have shown that proactive and reactive encounters have a different phase structure in terms of problem solving when sets of utterances are analyzed, and that officers use somewhat different decision patterns in proactive and reactive encounters.

12. We have shown that police probably are helpful in interrupting and preventing civilian-civilian confrontation.

13. We have shown that interactional as well as structural variables have an effect on seriousness of outcome.

14. We have shown that many of George Herbert Mead's concepts including the tripartite relationship, role-taking, and social act can be operationalized and measured using a second-order Markov model.

15. We have developed methods for quickly analyzing process data using both matrix algebra and log-linear models. Only when investigators have more frequently used such techniques will they get used to reading and interpreting them, and no longer have the feeling of being overburdened by method. It takes some time (we can testify ourselves) to get used to thinking about "Did what I said, before you said what you said, affect both what you said and what I am saying now?" in mathematical terms.

A NEW PERSPECTIVE ON POLICING

All of these findings lead us to conclude that a new perspective on policing better fits the data and is more likely to be both scientifically and practically productive than the current dominant perspective. Because police and civilians do not have access to the private thoughts of one another, we believe that perspectives which emphasize inner mental and emotional states are not useful. Police and civilian transactions occur primarily at the cultural and sociological, the noninterpersonal not interpersonal, level (Miller and Steinberg, 1975:79).

This new perspective emphasizes that *both* actors in a relationship share responsibility for how the relationship develops. This is the fundamental meaning of the terms "second order," "tripartite," or "transaction." For this reason we seriously doubt the validity of perspectives which see police or civilian behavior as independent, and attributable to static rather than dynamic variables. Neither the maintenance of order nor the contagion of a riot can be attributed exclusively to police or civilians. Together they "bring out" responses in each. Most of these responses are cooperative because both behave in such a way as to bring out such cooperative responses in the other. However cooperatively both may normally act, the "wrong" set of acts by one may bring out what appears to be an uncharacteristic response of the other. In reality it is not uncharacteristic at all, merely the outcome of an unusual transaction.

We conclude it is inefficient to change attitudes of officers. It is more effective to expose officers through role-playing, simulation, or "maneuvers" to unusual patterns of responses, and to rehearse in such situations those patterns of responses by police which the public believes to be most in their interest. Officers should have a choice of responses to use in unusual situations. Each pattern would be based on simulation of the interaction of such a pattern with a particular civilian pattern, and a study of the outcome structure of the combination. In choosing officers, it is likely that their typical interaction pattern should be elicited in testing situations and those whose typical responses are likely to combine with the normal patterns of civilians to produce violent or disordered situations eliminated as candidates.

One implication of this perspective is that the response propensities of categories of particular groups of civilians need much further exploration. While we believe there is a wide range of individual differences in response propensities within any particular group, we believe there may be subcultural patterns of response propensities. These may be based on age, gender, social class, ethnicity, or even membership in a social movement that encourages particular modes of interaction, such as Quakers versus terrorists. There is little that can be done about a person's membership in most such categories. On the other hand, if it is known that, for instance, young men of a particular class and ethnicity normally possess certain interaction propensities, then officers interacting with them can be taught the interaction strategies that are most likely to result in bringing out "the best," as the best is decided by the public, in both. It is also likely we will discover that prejudice or status is merely a "cover" variable for certain patterns of communication which precipitate violence, brutality, and disorder.

We believe that a social-behaviorist perspective will focus attention away from a preoccupation by scholars, police, and civilians with violent coercion, and focus attention on those response propensities that are more fundamental in "producing" cooperation or violence. Police should be taught to be, above all, persuasive, and sensitive to the meanings others are communicating. Above all, they should be able to take charge, regulate, and solve the typical problems they confront by talking. In most (but not all) cases they should learn how to talk first and also ask questions afterwards.

We believe that the aspect of the social-behaviorist perspective which focuses on the encounter as a volatile working group may also be useful. It is more appropriate in a democratic society to think of officers as experienced supervisors with an agenda of problems to solve—problems, for the most part, brought to their attention by civilians—than to think of them as an army of occupation. While police are sometimes corrupt, brutal, and inept, they are necessary. They are reinforcers of both formal and informal, public and private norms. Their function is to provide support when the private, internalized norms on which social order must normally depend break down. Their function is to use many means to reinforce these norms, not merely physical or deadly force. In a democratic society their authority should, insofar as possible, be moral, or calculative, not coercive.

We have found that by thinking of officers as supervisors of volatile working groups with three goals to achieve, policing is both more understandable and more amenable to rational analysis. Each encounter is seen as a series of problems: What happened? Who did what to whom? What should be done? Focus on the specific techniques officers, as supervisors, use to accomplish their goals. Focus on the mouth and the ears, not the gun and the badge. In a democratic society, policing should not mean "warring." Our approach is less legalistic than is that of many who emphasize professionalism. Law is unable to accommodate the many private social orders that exist in a complex society. Law is a source of both legitimacy and a resource, but it must be enforced with common sense. In normal peacekeeping it is of secondary importance.

In advocating this perspective we do not wish to downplay the unacceptably high rates of crimes against both persons and property in the United States. For reasons outside their control, police are unable, alone, to prevent such crime. They meet most civilians as peacekeepers, bureaucratic functionaries, taking reports, as unhappy witnesses to the pain of many victims, and as maintainers of public order. All of these activities are approached more realistically by those who consider themselves as supervisors of amateurs, with some problems to solve and decisions to make, and occasionally as persons offering support, when other friends are absent. In this regard their work is much like professionals and paraprofessionals in many helping vocations. Officers themselves might be more patient with civilians if they viewed them as merely incompetent rather than recalcitrant supervisees. In short, we wish to demystify and secularize policing not only for scholars, but for most police and civilians.

NEEDS FOR FURTHER RESEARCH

These data were collected in one, medium-sized, midwestern city. Analyses used separate sets of the data. These separate sets show similar forms of order. Earlier study of data from a somewhat larger midwest city by the first author displayed similar forms of order (Sykes, 1974). Nonetheless, many of these findings should be tested using data gathered in other American communities. Most policing is by local departments. Communities differ in wealth, heterogeneity, regional culture, ethnic subculture, and local leadership. These factors may affect not only the extent to which police activities are believed locally to be legitimate, but also how they are conducted. Specifically:

1. The second-order contingency needs to be examined further especially to determine its scope.
2. Much more research is necessary on the effects of personal, demographic, and situational factors on the acts of interactants; on the effect of prior acts on following acts; and of both on outcomes. The validity of most police research including our own will be unknown until such research is done.
3. Study needs to be done on whether second-order contingencies, interpreted as response propensities, do, in fact, characterize the responses of individuals as well as aggregates.
4. Study needs to be done on whether role-taking is accurately operationalized as a first-order probability distribution.

These data pertain only to uniformed police. Their relevancy to plainclothes police and to specialized squads dealing with prostitution, drugs, or gambling is unknown. We have not sought to address the nature or legitimacy of many local "undercover" police operations.

Scholars also need to compare the police-civilian encounter to other volatile working groups. There are many such working groups, all of which include one or more integral positions and one or more situated positions. These include a wide range of health professionals or paraprofessionals and their clients; social workers and recipients of social-welfare services; parole officers and parolees; investigators from many administrative agencies and civilians, including the Internal Revenue Service; professional and paraprofessional legal advisers and their advisees; teachers and students; and even coaches and their teams. In most of these cases professionals or paraprofessionals routinely supervise amateurs.

It would also be valuable to compare American police to police in other nations. Bayley (1979) has made an especially valuable contribution to comparative policing, though not from the perspective advocated here. Such comparisons would be especially useful if they could include valid data on whether police in other societies are legitimated by citizens; whether they perform as few law-and-order and as many peacekeeping activities as American police; whether they too do their job by talking; and how extensive is their resort to violence. These areas of research are of fundamental import to social psychology and to the understanding of social control, as well as to the study of policing.

Appendix
Bibliography
Index

Appendix: Social Psychologists at Work

In 1969 police were the focus of public outcry. They had played a prominent role in the events of the previous decade. Birmingham, Watts, and the Chicago Convention attracted public attention to the techniques with which police did their work. The public were polarized. Many shouted "pigs!" at squads as they passed. Others put bumper stickers on their cars advocating "Support your local police." Some officers were shot from ambush. Police put bumper stickers on their squads, "The next time you need help, call a hippie."

Apart from the collective violence, the extent of police and civilian violence, as well as the precise process of police-civilian interaction in normal small-group encounters was debated. At the time the scientific results of Reiss's study had not been published. Other studies documented cases of police brutality (Chevigny, 1969), but their incidence relative to the total number of police encounters was not documented, nor was the extent of civilian "brutality."

It was in this context that the Center for Studies of Crime and Delinquency agreed to sponsor a field study of police-civilian interaction in two major cities and several suburbs in the Midwest. The first author was principal investigator and John P. Clark was coprincipal investigator. While the first author had not previously studied police, the initial idea for the study had been his, based on three years' previous experience developing and applying techniques of systematic field observation to work groups. His notion was that those techniques could possibly be applied to police. Because of a decade of activity in the civil-rights movement, he had developed a special interest in the prevalent disputes between police and minority groups. Clark had possessed a scholarly interest in police well before the topic became "popular" in the late sixties (see Clark, 1965); had practical experience with officers; and was then serving as a consultant to one of the big-city departments that might be a focus of the study.

The challenge of the study was not just substantive, but methodological. Bales and his students had developed interaction process analysis as a generic method as well as a particular category system. Three important methodological problems needed to be tackled: (1) Could interaction process analysis as a generic method be used in the shifting, moving, open situations involving police? (2) If the method *could* be used, would police and civilians allow it to be used? (3) Would it be possible to sample police activities so that generalizations might be made to the universe of such activities? At the time we began these were open questions.

Much interaction process analysis had been done on either experimental or enclosed groups, but almost no spontaneous analysis in the unpredictable circumstances of workers on the move. Many participant observation studies had been done by criminologists, but, except for our own previous experience, little was known about how the average person would respond to an observer carrying the portable, electronic encoding equipment that had been invented to make field observation possible. How, moreover, could one enter into a process of activities being carried out by numerous officers in the area of an entire city when those officers were highly mobile, and were responding to radio dispatchers' orders that could not possibly be known to anyone in advance? Each of these questions generated many more specific problems.

The problems posed could not be solved "theoretically" or entirely before the fact. A method must be *used*. It is sometimes necessary to discover what is possible through action. This research had a processual and developmental dimension to it. It was truly an *act* in the Meadean sense. In no sense did it involve developing ahead of time a design, plan, or blueprint that was strictly adhered to throughout the study. To claim otherwise would not only be untruthful, but would gloss over what made it such an interesting project—its continuous development and growth in light of never-ending contingencies of real life.

DATA COLLECTION

When we speak of interaction process analysis in its *generic* sense, we mean the methodology of categorizing units of verbal behavior into one of a set of exhaustive and exclusive categories. To determine tentatively whether this could be done before the official start of data collection, we had to combine our previously gained expertise with a look at policing.

During the previous three years the first author had done systematic field observation in the context of about fifty work groups. Almost all of these groups had a stable membership and were located in enclosed places such as offices where there was limited movement. A special supervisor-worker interaction category system had been developed related to the substantive interests of that project.

During that project, electronic, portable encoding equipment was also invented (Sykes and Whitney, 1969; Sykes, 1977b), which was called MIDCARS (Minnesota Interaction Data Coding and Reduction System) and later renamed Datamyte by its commercial manufacturer. Apart from problems associated with early models of the equipment itself, we had no way of knowing how civilians would respond to an observer accompanying police, and electronically coding behavior as it occurred. Previous uses of the equipment under field conditions had involved subjects who had been carefully briefed ahead of time. No extant category system was designed for the study of police-civilian behavior. In preparation for developing such a system, the first author began to ride with police six months before the study was funded, and to review the literature on police. He also kept in mind the relevant findings, in the small-groups literature that needed testing for external validity. Duane Wallen, a graduate student who had experience with the previous studies, also rode with police until his indictment for refusal to accept military service (a charge of which he was later acquitted) made the human relations of riding with police impossible. Nonetheless, he made important contributions to the project. After the first four observers were hired, they also made suggestions based on their preliminary experience riding with officers. From all of these sources the first author created the first category system, Police I, in June 1970. This code attempted to combine previous experience in systematic observation, important variables in policing based on both experience riding and the literature, and important variables in the actual Bales IPA category system (Bales, 1950). Because the encoder had a numeric keyboard like an adding machine, each category had to be learned as a numeric code.

From previous experience we knew that actors could not be personally identified. In small groups they may wear signs with an assigned number, or be personally known to the observer. Quite apart from our sociological orientation to positions rather than persons, we knew that at the beginning of most encounters both the situated and personal identities of citizens were unknown to officers. Indeed, a vital process in these encounters was the gradual emergence of these identities from the interaction. Initially, a citizen could only be identified as such, not as a complainant or suspect. We chose to begin each interaction code with a "role ascription," which was to be as specific as possible but which possessed the capacity for *emergence*. As situated identities became evident, the process of their differentiation was to be specified by the observer.

We also knew from experience that the coding of every actual or implied simple sentence as in the Bales's code was impractical under field conditions using spontaneous coding. The burden was too great on the observer. People in real life not only do not speak in either complete or simple sentences, but use abbreviated expressions indexical to the situations. They do not respond primarily to simple sentences, but to the whole of what the previous speaker has said, or, alternately they select from it that which is salient to them. For this reason, we choose as the unit of analysis the *utterance*, all that one speaker said in one burst of speech. Usually an utterance is followed by a change of speaking turns, and thus is bounded by the set of nonverbal signals which marks such a change in turns. Occasionally, the utterance is rather involuntarily bounded by an interruption.

Uniformed police work is somewhat unusual in that it consists of long periods of patrolling punctuated by short bursts of activity with civilians, most lasting less than ten minutes each. Out of an eight-hour shift, officers will probably not spend much more than one hour in interaction with civilians. Only in the case of an arrest, when they must take the suspect to jail, will a longer period of time be spent in interaction.

The argot of police clearly differentiates these activities into a relatively specific set, each having a characteristic name. In the first jurisdiction studied the argot was used by dispatchers in sending officers to the scene of complaints. "NVA," "DOA," "DOGS," "Take a report," "Burglary in progress" are but a few of the terms in the argot. In some jurisdictions studied later a slightly different argot was used. In still other jurisdictions statute numbers were used.

It was necessary to delineate the type of activity; the manner in which police became aware of the activity; and the time the activity began and ended. A category system incorporating these variables was developed. Since there were too many different activities for observers to learn a number for each by heart, some more general rubric had to be found.

Based primarily on Reiss's work (1971) (see also McCall, 1978; Black, 1980), a distinction was made between initiators of activities:

Category	Code
Citizen initiated	456
Police initiated	123

General activity categories were developed:

Category	Code
Alleged crime against person	1
Alleged crime against property	2
Violation of private decorum	3

Violation of public decorum	4
Service	5
Motor-vehicle violation	9
End of encounter	0

Activity codes constituted preliminary definitions of the situation. These might be modified in important ways. Thus "Heavy domestic" meant a dispute between intimates in which potential or actual violence was involved and implicitly meant to the officers that they should proceed with emergency speed and be on guard against danger in the form of a possible weapon. On the other hand, "Take a report, burglary" meant a very routine, essentially bureaucratic activity. These modifications to the basic activities were important to officers and thus needed categorizing.

Category	Code
Emergency speed used	1
Danger reported likely	2
Ministerial function	3
Report-taking	4
Routine call	5

The observer, hearing the dispatcher direct his squad to investigate a complaint about a dispute between neighbors encoded "45645," signifying a citizen-initiated allegation of a violation of public decorum of a normal or routine kind.

When that number was encoded, the Datamyte automatically registered the time. At the end of the encounter the observer entered "4560," signifying the end of the encounter. Again, the time was automatically registered. The difference between time one and time two was the duration of the encounter.

Ultimately eighty-seven different types of police activities were identified. While the exact activity was recorded on a handwritten schedule, it was impossible for the observers to learn a separate code for each activity. They had to learn under which of the more general activity rubrics each more specific activity was to be coded. Initially, of course, many of the eighty-seven activities were not known to us despite our preliminary work.

Weekly staff meetings were held to review coding problems. An observer would report: "I had a purse snatch in which the woman was knocked down the other night. Is that a crime against person or property?" The ultimate decision was the principal investigator's. All such decisions were recorded and a memo was distributed to the staff specifying these coding conventions.

A general principle of quantitative, systematic field observation is that no matter how much preliminary fieldwork is done, unanticipated events will occur for which no coding rule exists. Although we found discussions of solutions to difficult categorization problems sensitizing, we did not find the solutions very useful. We were doing a large-scale study involving the statistical analysis of aggregate data. Unusual cases were generally *so* unusual that there was not a sufficient number for analysis. Many, in fact, occurred only once.

In the second stage of the study, what might be termed an "asterisk" was included in the code. An observer used it whenever an event occurred that was not covered by the code, or that was either novel, or that might later facilitate reconstruction of the interaction. The meaning of each asterisk was documented in longhand on the observation schedule in order of occurrence.

The work of Stinchcombe (1963) showed the importance of the distinction between public and private places for police. *Where* people do some things is sometimes more important than *what* they do. The existence of private places also limits police access to information. The second set of categories distinguished between private homes, apartments, nonresidential buildings, and the public streets and open spaces. It also specified whether police access to the locations was by permission of the occupants, by stealth, or by force. This code was entered at the time the patrol arrived on scene. The time of this code, less the initial activity code time, provided an approximation of response time.

We also hypothesized that the state of the citizens at the

time police arrived would affect their initial conduct. If a dispute was occurring at the time the police arrived, they would first move to restore order. This would take precedence over the collection of information. Observers categorized the initial situation as ordered, or, if not, whether a verbal or physical dispute was occurring.

At the time we began our study, labeling theory was ascendant. Some scholars claimed that police harassed known past offenders and in this way encouraged secondary deviance. We included a history category. Observers indicated whether or not the civilian(s) in the encounter were previously known as "troublemakers" by the particular police being observed and, if so, what the specific nature of the previous contact had been.

Sometimes the information exchanged at the beginning of the encounter, or even a chance remark much later, resulted in a complete redefinition of the situation. At such time as the original activity definition seemed confirmed, and at any time the situation was redefined, the observer entered a confirmation of original definition, or redefinition code. For instance, a call that was originally defined as a service call, a request to check on the well-being of an old woman who had not been seen for several days, might turn into a DOA (dead on arrival), still a service call; but in light of evidence noticed later, it might be redefined as a homicide. Similarly, many emergency runs to fights, assaults, and domestics became report-taking situations because the alleged violator was no longer at the scene when the police arrived. Analysis of the process of situation redefinition was possible given the demarcators: original definition; redefinition.

Encounters have outcomes. After the code was entered indicating the end of the encounter, an outcome code was necessary. Our preliminary work had indicated a much larger set of specific outcomes than we felt observers should memorize. The same procedure was followed as with the activity code. On their schedules the observers wrote the exact outcome, often in the words used by the officer when he reported back to the dispatcher. Each specific outcome was placed and encoded into a broader category: arrest-felony; arrest-misdemeanor; ticket; report taken; officer-imposed nonarrest resolution; mutually negotiated resolution; standoff—no resolution; resolution implicit in the interaction.

This set of types of categories provided a framework within which to view the process of the encounter. The preliminary definition of the situation and initiator of officer intervention were coded, followed by codes indicative of the space in which the interaction occurred and the state of the civilians when the officers arrived. When a point in the interaction was reached where the original definition was confirmed or redefinition took place, another code was entered. Codes were used to indicate previous contact between police and the civilian; to signify the end of interaction; and to classify the outcome of the encounter. Interaction took place within these structural markers.

Process Codes

Based on the police and small-groups literature as well as our own experience, four sets of categories were developed with which to classify utterances. These sets pertained to role of speaker; semantic function of utterance; structural function of utterance; and rank of civility of utterance. The observer categorized every work-related utterance with all four codes. Nonwork-related utterances were coded using only role ascriptions. Thus a work-related utterance might be coded "0365," signifying that the officer had asked a question about the activity in a civil manner.

As long as the sequence of utterances pertained to the same topic the continuous series of statements and questions was coded using what was termed an "operator," somewhat similar to ditto marks.

0365
19
09
19

signified a series of utterances constituting a string or a set of utterances (see Chapter 4). The topic of the string was established by the question or statement, which is indicated by the

Table A.1. **The interaction code for process**

Role Ascriptions	Semantic Function	Structural Function	Rank of Civility
0 (Officer)	3 (Subject activity-related)	4 (Statement)	3 (More than norm)
1 (Civilian)	5 (Procedural-related)	6 (Question)	5 (Norm)
2 (Civilian)	7 (Officer-civilian relations-related)	8 (Suggestion or order)	7 (Less than norm)
6 (Civilian)		0 (Accusation)	

first full code. The codes 19, 09, . . . mean that the citizen answered the question and that the dialogue related to the topic continued (semantic as well as structural contingency: see Chapter 11). When a new topic was introduced, a full, four-digit code was used again.

If the response to the question was negative then a different operator was used.

0365
147

signified that the officer asked a question in a civil manner, but the civilian refused to answer (14) in an uncivil manner (7).

Strings were of varying lengths ranging from 1 to nearly 100 codes (in a few cases). If length is disregarded, then strings can be summarized taking into account the initial full code (stringhead), and considering whether the interactants are (1) entirely cooperative; (2) occasionally uncooperative but cooperative eventually; (3) uncooperative; and whether the interactants are (1) mutually civil or more than usually civil; (2) unilaterally or mutually uncivil at some point in the encounter. The analysis of strings utilizes these summaries. The string

0365
19
09
19

Table A.2. **Typology of string summaries**

	Entirely Cooperative	Partly Cooperative	Uncooperative
Civil	Amity (1)	Ambivalent amity (2)	Passive resistance (3)
Uncivil	Defensiveness (4)	Ambivalent hostility (5)	Hostility (6)

would be summarized for some analyses "03651," meaning that an officer initiated a topic related to the activity which was the reason for the encounter; that the officer initiated the string in a civil manner; and that both officer and civilian were entirely cooperative and civil during the whole of the string.

It should be noted that certain codes perform an explicit function related to the situated identities of the civilians. The code "0305" is an accusation made in a civil manner by an officer to a civilian. It altercasts the civilian in the situated identity of suspect or alleged violator.

A second set of process categories termed *action* codes was developed for specific acts that research suggested were the special focus of interest for many students of police. These codes included: the threat of physical violence; the use of physical violence; the use of physical restraints (usually handcuffs); the threat of deadly force; the use of deadly force (discharging a gun); the threat of arrest; the statement of arrest; the Miranda warning. Action codes were used concomitantly with interaction codes when such behaviors occurred, and were ascribed to the source of the behavior. At the end of each encounter observers were required to enter a *default* action code if no "action-codeable" event had occurred. This served as a double check on the accuracy of the observers.

Table A.3 displays an encounter that includes both the structural and process codes. It is from data such as these that our analysis has been derived.

This is a *summary* of a very long and detailed process of code development. The "act" of research actually involved *four* different codes. The first code (Police I) was used approximately three months. Its revision was used a year (Police II). The revision of the revision (Police III) was never used except

Table A.3. **An example of these data: observation number 7008**

45627	Assist at crime against person	0305	Accusation by officer
555	See schedule for more info		Denial
7008	Observation #	14	String 6
0800	8:00 p.m. when call received	09	
		14	
731	Encounter in public space	09	
76	No physical or verbal conflict at time of arrival	14	
		0365	String 7—question
		19	
00345	String 1—two civilians in an encounter-related discussion	0585	String 8—behavioral order
		19	
009		0	String 9—nonwork
65378	Redefined as domestic-related, report-taking situation	1	
		134365	Complex code
		0345	Statement of information and discussion
0	Nonwork chit chat	19	
1		09	String 10
0365	Information seeking by officers	19	
		097	
19	String 2	19	
500	Who's the observer?	0385	Suggested resolution
09			String 11
19		19	Agreement
09		0345	Statement of information and discussion
19			
09		19	String 12
19		0	
0305	Accusation by officer	1	Ritual departure
	String 3	00	
19	Admission	45603	End of interaction. All information from verbal testimony
0365	Information seeking		
19	String 4		
030545	Complex code (accusation plus info about procedure)	8523	Prior history of domestic disputes
		90	No action code appropriate
1345	Statement by civilian and discussion	9637	Much of outcome contained in interaction itself
09			
19	String 5		
09		9634	Report taken (citizen advised)
19			

for experimental purposes. The revision of the revision of the revision (Police IV) was used for four months. It is this latter code which is summarized here. The handbook by Wallen and Sykes (1974) describes it in detail. Most data were collected with Police II and Police IV. Not all, but many parts of the codes are compatible with each other.

One major difference (not the only one) between Police II and Police IV should be stated. Police II contained an abbreviated Bales code, specifically the categories: question of information; gives information, gives order, and gives opinion. We found that in much police-civilian interaction it was almost impossible to differentiate between information and opinion. Many statements seemed to be mixed, or to fall in a gray area between the two.

Police IV included categories that were less universal than the Bales code, but, we felt, more substantively important for the study of police, especially the semantic function codes. Talk about the reason for the encounter, about police procedures, and police-civilian relations was distinguished by separate categories. No attempt was made to distinguish fact from opinion. These can be approximately equated to Bales categories or combinations of those categories. The revision also permitted the identification of strings, a unit not present in Bales-type data.

TRAINING AND RELIABILITY

Three techniques of observer training were used during the first phase of the study:

First, all observers rode with police for several weeks prior to beginning systematic collection of data. Not only did this familiarize them with police work and sensitize them to the interpersonal skills necessary for maintaining rapport with officers and civilians, but it provided them with background that was invaluable during the training sessions themselves. Several of the observers ultimately rode for more time with officers than had been ridden in any other study known to us except possibly for Rubinstein's (1973). They put in nearly as many hours riding as would a police officer in six to nine months of work.

Second, part of each training session was devoted to "finger drills." Since the data were to be encoded on a device rather like a calculator it was vital that observers utilize the keyboard with the skill of a good typist or pianist. This in itself required hours of practice.

Third, during the first phase of the study the most-often used training technique was role-playing. Research staff, including some observers, would role-play a particular type of encounter. Their concurrent experience riding with officers greatly assisted them in providing a realistic base for the role-playing. Each skit was videotaped. It was then replayed to check coding done during the original role-playing, and served for further practice when needed. After each coding the observers would discuss their problems. Gradually group consensus was developed over coding conventions with the principal investigator serving as final arbiter. During the first phase of the study the observers contributed many ideas to both Police I and Police II and took an active part in determining coding conventions.

Observers trained for three months. At the end of that time they were tested for reliability. Reliability was about .70 using Cohen's K, coding a very routine encounter from videotape. Using such an encounter did not seem inappropriate since about 90% of police work is similarly routine (Reiss, 1971).

Such figures do not mean much. In the first place, Police I and Police II were very complex category systems. During an encounter many different types of codes—activity, place, state, interaction, action, and outcome—were used. Not only did the events to which they applied occur at very different speeds, but their referents differed in their clarity. It is not difficult to classify most of the eighty-seven different activities into the correct category, nor to differentiate a home from a public street, but there is a gray line between being civil although in a rough sort of way, and being uncivil. Consequently no single figure can possibly mean anything. Reliability was further complicated by the fact that each utterance was coded by role, semantic function, structural function, and civility. These codes differed widely in reliability. The role ascription code was nearly 1.00 in reliability. The civility code was about .70, and the semantic function code less.

If all four interaction codes were used in an analysis and one of the codes was wrong, then the other three did not count and reliability became very low. Since there was a written record of the activity code, it could be checked with the coded record. After phase one, this was done. Some, though not a great many, activity codes were changed. The result was that nearly 1.00 reliability was obtained on the activity codes and other structural codes. Reliability varied by observer, conditions of observation, and speed of interaction for the interaction and action codes.

Reliability problems were made even more complex by the presence of an extraneous factor—finger dexterity. Observers differed widely in their ability to encode correctly the numbers they intended to encode. This contributed to characteristic differences between observers rather like the differences between laconic and wordy individuals. Observers who were good with their fingers encoded more of the interaction while those who were slow settled for the high points.

At the end of the first phase of the project these problems were communicated to its sponsors. They kindly supported a concentrated effort to improve reliability during the second phase of the study. This effort included: revision of the code twice, eventuating in Police IV; and the development of a project team that wrote, produced, and directed over fifty police-civilian encounters to be used during training. Employing professional actors, and utilizing a police consultant, these were videotaped by professional technicians at various sites throughout a metropolitan area. The encounters were created very deliberately to provide a wide range of activities and to serve as examples for all subsets of the code. These tapes were then coded by Duane Wallen, again available to the project, and the principal investigator. At the same time, an extensive observer training program was developed integrating finger practice, the videotaped encounters, and lectures and other study materials into a comprehensive training package. When observer training began for phase two, the training was much more structured, and performance was more carefully monitored than during phase one.

For phase two a completely different group of observers was used. Deliberately, twice as many observers were hired than were needed. Each day they drilled using the keyboard, this time entering the actual code numbers from videotaped slides. The code numbers gradually grew longer and the rate of presentation faster. After each day, the accuracy scores of all observers were publicly posted. Again, a wide difference was evident in finger dexterity. A training assistant who was an expert typist got nearly 100% correct each time. Some others could not exceed 60%. Seeing the handwriting on the wall, a number of poor performers gradually quit by absenting themselves from the training sessions. The four observers who were retained for the study were a mixed lot. Two had excellent finger dexterity and two had only fair dexterity. One of those who had only fair dexterity was highly reliable in his use of the code and also had excellent rapport with the police. Each had strengths and weaknesses that were important. Until ideal observers are cloned the writers see no way to achieve as much accuracy and reliability with a complex code as would be desired. On the other hand, the attempt to achieve better reliability leads to improved observational field studies, since in the past most were conducted on a qualitative basis by single individuals. To our knowledge, this study is the only observational study of police that attempts to provide any reliability measures.

Reliability problems may not be as serious as we have indicated. Data may be examined for reliability in two ways. The first and conventional way is to compare the protocols of two observers coding the same encounter and compare them code for code. It is this form of reliability that is not as high as is desirable. It can only be calculated during training, since two observers cannot normally ride with officers.

The second form of reliability is like that measured by many current psychometric techniques. Instead of looking at the surface similarity between two protocols one looks at the similarities and differences in the relationships between variables in aggregated data comparing across observers. Each observer is assumed to be an instrument measuring the relationship between the two particular variables, for instance between the amount of incivility and the type of outcome. While there are several technical statistical problems that remain to be solved it is interesting that in both phase one and phase two data the relationships between variables are remarkably similar for all observers, and that they are also very similar for the data gathered by one group of observers in one city and by another group of observers in a different city. In another place, the first author hopes to show that reliability of data gathered by quantitative, systematic field observation needs to be reconceptualized, and measured differently. Conventional coefficients are insufficient. At the very least the method must take into account as well as take for granted the "personal equation," as astronomers were the first to do a century and a half ago.

Validity

Many of the codes possess face validity. If a person in a blue uniform and wearing a gun is talking, chances are that categorizing him as a police officer is valid. The project did make an additional attempt to test the validity of that part of the code pertaining to civility. A questionnaire consisting of 1,000 examples of dialogue was prepared. A convenience sample of the public was taken as well as of police officers. They were asked to rate the degree of civility of statements in a sample of 200 of the 1,000 examples. The observers completed the questionnaire containing all 1,000 items over a period of several days, but independent of each other. There was high agreement between the public, the police, and the observers, though there was greater consensus among the observers than among the others. Disagreement was often related to the difference between the spoken and written word. Since all statements were written, but were amenable to different "readings," disagreements often appeared to arise from different imaginings of how the statement was said. This test did give us confidence that the public as well as the police tended to have the same standards of civility and incivility as our observers.

GAINING AND MAINTAINING ACCESS TO POLICE AND CIVILIANS

Field research in organizations is different from survey research. Outsiders are given the privilege to observe ongoing, day-to-day, organizationally private activities. Such observations are threatening because they may expose the multitude of little ways in which employees ignore or bend organizational policy, loaf on the job, take shortcuts, and commit numerous small derelictions of duty. The most threatened are middle-level supervisors who feel that observers will learn about problems and activities they do not know about themselves. Since the typical route of entry into organizations is through top management, middle managers also fear that observers will be spies for their superiors. Lower echelon employees are often less defensive once they are assured that the observer is not a company spy, or will not cause them substantial extra work. Some even welcome the observer as a new face, a set of new opinions, a pleasant diversion from the routine of work.

Organizations have secrets that they do not wish the public to know. So do police. Organizations have ambitious employees who do not wish their careers threatened by exposure of derelictions and incompetencies. So do police. Researchers receive permission from top management to observe *lower* level employees. The police are no different. Employees typically "test" observers to discover whether they will report rule violations to managers. So do the police. Organizations have a small number of defensive, insecure, or vulnerable employees who do not wish to be observed. So do the police. Government organizations are especially concerned with their public im-

Appendix: Social Psychologists at Work

age and the political implications of the information observers collect. So are the police. Organizations have numerous employees who know little about science, are suspicious of university professors, and take pride in their realistic rather than intellectual or theoretical approach. So do the police.

Gaining and maintaining access to police organizations and police officers is like doing so in other organizations (with exceptions to be noted below). Typically, the researcher approaches management at its highest level. If possible, he will "legitimate" himself through introductions from persons he believes upper management respects. Sometimes upper management will personally know the researchers already. Once the project is cleared at the top, the scientist is typically assigned liaison at a lower level who will introduce him to the actual workers he wishes to observe and mediate any conflicts that develop. Seldom does the chief executive officer have time to spend arranging day-to-day details of research.

Eventually, the researcher finds himself with the lower echelon employees: workers and foremen. They will generally find room for him, perhaps after telling him that they do not really have a very high opinion of ivory-tower research, but that they have nothing against the researcher as a person. If he wants to waste his time in such ethereal pursuits, well, that's his business. Then comes the period of testing. Employees set out to discover two things: (1) Is he a "regular fellow"? (2) Can he be trusted not to rat to the boss?

A regular fellow is one who does not talk jargon all the time; whom employees can talk to; who likes to rap informally like most people; and who is not hung up on all the formal rules and regulations. Above all he is not an "effete intellectual snob" who thinks he is better than the people he is observing and looks down on them and their everyday behavior. An observer like a psychiatrist must be nonjudgmental.

Testing for trust occurs through displaying a graduated series of transparent instances of occupational deviance. One day the subject will do something that is obviously contrary to rules. He will do it casually, almost as a challenge, and then he will observe the observer's reaction narrowly and "put his ear to the ground." Will he hear anything about it from anyone in the organization? Gradually he will try out his repertoire of occupational deviancies, and listen, until he is sure that the observer isn't a rat. These acts are not necessarily routine practice. They are tests. Interestingly, every day he practices organizationally accepted deviancies that he does not consider tests because he takes them for granted. An outsider, unused to the customs of the organization, may notice them immediately, but the insider will forget about them unless the outsider calls his attention to them (which he should not).

Observers who witness transparent deviancies when they first observe a subject should take them in stride. We would hypothesize that many deviancies observed early in the process of studying an organization are deliberate tests, and they inflate the normal rate and distribution of types of deviance if counted.

Traditional organizational field research does not depend on the fully voluntary or informed consent of the observed subjects. Approval by management means that for all intents and purposes the study is imposed on employees. This is especially true if the project is one from which the organization hopes to secure useful information. It is impossible to avoid a subtle coercion if the study is important to management.

At the time the police study began, the Department of Health, Education, and Welfare was instituting its policies for the protection of human subjects for the first time. The research was approved by top management of the first major department we were to study several months before the study began. Their approval was probably influenced by three factors: (1) personal friendship with and confidence in the coprincipal investigator; (2) the election of a police officer as mayor, thus making them less vulnerable politically, since the chief is appointed by the mayor; (3) a belief that actual observation of their officers would demonstrate the legitimacy of their activities.

The chief was willing to support the project but was doubtful about ordering his officers to cooperate. His officers, as the actual subjects of observation, had more to lose, and were more inconvenienced. They also had more doubts about the value of the study. Among the serious worries of the officers, three were important: (1) if an observer were injured, the officer might be liable for damages, especially in the case of a motor-vehicle accident; (2) if an observer were to be present in dangerous situations, the officer would feel obliged to protect him and perhaps endanger himself; (3) if an officer were to make an error, the observer might either report him to his superiors or voluntarily or involuntarily serve as a witness in disciplinary proceedings or in court. One *difference* between a police officer and most other workers is that some civilians are in an *adversary* relation to him, and the presence of a witness may be used by the adversary against him, either legitimately or for purposes of harassment.

At that time this department had a "ride-along" program and almost any civilian might request to ride with officers for all or part of one shift. Such ride-alongs were arranged well in advance and served a public-relations purpose. It is an index of the confidence of the department that it opened its activities to public scrutiny at a time when most departments in the country were very defensive. That the ride-along program was not *just* public relations is evident. At least one young woman passenger was seriously injured in an accident during a high-speed chase. Her injury had accentuated the problem of liability. Another found himself involved in a gun fight at an aborted robbery. Ride-alongs did not see all of police work but did get some idea of routine police activities.

Police were correct in gauging the public-relations value of the ride-along program, a value that could be achieved with little or no deception. Many of the persons police routinely deal with are lower class, and display or are victims of many behaviors condemned or disapproved by the middle- and "respectable" working class: drunkenness, profanity, disorganization, ignorance, disregard for cleanliness and other norms of interpersonal conduct, and violence. Since most ride-alongs are "respectable," middle-class citizens, they naturally come to sympathize with police in their work. The same is true of almost every social scientist who has ridden with police for any period of time. It does not take long to learn that "a policeman's lot is not a happy one."

The research project was assigned liaison through the ride-along program of the department. Since that program already had the personnel and experience maintaining contact with the precincts, that was appropriate. The study was to last at least a year, operating on a seven-day per-week, twenty-four-hour per-day basis. The duty of liaison would require time. It would have been unreasonable to expect the department to assign extra personnel to the project.

The project *was not* part of the ride-along program, but organized entirely differently. The chief did not feel he could formally *order* officers to cooperate, nor would federal human-subject regulations permit it. He could *strongly encourage* them to cooperate, but leave them the right to refuse. This amounted to covert pressure to cooperate. He made every precinct roll call in the city available to the investigators. They appeared at roll call; the memo indicating the chief's support was read; the investigators described the study; and questions were solicited. The reaction was varied; some officers did not like the idea of the study at all, while others were quite friendly. Because of the organization of shifts, approximately one-third of the men on a shift were always absent from roll call on vacation. Though the investigators appeared at every roll call (fifteen in all), they unavoidably missed that third of the officers and they were never officially briefed.

Once the study began, access to squads was very direct. The department had provided a list of cars (by number) that were usually on the streets during a particular shift. Each observer had been provided with a special identification card, including his photograph, signed by the chief. Every precinct received a memo describing the study, mentioning the card, and ordering the precinct (if not the individual officers) to cooperate. Using a stratified random shift sample design, car shifts were chosen randomly and assigned to an observer. Police were not notified in advance of the choice. The observer merely showed up at the precinct station at the beginning of the sampled shift, presented his ID, and asked to ride on the sampled car. In a very high percentage of the cases he did so.

Observers did have problems. Off and on during the study the duty sergeant would raise questions or refuse to cooperate despite the special ID. This was directly contrary to the chief's orders. The sergeant was required to cooperate. He was not a subject of the research but an administrator. In most cases at this level noncooperation was merely normal bureaucratic conservatism or ineptitude. Sergeants had difficulty getting used to the fact that a researcher could merely walk into the precinct unannounced and ride. Many sergeants had not been present at the roll-call briefing and knew nothing about the study. Many were older men nearly ready for retirement. They did not understand research. If they had had their day off when the chief's memo arrived, they had not read it. As months passed and memos on other matters were issued, the research memo came to rest at the bottom of one and ultimately two stacks of memos a couple of inches thick. The sergeants could not find it.

When problems were encountered at this level, observers were instructed to explain their ID, refer the sergeant to the memo, and persuade him to cooperate. Sometimes the observer would find a patrolman with whom he had ridden previously who would vouch for him, or the precinct commander would come to his aid. Above all, the observer was instructed *not* to start any arguments. If denied cooperation by the sergeant, the observer was to leave. The next day the project administrator would contact the precinct and if necessary the liaison at the ride-along program. They would insure that the sergeant understood the program and cooperated in the future.

Normally, the sergeant would inform the patrolmen of the selected squad that an observer would ride with them during the coming shift. Occasionally, one or both officers would refuse, or that particular car would not be on the street owing to a shortage of manpower, need for repairs, or very occasionally because it was being used for a stakeout. The observer carried an alternate number, also randomly chosen for this contingency.

Observers were instructed *not* to argue with uncooperative officers. They reported back to the project and the project administrator would visit the precinct and do a little public relations, or contact the ride-along liaison to secure official support. Occasionally, a rumor or an actual incident would occur or be used as a pretext by a few officers in a precinct to withhold cooperation. We would avoid argument and withdraw all observers from the precinct for a few days until tempers had cooled, and until a quiet combination of public relations and official but informal pressure to cooperate could be applied.

There is no way of knowing what the *real* reasons for noncooperation were. In some cases officers complained that an observer had behaved improperly. Another source of complaints, though of few refusals, was the backup shift. This was a small shift that was deliberately oversampled because its members handled more exciting and difficult calls. Officers on the shift complained that they were observed much more frequently than others, which was true. On the whole they were cooperative and friendly. As time passed, these officers and our observers grew to know each other quite well.

A few officers were just disagreeable. One we never rode with. All squads consisted of two officers. This particular officer could not get along with anyone and rode alone.

In some cases, being chosen on a particular night was inconvenient for the particular officers, or they were on special assignment. The inconvenience might be related to their work, but it might also be related to something as simple as a very unofficial date with a young woman during a quiet period of the late shift. In our own opinion, most refusals had little to do with any intent to keep observers away from police activities of scientific interest to the investigators, that is, police-civilian interaction during normal policing by uniformed patrol. In any event, refusals amounted to less than 10% of sampled car shifts.

These problems did not affect the study in other jurisdictions. The department in the other major city studied was not organized by precinct, but centrally. Top management was very firmly committed to the project. Since all officers operated out of the same headquarters, they were more subject to administrative pressure. They formally possessed the right to refuse, but they never exercised it. The city had never had a ride-along program so the presence of nonpolice was considered unusual by both officers and civilians. One benefit of a publicly known ride-along program in the first city was that both officers and civilians were somewhat used to the presence of nonpolice in squad cars. Observer-officer relations in suburbs were uneventful.

Observers had to be diplomatic in order to avoid imagined or real behaviors that might lead to incidents which would threaten the project. During the preliminary study, an observer was riding when the squad overtook and pulled over a driver in a car that at first appeared to be trying to escape from them. They approached the car with guns drawn, ordered out the lone driver, and threw him in the back seat of the squad. The driver had been dragging, and at the time he accelerated had not known a squad car was in the blind spot just to the left rear of his car. He was frightened and afraid the officers would hurt him. He appealed to the observer sitting in the back seat with him for protection and support. After the incident was over, the observer asked as a matter of information whether the officers often drew their guns when approaching cars they had curbed. The officers interpreted the question as a criticism and filed a false complaint with their superiors about the observer's conduct. From this and other incidents we learned to avoid even the appearance of criticism.

An observer was riding with two officers who had confiscated a gun during the previous encounter. They were "playing" with it recklessly enough so that the observer threw himself on the floor out of fear of getting shot. The gun accidentally discharged shooting a hole in the front windshield. The observer supported the officers' contention that a stone had hit the windshield.

An observer started what he thought would be a routine ride. The two officers did not like each other and disagreed about how to handle their work. Ultimately they got into a fight. One officer drove the other back to the station and threw him out of the car, refusing to ride with him. The next morning the sergeant called the observer to get his version of what had happened between the two officers. He refused to tell the sergeant anything about the altercation.

During the entire study the observers found only one officer whom they unanimously agreed was a bad officer. Independently, they came to the conclusion that this officer deliberately baited people into violence and then often had to call on his fellow officers for help, thus acting as a menace to both civilians and his fellow officers. Although they privately called him "the Nazi," the observers continued to ride with him throughout the study without ever disclosing their opinion.

The greatest source of strain between officers and observers was undoubtedly the Vietnam war. The first phase of the study took place during the height of antiwar protests. The day that the observers were scheduled to begin their initial riding experience turned out to be the day after the Cambodian incursion ordered by President Nixon. Ten thousand people gathered on and near the campus, where a riot ensued that finally resulted in the calling out of the National Guard.

Police officers did not necessarily favor the war, but the demonstrations led to long hours of overtime under very stressful circumstances. Even if there were not ideological differences between officers and observers, the initiation of a study associated with the university, on top of all the other events of the day, required exceptional restraint.

The observers frequently found themselves in the midst of demonstrations while in their role as observers. They were not studying collective behavior and the code was not designed to deal with it. Officers seemed unable to handle demonstrations because they were used to dealing with individuals on an interpersonal basis. The observers found themselves in the middle, almost literally. Not dressed as officers, they were not quite defined by civilians as such. On the other hand, the only officers who knew them not to be demonstrators were those they rode with. Their identity in the midst of a demonstration was precarious to themselves, to the demonstrators, and to most police. Like a press camera to a reporter, this was one situation in which the coding equipment was useful as a badge of some mysterious third identity.

Observers suffered from culture shock. They might disapprove of police behavior, but it was usually in response to an act by a civilian that was, if anything, worse. Officers beat up a man who had beaten up his wife and daughter, had his daughter's boyfriend's car towed away by police, had insulted and then threatened to pull a gun on police, and had resisted arrest. This was not his first such offense. The officers invited the observer to help them beat the man. The observer, a pacifist, refused. He confessed later that he was tempted and could understand if not approve of the officers' actions. The breaking down of simple stereotypes of good guys and bad guys left most observers under continuous psychological stress. Periodically, an observer would say he could not stand it any more. For rest and rehabilitation he would be assigned for a couple of weeks to observing suburban police.

Police objections to being observed were met in other ways. In order to free officers from the worry of being sued in case an observer were injured, all observers signed blanket waivers. They gave up their rights to sue. They also were secured workman's compensation coverage, since observing was their occupation.

Officers had the right to order observers to stay in the squad cars if they thought the situation was too dangerous. This right was very seldom exercised. An observer came back from a ride. He said with a big smile that the officers had let him hold the flashlight in a dark hallway while they broke down a door. Observers frequently went along on bomb searches, high-speed chases, and to bar fights. The inside back doors of squad cars do not have door or window handles. Every observer carried his own handle to let himself out. Suburban police typically rode alone. One source of tension was that the officer wanted the observer to "ride shotgun," that is, to cover an officer sometimes as he approached a suspicious car. It was necessary to forbid such activity.

The only "intervention" observers were permitted was first aid. They had gone through the first-aid section of the rookie training program in one department. An observer reported back to the office after riding that a small child hit by a car had suffered a punctured lung. Because that type of injury had been covered in the first-aid course, the observer was able to administer first aid correctly, a source of great satisfaction to him.

In the course of the study about 15,000 civilians were observed. Considering the nature of the encounters, it was impossible to obtain their informed consent. Observers did their job in homes, apartments, stores, warehouses, lawns, cars, and in the public street. Civilians asked about them (see Sykes, 1978) but almost never objected. Where delicate negotiations or very private matters were to be discussed, as during the taking of a rape report, they voluntarily absented themselves. The most obstreperous civilian was a drunk thrown out of a tavern, who threatened to sue if the observer published his name in "your newspaper."

Observers were instructed to answer citizens' questions. If time did not permit, or there were further questions, the observers gave the civilian a calling card containing the names of the investigators and their phone number and instructed them to call the investigators. No one ever called. As a matter of policy, we collected no information about the personal identities of civilians or officers. The data are anonymous.

To avoid involvement in litigation, observers were not listed in official reports as having been present. Only once was an observer subpoenaed, and fortunately that was in regard to events he had witnessed together with about 1,000 other people.

THE SAMPLING DESIGN

Previous field studies of police did not use random sampling techniques. Reiss's (1971) observers rode solely in high-crime-rate precincts of three major cities. Even there, most police work is routine. In most other places it ranges from tedious to boring. We elected to utilize a stratified, random shift sampling design both to maximize the selection of nonroutine activities and because of its statistical advantages.

Typically, police departments mount three major watches: day (7:30 a.m.–3:30 p.m.), middle (3:30 p.m.–11:30 p.m.), and dog (11:30 p.m.–7:30 a.m.). In some departments officers are permanently assigned to a particular watch. In other departments they rotate shifts every thirty days. Often those with the least seniority work the busiest watch. Other variations exist. One department experimented with a ten-hour day, four-day week at the time of our observations. Departments not uncommonly mount special watches to provide extra help at the busiest times or to perform special duties.

The busiest time of day is from about 8 p.m. to 12 midnight. The busiest evenings are Friday and Saturday. By stratifying our sample so as to saturate the busiest times, we increased the frequency of nonroutine encounters. Despite this, we observed more routine encounters than we desired. During the second phase of the study we stratified not only by time but by car. The department made available to us the activity rates for all their cars for the previous twelve months. The cars were ordered by activity rate and the busiest cars oversampled. We were still unsuccessful in observing as large a number of nonroutine encounters as we would have wished.

Suburbs were sampled in the same way. Our observers found that suburban police had very little to do compared with police in high-crime-rate districts of the central cities. If in the cities observers contended with culture shock, in the suburbs they contended with boredom. There were exceptions to the lack of activity if not to the boredom. An observer arrived back at the office after a suburban, daytime ride, dog tired. The officer with whom he had ridden for the first time had given out thirty-eight moving-violation tags during the eight-hour shift, about eight times the norm. We concluded he was insecure being observed while inactive and that he had tried to impress the observer by his activity. Thereafter, observers in that department went out of their way to assure the officers that they were not looking for unnecessary activity or excitement.

Invariably, random shift samples were derived from an enumeration of the universe of cars reputed to be on the street during a particular shift. At the time the study began we intended to assign observers to car shifts on a random basis. Although this was desirable in principle, it was necessary to compromise. During many months of observing, human factors such as class schedules, illnesses, and vacations, and chance occurrences such as being assigned two consecutive ten-hour shifts, made it impractical. We also found it helpful to overassign a particular observer to a particular suburb or precinct. That observer soon got to know the personnel well enough to assist handling any problems that arose affecting himself or the other observers. He was better able to judge the possibility of particular problems arising, of particular officers causing the project trouble, and to find out through informal contacts what the effect of an unforeseen event such as a large demonstration might be on our sampling design.

More than most other research, field research necessitates an interaction of the abstractly desirable with the practicalities of dealing with the contingencies impinging upon people and organizations in the real world. The road to compromise is paved with good intentions.

The design randomly sampled not encounters but shifts. In large metropolitan areas randomly sampling encounters is either impractical or impossible. If observers rode separately to encounters randomly sampled over the police radio, they could not be sure of arriving on time, and in a large department they would have trouble identifying themselves to strange officers. If they rode in shifts, but took data only on a random subsample of activities enormous expense would be involved. The encounters observed during a shift are *not* dependent on other encounters, nor on the officers, but on the car/shift itself, which is the basic deployment unit of police.

We were probably unsuccessful in getting a random sample of activities (and thus of other structural and interaction variables) by observer, despite the stratified random sample design. Since written records were maintained on all activities, these could be compared to their coding after the fact and any errors corrected. Nearly 1.00 reliability is attained in this manner. Despite 1.00 reliabilty, a cross-tabulation of more than 4,000 encounters by the ten observers involved in both phases of the study manifests significant differences. These are probably due to differences in car/shift or precinct assignments of the observers attributable to the human factors previously discussed. Activity rates vary greatly by car/shift and precinct or community. Even if the sampling had been perfect, it would be possible to generalize only to the universes of encounters in the particular communities studied. No true national random sample of police activities has ever been tried or taken. The data on police activities are largely a collection of community case studies. This is unavoidable. Readers wishing to read about other perspectives on the study and additional detail on the methodology may consult Fox and Lundman, 1974; Lundman and Fox, 1978; Bell, 1979; Lundman and Fox, 1979; and Sykes, 1977b and 1978.

Bibliography

American Bar Association
1972 *The Urban Police Function: Report of an Advisory Committee on the Police Function, Frank J. Remington, Chairman.* Chicago: American Bar Association, 12.
Anderson, Theodore W., and Leo Goodman
1957 "Statistical Inference about Markov Chains." *Annals of Mathematical Statistics* 28:89–110.
Armor, David F.
1974 "Theta Reliability and Factor Scaling." In Herbert Costner, ed., *Sociological Methodology 1973–74.* San Francisco: Jossey-Bass.
Ashby, Ross W.
1956 *An Introduction to Cybernetics.* London: Chapman and Hall.
Bales, Robert F.
1950 *Interaction Process Analysis: A Method for the Study of Small Groups.* Cambridge, Mass.: Addison-Wesley.
Bales, Robert F., and Fred Strodtbeck
1951 "Phases in Group Problem Solving." *Journal of Abnormal and Social Psychology* 46:485–495.
Bayley, David H.
1979 "Police Function, Structure, and Control in Western Europe and North America." In Norval Morris and Michael Towry, eds., *Crime and Justice: An Annual Review of Research*, Vol. 1. Chicago: University of Chicago Press.
Becker, Howard S.
1963 *Outsiders: Studies in the Sociology of Deviance.* London: Free Press.
Bell, Daniel J.
1979 "Maintaining Access to Organizational Research." *Criminology* 17:112–118.
Bertalanffy, Ludwig von
1968 *General Systems Theory: Foundations, Development, Applications.* New York: G. Braziller.

Birch, M. W.
- 1963 "Maximum Likelihood in Three-Way Contingency Tables." *Journal of Royal Statistical Society (Series B)* 25:220–233.

Bishop, Yvonne M., Stephen E. Fienberg, and Paul W. Holland
- 1975 *Discrete Multivariate Analysis: Theory and Practice.* Cambridge, Mass.: MIT Press.

Bittner, Egon
- 1967a "Police Discretion in Emergency Apprehension of Mentally Ill Persons." *Social Problems* 14:278–292.
- 1967b "The Police on Skid-Row: A Study of Peace Keeping." *American Sociological Review* 32:699–715.
- 1970 *The Functions of the Police in Modern Society: A Review of Background Factors, Current Practices, and Possible Role Models.* Rockville, Md.: National Institute of Mental Health (DHEW publication: No. (ADM) 75–260).
- 1974 "Florence Nightingale in Pursuit of Willie Sutton: A Theory of the Police." In Herbert Jacob, ed., *The Potential for Reform of Criminal Justice.* Sage Criminal Justice Systems Annals, 3.

Black, Donald
- 1968 "Police Encounters and Social Organization: An Observation Study." Doctoral dissertation. Department of Sociology, University of Michigan.
- 1970 "Production of Crime Rates." *American Sociological Review* 35:733–748.
- 1971 "The Social Organization of Arrest." *Stanford Law Review* 23:1087–1111.
- 1972 "The Boundaries of Legal Sociology." *Yale Law Review* 81:1086–1100.
- 1976 *The Behavior of Law.* New York: Academic Press.
- 1980 *The Manners and Customs of the Police.* New York: Academic Press.

Black, Donald, and Albert Reiss
- 1970 "Police Control of Juveniles." *American Sociological Review* 35:63–77.

Blumer, Herbert
- 1969 *Symbolic Interactionism: Perspective and Method.* Englewood Cliffs, N.J.: Prentice-Hall.

Cappella, Joseph N.
- 1979 "Talk-Silence Sequences in Informal Conversations I." *Human Communication Research* 6:1–16.

Chapple, Eliot D., in collaboration with Conrad M. Arensburg
- 1940 *Measuring Human Relations: An Introduction to the Study of the Interaction of Individuals.* Provincetown, Mass: The Journal Press.
- 1953 "The Standard Experimental (Stress) Interview as Used in

Interaction Chronograph Investigations." *Human Organization* 12:23–32.
Chevigny, Paul
  1969 *Police Power: Police Abuses in New York City.* New York: Pantheon Books.
Clark, John P.
  1965 "Isolation of the Police: A Comparison of the British and American Situations." *Journal of Criminal Law, Criminology, and Police Science* 56:307–319.
Cohen, Jacob
  1960 "A Coefficient of Agreement for Nominal Scales." *Educational and Psychological Measurement* 20:37–46.
Coleman, James S.
  1973 *The Mathematics of Collective Action.* London: Heinemann Educational Books.
Cortes, F., A. Przeworski, and J. Sprague
  1974 *Systems Analysis for Social Scientists.* New York: Wiley.
Cronbach, Lee J.
  1951 "Coefficient Alpha and the Internal Structure of Tests." *Psychometrika* 16:297–334.
Cronbach, Lee J., G. C. Gleser, and N. Rajaratnam
  1972 *The Dependability of Behavioral Measurements: Theory of Generalizability for Scores and Profiles.* New York: Wiley.
Crozier, Michael
  1964 *The Bureaucratic Phenomenon.* Chicago: University of Chicago Press.
Cruse, D., and J. Rubin
  1973 "Police Behavior." *Journal of Psychiatry and Law* 1:167–222.
Dalton, Melville
  1959 *Men Who Manage.* New York: Wiley.
Deising, Paul
  1971 *Patterns of Discovery in the Social Sciences.* Chicago: Aldine.
Dewey, John
  1922 *Human Nature and Conduct: An Introduction to Social Psychology.* New York: Modern Library.
Donohue, William A., Leonard C. Hawes, and Timothy Makee
  1981 "Testing a Structural-Functional Model of Group Decision-Making Using Markov Analysis." *Human Communication Research* 7:133–146.
Ellis, Donald G.
  1979 "Relational Control in Two Group Systems." *Communication Monographs* 46:153–166.
Ellis, Donald G., and B. Aubrey Fisher
  1975 "Phases of Conflict in Small Group Development: A Mar-

kov Analysis." *Human Communication Research* 1:195–212.

Etzioni, Amitai
1961 *A Comparative Analysis of Complex Organizations: On Power, Involvement and Their Correlates*. New York: Free Press.

Feller, William
1968 *An Introduction to Probability Theory and Its Applications*. New York: Wiley.

Fisher, B. Aubrey
1970 "Decision Emergence: Phases in Group Decision-Making." *Speech Monographs* 37:53–66.
1982 "The Pragmatic Perspective of Human Communication: A View from System Theory." In Frank E. X. Dance, ed., *Human Communication Theory*. New York: Harpers.

Fox, James, and Richard Lundman
1974 "Problems and Strategies in Gaining Research Access in Police Organizations." *Criminology* 12:52–69.

French, J. R., and B. H. Raven
1959 "The Basis of Social Power." In D. Cartwright, ed., *Studies in Social Power*. Ann Arbor: University of Michigan Press.

Garrett, M., and J. F. Short
1975 "Social Class v. Personal Demeanor in Police Stereotypes of Juveniles." *Social Problems* 22:368–383.

Glaser, Barney G., and Anselm L. Strauss
1967 *The Discovery of Grounded Theory: Strategies for Qualitative Research*. Chicago: Aldine.

Goffman, Erving
1956 "The Nature of Deference and Demeanor." *American Anthropologist* 58:473–502.
1961a *Asylums: Essays on the Social Situation of Mental Patients and Other Inmates*. Garden City, N.Y.: Anchor Books.
1961b *Encounters: Two Studies in the Sociology of Interaction*. Indianapolis: Bobbs-Merrill.

Goldstein, Herman
1967 "Administrative Problems in Controlling the Exercise of Police Authority." *Journal of Criminal Law, Criminology, and Police Science* 58:160–172.
1977 *Policing a Free Society*. Cambridge, Mass.: Ballinger Publishing Co.

Goldstein, Joseph
1960 "Police Discretion Not to Invoke the Criminal Process: Low Visibility Decisions in the Administration of Justice." *Yale Law Review* 69:543–594.

Gorsuch, R. L.
1974 *Factor Analysis*. Philadelphia: Saunders.

Harre, Rom, and Paul Secord
1972   *The Explanation of Social Behavior.* Totowa, N.J.: Rowman and Littlefield.
Hatfield, John D., and Deborah Weider-Hatfield
1978   "The Comparative Utility of Three Types of Behavioral Units for Interaction Analysis." *Communication Monographs* 45:44–50.
Hawes, Leonard C., and Joseph M. Foley
1973   "A Markov Analysis of Interview Communication." *Speech Monographs* 40:208–219.
1976   "Group Decisioning: Testing a Finite Stochastic Model." In G. R. Miller, ed., *Explorations in Interpersonal Communication.* Beverly Hills, Calif.: Sage Publications.
Heider, Fritz
1958   *The Psychology of Interpersonal Relations.* New York: Wiley.
Hernes, G.
1976   "Structural Change in Social Processes." *American Journal of Sociology* 82:513–547.
Hewes, Dean E.
1975   "Finite Stochastic Modeling of Communication Processes: An Introduction and Some Basic Readings." *Human Communication Research* 1:271–283.
1979   "The Sequential Analysis of Social Interaction." *The Quarterly Journal of Speech* 65:56–73.
1980   "Stochastic Modeling of Communication Processes." In P. R. Monge and J. N. Cappella, eds., *Multivariate Techniques in Human Communication Research.* New York: Academic Press.
Howard, R. A.
1971   *Dynamic Probabilistic Systems.* New York: Wiley.
Hudson, J. R.
1970   "Police-Citizen Encounters That Lead to Citizen Complaints." *Social Problems* 18:179–193.
Hughes, Everett C.
1958   *Men and Their Work.* Glencoe, Ill.: Free Press.
Isaacson, D. L., and R. W. Madsen
1976   *Markov Chains: Theory Applications.* New York: Wiley.
Jacobs, D., and D. Britt
1979   "Inequality and Police Use of Deadly Force: An Empirical Assessment of a Conflict Hypothesis." *Social Problems* 26:403–412.
Jaffe, Joseph
1978   "Parliamentary Procedure and the Brain." In Aron W. Siegman and Stanley Feldstein, eds., *Nonverbal Behavior*

and Communication. Hillsdale, N.J.: Lawrence Erlbaum Associates.

James, William
1907   *Pragmatism.* New York: Longmans, Green.

Kadish, Sanford H.
1962   "Legal Norm and Discretion in the Police and Sentencing Processes." *Harvard Law Review* 75:904–931.

Kania, R. E., and W. C. Mackey
1977   "Police Violence as a Function of Community Characteristics." *Criminology* 15:27–48.

LaFave, Wayne
1965   *Arrest: The Decision to Take a Suspect into Custody.* Boston: Little, Brown.

Liebow, Eliot
1967   *Tally's Corner: A Study of Negro Streetcorner Men.* Boston: Little, Brown.

Lingoes, J.
1973   *The Guttman-Lingoes Nonmetric Program Series.* Ann Arbor: Mathesis Press.

Little, Roger W.
1964   "Buddy Relations and Combat Performance." In Morris Janowitz, ed., *The New Military.* New York: Russell Sage.

Lundman, Richard
1974   "Routine Police Arrest Practices: A Commonweal Perspective." *Social Problems* 22:127–141.

Lundman, Richard, ed.
1980   *Police Behavior: A Sociological Perspective.* New York: Oxford.

Lundman, Richard, and James Fox
1978   "Maintaining Research Access in Police Organizations." *Criminology* 16:87–97.
1979   "Lundman and Fox Reply to Bell." *Criminology* 17:112–118.

Maas, Peter
1973   *Serpico.* New York: Bantam.

McCall, George
1978   *Observing the Law: Field Methods in the Study of Crime and the Criminal Justice System.* New York: Free Press.

McDonald, William F., ed.
1976   *Criminal Justice and the Victim.* Beverly Hills, Calif.: Sage Publications.

McNamara, John H.
1967   "Uncertainties in Police Work: The Relevance of Police Recruits' Backgrounds and Training." In David J. Bordua, ed., *The Police: Six Sociological Essays.* New York: Wiley.

McPhail, Clark, and Cynthia Rexroat

1979 "Mead vs. Blumer: The Divergent Methodological Perspectives of Social Behaviorism and Symbolic Interactionism." *American Sociological Review* 44:449–467.
Manning, Peter
1977 *Police Work: The Social Organization of Policing.* Cambridge, Mass.: MIT Press.
March, James, and Herbert Simon
1958 *Organizations.* New York: Wiley.
Mead, George H.
1932 *The Philosophy of the Present.* Ed. Arthur E. Murphy. Chicago: Open Court.
1934 *Mind, Self, and Society from the Standpoint of a Social Behaviorist.* Chicago: University of Chicago Press.
Miller, Gerald, and Mark Steinberg
1975 *Between People: A New Analysis of Interpersonal Communication.* Chicago: Scientific Research Associates.
Monge, Peter, and Joseph Cappella, eds.
1980 *Multivariate Techniques in Human Communication Research.* New York: Academic Press.
Muir, Jr., William Ker
1977 *Police: Streetcorner Politicians.* Chicago: University of Chicago Press.
Niederhoffer, Arthur, and Abraham Blumberg, eds.
1976 *The Ambivalent Force: Perspectives on the Police.* Hinsdale, Ill.: The Dryden Press.
Parnas, Raymond I.
1967 "The Police Response to the Domestic Disturbance." *Wisconsin Law Review* (1967):914–960.
Piliavin, Irving M., and Scott Briar
1964 "Police Encounters with Juveniles." *American Journal of Sociology* 70:206–214.
Polsky, Ned
1967 *Hustlers, Beats, and Others.* Chicago: Aldine.
Rausch, Harold L.
1965 "Interaction Sequences." *Journal of Personality and Social Psychology* 2:487–499.
1972 "Process and Change—A Markov Model for Interaction." *Family Process* 11:275–298.
Reiss, Albert
1971 *The Police and the Public.* New Haven: Yale University Press.
1974 "Discretionary Justice." In D. Glaser, ed., *Handbook of Criminology.* Chicago: Rand McNally.
Reynolds, Paul
1971 *A Primer in Theory Construction.* Indianapolis: Bobbs-Merrill.

Richardson, J. F.
  1974 *Urban Police in the United States.* Port Washington, N.Y.: Kennikat Press.
Roebuck, Julian, and D. Wood Harper
  1975 "The After-Hours Club: Notes on a Deviant Organization." In Simon Dinitz, Russell R. Dynes, and Alfred C. Clarke, eds., *Deviance: Studies in Definition, Management, and Treatment.* New York: Oxford.
Rolhf, F. James, John Kishpaugh, and David Kirk
  1972 *Numerical Taxonomy System of Multivariate Statistical Programs.* Stony Brook, N.Y.: State University of New York.
Roy, Donald
  1952 "Quota Restriction and Goldbricking in a Machine Shop." *American Journal of Sociology* 57:427–442.
Rubinstein, Jonathan
  1973 *City Police.* New York: Farrar, Straus and Giroux.
Rudner, Richard S.
  1966 *Philosophy of Social Science.* Englewood Cliffs, N.J.: Prentice-Hall.
Rumbaut, Ruben G., and Egon Bittner
  1979 "Changing Conceptions of the Police Role." In Norval Morris and Michael Towky, eds., *Crime and Justice: An Annual Review of Research,* Vol. 1. Chicago: University of Chicago Press.
Sacks, Harvey
  1972 "Notes on Police Assessment of Moral Character." In David Sudnow, ed., *Studies in Social Interaction.* New York: Free Press.
Sampson, Edward E.
  1976 *Social Psychology and Contemporary Society.* New York: Wiley.
Schegloff, Emanuel
  1968 "Sequencing in Conversational Openings." *American Anthropologist* 70:1075–1095.
Schutz, Alfred
  1970 *Alfred Schutz on Phenomenology and Selected Writings,* ed. Helmut R. Wagner. Chicago: University of Chicago Press.
Scott, Marvin B., and Stanford Lyman
  1968 "Accounts." *American Sociological Review* 33:46–62.
Sherman, Lawrence W.
  1976 "The Sociology and Social Reform of the American Police: 1950–1973." In A. Neiderhoffer and A. Blumberg, eds., *The Ambivalent Force.* Hinsdale, Ill.: The Dryden Press.
  1980 "Causes of Police Behavior: The Current State of Quantita-

tive Research." *Journal of Research in Crime and Delinquency* 117:69–100.

Simmel, Georg
1950 *The Sociology of Georg Simmel*, trans. Kurt H. Wolff. Glencoe, Ill.: Free Press.
1955 *Conflict and the Web of Group Affiliations*, trans. Kurt H. Wolff and Reinhard Bendix. New York: Free Press.

Simon, Herbert
1955 "A Behavioral Model of Rational Choice." *Quarterly Journal of Economics* 69:99–118.

Skolnick, Jerome
1966 *Justice without Trial*. New York: Wiley.

Sneath, P. H. A., and R. R. Sokal
1973 *Numerical Taxonomy*. San Francisco, Calif.: Freeman.

Sokal, R. R., and P. H. A. Sneath
1963 *Principles of Numerical Taxonomy*. San Francisco, Calif.: Freeman.

Spradley, James P.
1970 *You Owe Yourself a Drunk: An Ethnography of Urban Nomads*. Boston: Little, Brown.

Stinchcombe, Arthur L.
1963 "Institutions of Privacy in the Determination of Police Administrative Practice." *American Journal of Sociology* 69:150–160.

Sudnow, D.
1965 "Normal Crimes." *Social Problems* 12:255–276.

Suttles, Gerald
1968 *The Social Order of the Slum*. Chicago: University of Chicago Press.

Sykes, Richard E.
1974 "A Preliminary Markov Model of Interaction Between Police and Citizens Considered as General Systems." Unpublished paper given to the annual meeting of the International Communications Association, April.
1977a "A Regulatory Theory of Policing: A Preliminary Statement." In David H. Bayley, ed., *Police and Society*. Beverly Hills, Calif.: Wiley.
1977b "Techniques of Data Collection and Reduction in Systematic Field Observation." *Behavior Research Methods and Instrumentation* 9:407–417.
1978 "Toward a Theory of Observer Effect in Systematic Field Observation." *Human Organization* 37:148–156.

Sykes, Richard E., and John P. Clark
1975 "A Theory of Deference Exchange in Police-Citizen Encounters." *American Journal of Sociology* 81:584–600.
1976 "Comparative Characteristics of Routine Police-Minority

and Police-Majority Citizen Contacts." Unpublished paper.
Sykes, Richard E., John P. Clark, and James Fox
1976 "A Socio-Legal Theory of Police Discretion." In A. Niederhoffer and A. Blumberg, eds., *The Ambivalent Force*. Hinsdale, Ill.: The Dryden Press.
Sykes, Richard E., and Fraine Whitney
1969 "Systematic Observation Utilizing the Minnesota Interaction Data Coding and Reduction System." *Behavioral Science* 14:167–169.
Tapp, June L., and Lawrence Kohlberg
1971 "Developing Senses of Law and Legal Justice." *Journal of Social Issues* 27:65–91.
Tapp, June L., and Felice J. Levine
1977 *Law, Justice and the Individual in Society: Psychological and Legal Issues*. New York: Holt, Rinehart and Winston.
Thomas, William I.
1923 *The Unadjusted Girl—With Cases and Standpoint for Behavior Analysis*. Boston: Little, Brown.
Toch, Hans
1969 *Violent Men*. Chicago: Aldine.
1977 "Police, Prisons, and the Problem of Violence." In *DHEW Crime and Delinquency Issues: A Monograph Series*.
Van Maanen, John
1978 "The Asshole." In P. K. Manning and J. Van Maanen, eds., *Policing: A View from the Street*. Santa Monica, Calif.: Goodyear.
Waitzkin, Howard, and John D. Stoeckle
1972 "The Communication of Information about Illness: Clinical, Sociological, and Methodological Considerations." *Advanced Psychosomatic Medicine* 8:180–215.
Wallen, Duane, and Richard E. Sykes
1974 *Police IV: A Code for the Study of Police-Civilian Interaction*. Minneapolis: Minnesota Systems Research.
Wambaugh, Joseph
1972 *The Blue Knight*. Boston: Little, Brown.
Weinstein, Eugene, and Paul Deutschberger
1963 "Some Dimensions of Altercasting." *Sociometry* 26:454–466.
Westley, William A.
1953 "Violence and the Police." *American Journal of Sociology* 59:34–41.
1970 *Violence and the Police: A Study of Law, Custom, and Morality*. Cambridge, Mass.: MIT Press.
Whyte, William Foote
1955 *Street Corner Society: The Social Structure of an Italian Slum*. 2nd ed. Chicago: University of Chicago Press.

Wiley, M. G., and T. L. Hudik
   1974   "Police-Citizen Encounters: A Field Test of Exchange Theory." *Social Problems* 22:119–129.

Wilson, J. Q.
   1968   *Varieties of Police Behavior*. Cambridge, Mass.: Harvard University Press.

Wiseman, Jacqueline P.
   1970   *Stations of the Lost: Treatment of Skid Row Alcoholics*. Englewood Cliffs, N.J.: Prentice-Hall.

Index

absorbing states, 222
accounts, 77
accusation, 92, 151; activity-related, 81, 86, 93; behavioral, 82, 93
activity-related accusation, 81, 86, 93
activity-related answer, 111
activity-related question, 111
activity-related suggestion, 82, 86, 93
acts: confirming (*see* confirming acts); controlling (*see* controlling acts); definitional (*see* definitional acts); resistant (*see* resistant acts); social (*see* social acts)
age of complainant, 134
American Bar Association, 14, 293
Anderson, Theodore W., 126
aperiodic, 161
argot, 31, 32, 265
Armor, David F., 216
arrest, 75, 76, 89, 109
Ashby, Ross W., 3, 5, 59
attributions, 4
authority, 14, 16, 23, 56–57, 73, 157, 199; coercive, 14, 69; degree of, 91; legitimate, 57, 59, 70, 198, 249; supervisory, 57

balance, principle of, 155
Bales, Robert F., 4, 55, 78, 80, 87, 240, 250, 262, 264, 273
Bayley, David H., 18, 25, 28, 257
Becker, Howard S., 26
behavioral accusation, 82, 93
Bell, Daniel J., 291
Bertalanffy, Ludwig von, 5
Birch, M. W., 126

Bishop, Yvonne M., 7, 118
Bittner, Egon, 1, 11–18, 20–22, 25, 198
Black, Donald, 18, 23, 28, 75, 101–102, 145–147, 160, 201, 209, 217, 265
Blumberg, Abraham, 75, 248
Blumer, Herbert, 227–228, 231, 235
Brent, Jr. Edward E., xviii
Briar, Scott, 101, 209
Britt, D., 20

Cappella, Joseph N., 110
Chapple, Eliot D., 179
Chevigny, Paul, 25, 199, 248, 261
Clark, John P., 33, 56, 59–60, 75, 101–102, 209, 261–262
closing utterances, 172, 173, 175
cluster, 38, 41, 43; analysis, 35, 39; tree, 39
coerce, 29
coercion, 12, 14, 16, 17, 18, 19, 21, 23, 24, 25, 27, 29, 68, 254; physical, 13
coercive, 13, 22; contacts, 23
Cohen, Jacob, 274
Cohen's k, 274
Coleman, James S., 163
command, 82, 92, 93, 111
communication, 4, 5, 254; nonverbal, 2, 4; problems, 197, 203, 204, 206, 207
complexity, 91, 95, 96, 109
compliance, 24
compliant act, 109
conclusions, 221–223
confirming acts, 107, 108, 109, 125, 144, 151
confrontation, 197

305

context hypothesis, 210
contingency, 117, 149, 151, 154, 238, 242; relation, 105; semantic, 239; structural, 239
contingent, 110; mutually, 114; other-, 114, 238; self-, 114, 238
control, 58
controlling acts, 107, 109, 125, 144, 151
cooling out, 14
cophenetic correlation, 39
Cortes, F., 105
cost, 64
Cronbach, Lee J., 39, 216
Cronbach's alpha, 216
Crozier, Michael, 70
Cruse, D., 23, 95, 108

Dalton, Melville, 26
Datamyte, 263, 266
deference, 102, 104, 199; approach, 102; exchange, 101, 109
deference-incivility scale, 102
defiance of authority, 199
definition of the situation, 2, 9, 32, 48, 66, 78, 87, 90–92, 158, 252, 268; confirmation, 47, 82; covert, 32; original, 47, 48, 266, 268, 269; redefinition, 47, 80, 82, 84, 268
definitional acts, 106, 108, 109, 125, 144, 151
Deising, Paul, 228
demeanor, 101
demonstrations, 197, 198, 286. *See also* riots
demonstrators, 199, 200
dendogram, 39
Deutschberger, Paul, 62
Dewey, John, 231, 234
digraphs. *See* directed graphs
dimensions of interaction: demeanor, 101; symbolic content (*See* symbolic content)
directed graphs, 150, 155, 174
discretion, 4, 12, 69, 75–77, 87, 89, 209, 251
discretionary, 26, 87; decisions, 76, 77; typifications, 78
dispatch encounters. *See* proactive encounters
disturbance, 58, 59, 63, 64, 66; to goal of order, 63; to goal of resolution, 63; to goal of respect, 63
Donohue, William A., 110
dramaturgical perspective, 15
dyad: dissolution, 177; formation, 177, 191
dynamic, 5, 6

ecological fallacy, 142
eigenvalue, 150, 160, 161, 202, 203, 207
eigenvector, 150, 160
Ellis, Donald G., 87, 110
encounter, 2, 53
equilibrium, 94, 108, 117, 160, 161, 171, 200, 203, 207; distribution, 116, 117, 130, 131, 140, 141, 143, 144, 149, 161, 162
ergodic, 130, 161
Etzioni, Amitai, 24, 57
evolving: situation, 47; structures, 211–213, 222
expectations, 103, 236
externalization, 56, 90, 237

factor analysis, 35, 37, 215, 216
feedback, 6
Feller, William, 110, 127, 130, 160, 161
Fienberg, Stephen E., 7, 118
Fisher, B. Aubrey, 6, 87, 110
Foley, Joseph M., 87, 110
force, 1, 12, 13, 15, 16, 19, 21, 29; actual use of, 63; brute or brutal, 12, 60, 261; deadly, 20; excessive, 13, 21; gross, 23; minimal, 13, 14; necessary, 13; situationally justified, 22; threat of, 63; unnecessary, 60
forms: Simmel's, 151; of social interaction, 4
Fox, James, 75, 209, 296, 297
French, J. R., 2

Garrett, M., 101
gender of complainant, 134
general systems theory, 6, 105. *See also* systems perspective
Glaser, Barney G., 228
Gleser, G. C., 39
goals, 64; order, 63, 69; resolution, 63, 69; respect, 63

Index

Goffman, Erving, 26, 52–53, 102, 229
Goldstein, Herman, 14, 18, 20, 75
Goldstein, Joseph, 75, 248
Goodman, Leo, 126
Gorsuch, R. L., 37

Harper, D. Wood, 26
Harre, Rom, 28
Hatfield, John D., 87
Hawes, Leonard C., 87, 110
Heider, Fritz, 155
Hernes, G., 105, 115, 149, 160
heterogeneity, 122, 125, 126, 127, 131, 132, 140, 141, 144, 149. *See also* homogeneity
Hewes, Dean E., 110
Holland, Paul W., 7, 118
homogeneity, 122, 141, 144; assumption, 115, 125, 134, 149. *See also* heterogeneity
Howard, R. A., 110
Hudik, T. L., 23, 103, 303
Hudson, J. R., 103, 198
Hughes, Everett C., 51

identity. *See* position
information, 79, 81, 82, 84, 103; goal (*see* tasks, information); legal (nexial) or activity-related, 79, 80, 84, 85–87, 93, 94; procedural or role-expectation-related, 79, 80, 84, 85–87, 93, 94; search, 87, 89; task (*see* tasks, information)
initial: acts, 46, 172, 188, 189, 251, 252; state vector, 118
integral identity. *See* position, integral
interact, 59
interaction coding system, 240–241, 263–273
interaction process analysis, 262, 263, 273
Isaacson, D. L., 110

Jacobs, D., 20
Jaffe, Joseph, 62
James, William, 234

Kadish, Sanford H., 75
Kania, R. E., 20
Kirk, David, 39

Kishpaugh, John, 39
Kohlberg, Lawrence, 2

LaFave, Wayne, 75
last social act, 172, 173, 175
last word, 172, 173, 175
law: scientific, 233
legitimacy, 23, 197, 198, 255, 256
legitimate, 23, 198, 257
levels of structure, 6, 105; output structure, 105, 143, 144, 149, 150, 175, 249; parameter structure, 106, 109, 143, 147, 149, 150, 175, 249; process structure, 105, 147, 149, 150, 151, 249
levels of structure and process, 163; opportunity structures, 163, 165, 174, 175; response propensities, 163, 168, 171, 174, 197, 201, 208; situation, 163, 165, 167, 174, 175, 184, 252
Levine, Felice J., 2, 56
Liebow, Eliot, 26
Lingoes, J., 43
Little, Roger W., 26
log-linear models, 6, 7, 118, 119, 122, 131, 132, 168, 190, 252
Lundman, Richard, 75, 291
Lyman, Stanford, 29, 77

Maas, Peter, 230
McCall, George, 265
McDonald, William F., 26
McNamara, John H., 103
McPhail, Clark, 228
Mackey, W. C., 20
Madsen, R. W., 110
Makee, Timothy, 110
Manning, Peter, 15, 17–19, 25, 76, 78
March, James, 58
Markov: models, 6, 7, 110, 111, 113, 119, 122, 124, 125, 127, 130, 131, 132, 140, 143, 149, 150, 160, 199, 222, 244, 248, 250, 252; process, 7, 94, 110, 114, 117, 118, 122, 125, 126, 134
mass disorder, 11. *See also* demonstrations
mathematical models, 5, 6. *See also* Markov
Mead, George H., 2, 4, 151, 154, 163, 174, 225–229, 233–237, 239–240, 242–244, 252, 262

metaprocess, 177, 193
MIDCARS, 263
military model, 13
Miller, Gerald, 250, 253
MINISSA, 43
models: "independent effects," 210, 221–223; "intervening variable," 210, 219; log-linear (see log-linear models); Markov (see Markov); mathematical (see mathematical models); military, 13; "no effects," 210; "spurious effects," 210
Monge, Peter, 110
Muir, Jr. William Ker, 16–18, 24–25, 57, 158
multidimensional contingency tables, 6, 7
multiple-position interaction, 177
multistep transition probabilities, 127, 130, 140, 149

natural settings, 5
negotiated settlement, 14
negotiation, 13, 27, 288
Niederhoffer, Arthur, 75, 248
nonroutine, 95–98
nonverbal communication, 2, 4
normative order. See orders, normative
NT-SYS, 39

observer: reliability, 274–276; training, 274–276
offense, 122, 124, 146
on-scene encounters. See proactive encounters
order, 114, 134, 145, 146, 184, 211, 245, 249, 255; zero, 114, 212; first, 108, 109, 119, 122, 132, 134, 140, 147, 163, 185, 212, 244, 256; second, 109, 114, 122, 125–127, 131, 132, 134, 140, 141, 143, 144, 147–149, 151, 154, 163, 184, 185, 192, 193, 213, 244, 250, 252, 253, 256; third, 122, 132, 134, 149; higher, 109, 219, 222
orders: formal, legal, 28; informal social, 27, 28; normative, 26, 27; private, 27–29. See also worlds
orthodox view of police, 19; objections to, 19
outcome, 78, 89, 92, 106, 209–213, 216–217, 219, 221–223, 252, 268; arrest (see arrest); nonarrest alternative, 76; severity, 216, 219
output, 106; vector, 115, 116, 117

paradox, 104, 251
parameter: estimates, 196; interaction, 213–216; values, 196
Parnas, Raymond I., 28
patterns of decisions, 91–92, 95–98
periodic, 127, 130, 161; aperiodic, 161
perspectives: deference (see deference approach); dramaturgical (see dramaturgical perspective); orthodox (see orthodox view of police); social behaviorist (see social behaviorist, perspective); supervisory (see supervision, perspective); symbolic (see symbolic approach); systems (see systems perspective)
phase structure or phase model, 78, 87, 89, 108, 252
phases, 3, 82, 84, 87, 89, 251; of group problem solving, 3
Piliavin, Irving M., 101, 209
Police Code, 111, 264, 272–273, 275
Polsky, Ned, 26
position, 240; integral, 52, 54–56, 141, 243; situated, 52, 54–56, 58, 77–79, 81, 82, 87, 89, 92, 95–97, 141, 243, 264
power, 27; legitimate, 2; coercive, 2, 23, 24
predictable, 71, 175, 243; unpredictable, 167, 176. See also uncertainty
predispositions to respond. See response propensity
proactive encounters, 66, 69, 83, 85–86, 90, 91, 92, 109, 252
probability, 93, 94, 111, 117, 212, 213, 240, 242, 251, 256; matrix, 113, 114, 242; vector, 115
procedural accusation, 86
procedural command, 86
process, 5, 6, 93
process structure, 108, 147
professionalism, 20
professionals, 13, 255, 257
Przeworski, A., 105

question, 151

Index

Rajaratnam, N., 39
Rausch, Harold L., 126, 145
Raven, B. H., 2
reactive encounters, 31, 66, 69, 81, 83, 85–86, 91, 252
regulate, 61, 67, 89
regulation. *See* supervision
Reiss, Albert, 14, 18, 20, 21, 23, 28, 31, 69, 75, 77, 95, 101, 147, 161, 209, 248, 249, 261, 265, 274, 288
reliability. *See* observer, reliability
repetition, 67, 70, 71
resistant acts, 107, 108, 109, 144, 151
resolution, 60, 63, 82, 83, 87
response propensity, 146, 150, 251, 253, 256
restore order, 142
Rexroat, Cynthia, 228
Reynolds, Paul, 233
Richardson, J. F., 199
riots, 195, 247, 253. *See also* demonstrations
Roebuck, Julian, 26
role taking, 2, 163, 225, 232, 242, 243, 251, 252, 256
Rolhf, F. James, 39
Roy, Donald, 26
Rubin, J., 23, 95, 108
Rubinstein, Jonathan, 15–19, 25, 29, 33, 61, 229–230, 274
Rudner, Richard S., 22
Rumbaut, Ruben G., 18, 21
runs, 127, 130; distribution of, 127, 140, 143, 149

Sacks, Harvey, 103
sample, 33, 45; convenience, 47; design, 33, 288–291; of encounters, 45; random shift, 33
Sampson, Edward E., 250
satisficing, 232
Schegloff, Emanuel, 229
Schutz, Alfred, 32
Scott, Marvin B., 29, 77
script (or strategy), 93, 94, 98, 232
second acts, 192
second thoughts, 192
second utterances, 192
Secord, Paul, 28
selective enforcement, 12

sensitivity, 195
set of utterances. *See* string
severity: of offense, 134; of outcome, 134
Sherman, Lawrence W., 75, 248
Short, J. F., 101
Simmel, Georg, 4, 151, 154
Simon, Herbert, 58, 229, 232
simulation, 195, 196, 199, 253
situated identity. *See* position, situated
situation. *See* levels of structure and process, situation
situational exigencies, 12, 20
Skolnick, Jerome, 18, 33, 229, 230, 248
smallest space analysis, 38, 43
Sneath, P.H.A., 39, 43
social acts, 151, 154, 156, 157, 173–175, 225, 243–244, 252; agreement, 151, 153, 155, 156, 160, 204; competition, 151, 153, 221; confrontation, 153, 156–159, 161, 175, 199, 200, 201, 203, 208, 219, 244, 251; cooperation, 153, 155–161, 171, 175, 200, 201, 206, 244, 251, 253; domination, 153, 161, 204, 244; evasion, 153; non-cooperation, 152, 153, 159, 161, 175, 204, 206; persistence, 153, 155–157, 159, 160, 175; reassertion, 153, 155–157, 159, 175, 244; redirection, 152, 153, 155, 156, 204; sanctioning, 152, 155, 160, 161, 221; tacking, 152, 155, 160, 175, 204, 217
social behaviorist: perspective, 4, 228, 234, 254; tradition, 4
social class, 124, 146, 147, 254; perceived, 122
socialization, 56
socialize, 57, 79
Socrates, 2, 61
Sokal, R. R., 39, 43
Spradley, James P., 26
Sprague, J., 105
SPSS, 112
stable distribution of states, 94
states, 6; absorbing, 222
state vector, 115
stationarity, 87, 117, 122, 141, 211; assumption, 115, 125, 134, 149; non-stationarity, 87, 124
Steinberg, Mark, 250, 253
Stinchcombe, Arthur L., 267

Stoeckle, John D., 70
strategies, 3
Strauss, Anselm L., 228
string, 3, 87, 89, 94, 270
Strodtbeck, Fred, 55, 78, 80, 87
structural equation analysis or models, 214–215
structure, 5, 6; evolving, 211–213, 222; levels (*see* levels of structure; levels of structure and process)
subordinate, 54, 55, 56
substitution hypothesis, 210–211, 221, 223
Sudnow, D., 32
suggestion, activity-related. *See* activity-related suggestion
superordinate-subordinate relation, 55
superordinates, 54, 55, 56
supervision, 57–59, 61, 64, 66, 69, 250, 251, 254; coercive, 63, 66, 72, 73; definitional, 61, 66, 67, 69, 72, 73, 151, 167; imperative, 63, 66, 67, 69, 71–73, 167; perspective, 66; processes of, 64; supervisor, 61, 70
Suttles, Gerald, 26
Sykes, Richard E., xviii, 26, 33, 56, 58–60, 75, 101–102, 109, 110, 209, 255, 263, 273, 288, 291
symbolic approach, 102
symbolic content, 102, 103, 104, 109, 113
symbolic interaction, 5, 227, 231, 250
system, 59, 105, 106
systematic quantitative observations, 4, 5
systems perspective, 105, 227, 229

take charge, 57, 104, 254
talking, 2, 9, 29, 99, 249, 251, 254
Tapp, June L., 2, 56
tasks: behavior, 60, 63; information, 60, 63, 76, 78, 79; resolution (*see* resolution); respect, 60, 63
temporal sequence, 105
Thomas, William I., 2
Toch, Hans, 25, 198, 199
transactions, 250, 252, 253
transition: matrix, 94, 106, 114–117, 126, 127, 130, 150, 160, 179, 204, 206, 244; probability, 71, 93, 94, 106, 108, 114, 126, 130, 132, 134, 140, 142, 144, 150, 171, 185, 186, 204, 212, 213
tripartite relationship, 113, 114, 225, 234–236, 241, 243, 244, 252, 253
typification, 77, 78, 89; discretionary, 78

u-terms, 119
uncertainty, 70, 208. *See also* predictable
units of analysis, 87; encounter (*see* encounter); interact, 59; string (*see* string); transactions (*see* transactions); utterances (*see* utterance)
utterance, 3, 87, 106, 231, 250, 252, 264, 269; set of (*see* string)

validity, 277
Van Maanen, John, 60, 78
violence, 21, 25, 257
volatile working group, 3, 49, 53, 72, 157, 249, 254, 256

Waitzkin, Howard, 70
Wallen, Duane, 263, 273, 275
Wambaugh, Joseph, 230
Weider-Hatfield, Deborah, 87
Weinstein, Eugene, 62
Westley, William A., 1, 25, 60, 229
Whitney, Fraine, 263
who-to-whom, 177–179, 181, 184, 193, 213
Whyte, William Foote, 26
Wiley, M. G., 23, 103
Wilson, J. Q., 18, 20, 248
Wiseman, Jacqueline P., 26
working group, 53, 54, 99; volatile (*see* volatile working group)
worlds, 229–231. *See also* orders
Wroclaw diagram, 43

zone: of agreement, 155; of disagreement, 155; of general cognitive structuring, 155; of more or less overt conflict, 155